W9-CKR-851

In Arabian Nights

Also by Tahir Shah

In Arabian Nights

A CARAVAN OF MOROCCAN DREAMS

TAHIR SHAH

Bantam Books

IN ARABIAN NIGHTS
A Bantam Book / January 2008

Published by Bantam Dell
A Division of Random House, Inc.
New York, New York

Copyright © 2008 by Tahir Shah
Interior illustrations by Laetitia Bermejo
Map by Michael Greer

Book design by Lynn Newmark

Bantam Books is a registered trademark of Random House, Inc.,
and the colophon is a trademark of Random House, Inc.

Library of Congress Cataloging-in-Publication Data
Shah, Tahir.
In Arabian nights / Tahir Shah.
p. cm.
ISBN 978-0-553-80523-9 (hardcover)
1. Shah, Tahir.   2. Morocco—Description and travel.
3. Travel writers—Morocco—Biography.   I. Title.

DT310.3.S43 2008
916.404'53—dc22
2007027812

Printed in the United States of America
Published simultaneously in Canada

www.bantamdell.com

10 9 8 7 6 5 4 3 2 1
BVG

This book is for my aunt Amina Shah,
Queen of the Storytellers

Here we are, all of us: in a dream-caravan.
A caravan, but a dream—a dream, but a caravan.
And we know which are the dreams.
Therein lies the hope.

–Sheikh Bahaudin

Nasrudin was sent by the King to find the most foolish man in the land and bring him to the palace as Court jester. The Mulla traveled to each town and village, in turn, but could not find a man stupid enough for the job. Finally, he returned alone.

"Have you located the greatest idiot in our kingdom?" asked the Monarch.

"Yes," replied Nasrudin, "but he is too busy looking for fools to take the job."

—The World of Nasrudin *by Idries Shah*

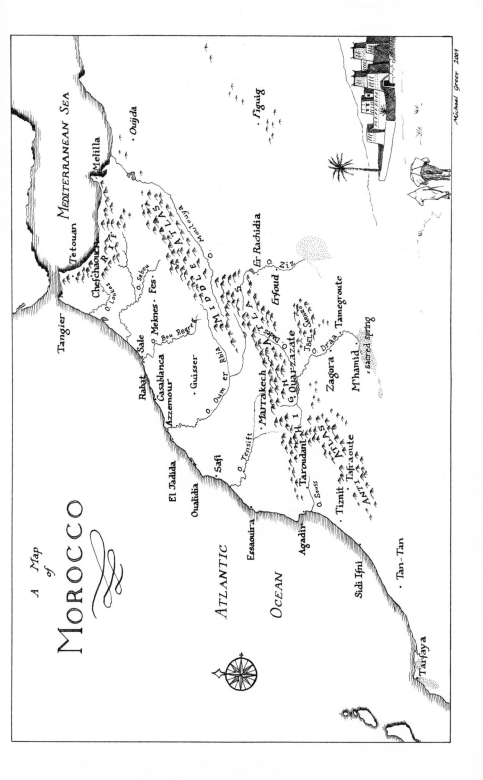

A Map of
MOROCCO

Michael Greer 2007

MEDITERRANEAN SEA

ATLANTIC

OCEAN

Tangier
Tetouan
Chefchaouen
RIF

Melilla
· Oujda

· Figuig

O. Loukos
O. Sebou
Fes ·
Meknes ·
Rabat · Salé
Casablanca
Azzemour
· Guisser

MIDDLE ATLAS

Moulouya
O.

Er-Rachidia
O. Ziz

Erfoud

El Jadida
Oualidia
Safi
Essaouira
Agadir

Marrakech ·
G. Ouarzazate
Taroudant ·
Tiznit ·
Tafraoute ·
ANTI ATLAS

HIGH ATLAS

O. Draa
JBEL SAGHRO
Zagora ·
Draa ·
Tamegroute ·
M'hamid ·
× sacred spring

Bou Regreg
O. Oum er Rbia
O. Tensift
O. Souss

Sidi Ifni
· Tan-Tan

Tarfaya

chapter one

Be in the World, but not of the World.

Arab proverb

The torture room was ready for use. There were harnesses for hanging the prisoners upside down, rows of sharp-edged batons, and smelling salts, used syringes filled with dark liquids and worn leather straps, tourniquets, clamps, pliers, and equipment for smashing the feet. On the floor there was a central drain, and on the walls and every surface, dried blood—plenty of it. I was manacled, hands pushed high up my back, stripped almost naked, with a military-issue blindfold tight over my face. I had been in the torture chamber every night for a week, interrogated hour after hour on why I had come to Pakistan.

All I could do was tell the truth: that I was traveling through en route from India to Afghanistan, where I was planning to make a documentary about the lost treasure of the Mughals. My film crew and I had been arrested on a residential street, and taken to the secret torture installation known by the jailers as "The Farm."

I tried to explain to the military interrogator that we were innocent of any crime. But for the military police of Pakistan's North-West Frontier Province, a British citizen with a Muslim name, coming overland from an enemy state—India—set off all the alarms.

Through nights of blindfolded interrogation, with the screams of other prisoners forming an ever-present backdrop to life in limbo, I answered the same questions again and again: *What was the real purpose of my journey? What did I know of Al-Qaeda bases across the border in Afghanistan* and even, *why was I married to an Indian?* It was only after the first week that the blindfolds were removed and, as my eyes adjusted to the blaring interrogation lamps, I caught my first burnt-out glimpse of the torture room.

The interrogations took place at night, although day and night were much the same at The Farm. The strip-light high on the ceiling of my cell was never turned off. I would crouch there, waiting for the sound of keys and for the thud of feet pacing over stone. That meant they were coming for me again. I would brace myself, say a prayer, and try to clear my mind. A clear mind is a calm one.

The keys would jingle once more and the bars to my cell would swing open just enough for a hand to reach through and grab me.

First the blindfold and then the manacles.

Shut out the light, and your other senses compensate. I could hear the muffled screeches of a prisoner being tortured in the parallel block and taste the dust out in the fields on my tongue.

Most of the time, I squatted in my cell, learning to be alone. Get locked up in solitary in a foreign land, with the threat of immediate execution hanging over you, a blade dangling from a thread, and you try to pass the time by forgetting where you are.

First I read the graffiti on the walls. Then I read it again, and again, until I was half-mad. Pens and paper were forbidden, but previous inmates had used their ingenuity. They had scrawled slogans in their own blood and excrement. I found myself desperate to make sense of others' madness. Then I knelt on the cement floor and slowed my breathing, even though I was so scared words could not describe the fear.

Real terror is a crippling experience. You sweat so much that your skin goes all wrinkly like when you've been in the bath all afternoon.

And then the scent of your sweat changes. It smells like cat pee, no doubt from the adrenaline. However hard you wash, it won't come off. It smothers you, as your muscles become frozen with acid and your mind paralyzed by despair.

The only hope of staying sane was to think of my life, the life that had become separated from me, and to imagine that I was stepping into it again... into the dream that, until so recently, had been my reality.

The white walls of my cell were a kind of silver screen on which I projected the Paradise to which I longed to return. The love for that home and all within washed out the white walls, the blood-graffiti, and the stink of fear. And the more I feared, the more I forced myself to think of my adopted Moroccan home, Dar Khalifa, the Caliph's House.

There were courtyards brimming with fountains and birdsong, and gardens in which Timur and Ariane, my little son and daughter, played with their tortoises and their kites. There was bright summer sunlight, and fruit trees, and the sound of my wife, Rachana's, voice, calling the children in to lunch. And there were lemon-colored butterflies, scarlet red hibiscus flowers, blazing bougainvillea, and the hum of bumblebees dancing through the honeysuckle.

Hour after hour I would watch my memories screened across the blank walls. I would be blinded by the colors, and glimpse in sharp detail the lives we had created for ourselves on the edge of Casablanca. With my future now in the balance, all I could do was to pray. Pray that I might be reunited with that life, a melodious routine of innocence interleaved with gentle calamity.

As the days and nights in solitary passed, I moved through the labyrinth of my memories. I set myself the task of finding every memory, every fragment of recollection.

They began with my childhood, and with the first moment I ever set foot on Moroccan soil.

The ferry had taken us from southern Spain, across the Strait of

Gibraltar. It was the early seventies. Tucked up in the northwest corner of Africa, Tangier was a mélange of life like none other. There were beatniks and tie-dyed hippies, drug dealers and draft dodgers, writers, poets, fugitives, and philosophers. They were all united in a swirling stew of humanity. I was only five years old, but I can remember it crystal clear, a world I could never hope to understand. It was scented with orange blossom, illuminated by sunshine so bright that I had to squint.

My father, who was from Afghanistan, had been unable to take my sisters and me to his homeland. It was too dangerous. So he brought us on frequent journeys to Morocco instead. I suppose it was a kind of Oriental logic. The two countries are remarkably similar, he would say: dramatic landscapes, mountain and desert, a tribal society steeped in history, rigid values, and a code of honor, all arranged on a canvas of vibrant cultural color.

The animated memories of those early travels were relived on the whitewashed walls of solitary, mile by mile. As I watched them, I found myself thinking about the stories my father told as the wheels beneath us turned through the dust, and how they bridged the abyss between fact and fantasy.

The interrogations in the torture room came and went, as did the jangle of keys, the plates of thin soupy *daal* slipped under the bars, and the nightmares. Through it all, I watched the walls, my concentration fixed on the matinees and the late-night shows that slipped across them. With time, I found I could navigate through weeks and years I had almost forgotten took place, and could remember details that my eyes had never quite revealed. I revisited my first day at prep school, my first tumble from a tree-climbing childhood, and the day I almost burned down my parents' house.

But most of all, I remembered the tales my father told.

I pictured him rubbing a hand over his dark mustache and down over his chin, and the words that were the bridge into another world:

"Once upon a time..."

SOMETIMES THE FEAR would descend over me like a veil. I would feel myself slipping into a kind of trance, numbed by the frantic debauched screams of the prisoner being worked over in the torture room. In the same way that a bird in the jaws of a predator readies itself for the end, I would push the memories out, struggle to find silence. It only came when the uncertainty and the fear reached its height. And with it came a voice. It would ease me, calm me, weep with me, and speak from inside me, not from my head, but from my heart.

In a whisper the voice guided me to my bedroom at the Caliph's House. The windows were open, the curtains swaying, and the room filled with the swish of the wind in the eucalyptus trees outside.

There is something magical about the sound, as if it spans emptiness between restraint and the furthest reaches of the mind. I listened hard, concentrating to the hum of distant waves and to the rustle of crisp eucalyptus leaves, and walked down through the house and out onto the terrace. Standing there, the ocean breeze cool on my face, I sensed the tingle of something I could not understand, and saw a fine geometric carpet laid over the lawn. I strolled down over the terrace and onto the grass, and stepped aboard it, the silk knots pressing against my bare feet. Before I knew it, we were away, floating up into the air.

We moved over the Atlantic without a sound, icy waters surging, cresting, breaking. Gradually, we gathered speed and height until I could see the curve of the earth below. We crossed deserts and mountains, oceans and endless seas. The carpet folded back its edge, protecting me from the wind.

After hours of flight, I glimpsed the outline of a city ahead. It was ink-black and sleeping, its minarets soaring up to the heavens, its domed roofs hinting at treasures within. The carpet banked to the left and descended until we were hovering over a grand central square. It was teeming with people and life, illuminated by ten thousand blazing torches, their flames licking the night.

A legion of soldiers in gilded armor was standing guard. Across from them were stallions garlanded in fine brocades, elephants fitted with howdahs, a pen of prowling tigers, and, beside it, a jewel-encrusted carousel. There were oxen roasting on enormous spits, tureens of mutton stewed in milk, platters of brazed camel meat, and great silver salvers heaped with rice and with fish.

A sea of people were feasting, entertained by jugglers and acrobats, serenaded by the sound of a thousand flutes. Nearby, on a dais crafted from solid gold, overlaid with rare carpets from Samarkand, sat the king. His bulky form was adorned in cream-colored silk, his head crowned by a voluminous turban, complete with a peacock feather pinned to the front.

At the feet of the monarch sat a delicate girl, her skin the color of ripe peaches, her eyes emerald green. Her face was partly hidden by a veil. Somehow I sensed her sadness. A platter of pilau had been put before her, but she had not touched it. Her head was low, her eyes reflecting a sorrow beyond all depth.

The magic carpet paused long enough for me to take in the scene. Then it banked up and to the right, flew back across the world over mountains and deserts, oceans and seas, and came to a gentle rest on our own lawn.

In my heart I could hear the hum of Atlantic surf, and the wind rippling through the eucalyptus trees. And in my head I could hear the sound of keys jangling, and steel-toed boots moving down the corridor, pacing over stone.

chapter two

Examine what is said, not him who speaks.

Moroccan proverb

On our childhood travels to Morocco, my father used to say that to understand a place you had to look beyond what the senses show you. He would tell us to stuff cotton in our nostrils, to cover our ears, and to close our eyes. Only then, he would say, could we absorb the essence of the place. For children the exercise of blocking the senses was confusing. We had a thousand questions, each one answered with another question.

At dusk one evening we arrived at Fès. As usual the family was squeezed into our old Ford station wagon, vinyl suitcases loaded on the roof, the gardener at the wheel. That evening I caught my first sight of the massive medieval city walls, impenetrable and bleak like the end of the world. There were figures moving beside them in hooded robes, carts laden with newly slaughtered sheep, and the piercing sound of a wedding party far away.

The car stopped and we all trooped out.

In the twilight my father pointed to a clutch of men, huddled on the ground outside the city's grand Imperial Gate.

"They're gamblers," said my mother.

"No, they are not," my father replied. "They are the guardians of an ancient wisdom."

I asked what he meant.

"They are the storytellers," he said.

FOR MY FATHER there was no sharper way to understand a country than listening to its stories. He would often line up my sisters and me, and enthrall us with episodes from *Alf Layla wa Layla, A Thousand and One Nights*. The tales worked in a special way, he said, diverting the mind while passing on a kind of inner knowledge. Listen to the stories, he would repeat again and again, and they would act like an instruction manual to the world.

As far as he was concerned, the stories and the ability to tell them were a kind of baton to be passed from one generation to the next. He used to say that many of the tales he related had been in our family for centuries, that they were fastened to us in some way, a part of us.

He would sometimes make me uneasy, stressing the grave duty, the burden of responsibility, sitting on my shoulders. My school friends used to love stories as much as me, but we differed. From before I could walk I was reminded that these tales were magical, that they contained wisdom, and that one day I would be expected to pass them on to my own children. Deep down I never really expected the time would come to pass the baton on.

But it did.

One night as I tucked her into bed, Ariane put her arms round my neck and whispered into my ear: "Tell me a story, Baba." I froze, for the words had been mine thirty years before.

I felt under-equipped to handle the duty of teaching with stories. Ariane and Timur enjoyed listening to my small repertoire, but when I tried to explain the many layers, they said they didn't understand, or that I was boring them. I thought back to how my father recounted the tales to us, how he had passed the baton on. I pictured myself in his study with my sisters, sitting in a line on his turquoise divan. He would be perched opposite, leaning forward cupped in a grand leather chair, fingertips pressed together, sunlight streaming in through French doors behind.

"Clear your minds," he would say. "Close your eyes. Listen to the sound of my voice."

We would be squirming at first, unable to keep still. Then the voice began, soft as silk, precise, calm... "Once upon a time in a kingdom far away..." Within a moment it had pulled us in, taken over, and we were lost in its realm. That was it. My father never told us how the stories worked. He didn't reveal the layers, the nuggets of information, the fragments of truth and fantasy. He didn't need to—because, given the right conditions, the stories activated, sowing themselves.

THE CALIPH'S HOUSE has the ability to suck you in and tantalize your senses. There are courtyards shaded by fragrant honeysuckle and blazing bougainvillea vines; fountains crafted from hand-cut mosaics, gardens hidden behind secret walls, terracotta tiled floors, carved cedarwood doors, and acres of Venetian plaster etched with intricate geometric designs.

When we bought Dar Khalifa, we were newcomers to the local culture and its layers of superstitious belief. But the learning curve was a steep one. Spend more than a few weeks living in Morocco and you understand that daily life is inextricably linked to an ancient Oriental system. A good way to make sense of the society, which at first seemed so daunting, so incomprehensible, was to read it as if it were a kingdom from the time of Harun ar-Rashid. From the first day, I found the reality of our new lives mirroring the make-believe world of *A Thousand and One Nights*.

Almost as if through some medieval right of sale, we inherited three guardians with the Caliph's House. Their leader was Hamza.

He was tall, solemn, and stooped, as if the world's burdens were laid on his shoulders. Then there was Osman. He was the youngest and had worked at the house since his childhood. He had a smile that was permanently fastened to his lips. The third guardian was called

Mohammed, but known by all as the Bear. He was strong as an ox, had enormous hands, a hooked nose, and a nervous twitch.

Hamza, Osman, and the Bear spent most of their time skulking in the stables at the bottom of the garden, hoping that I would forget about them. On the rare occasions that they ever spoke to me, it was to remind me of the grave dilemma, the predicament of the Jinns.

In the West, a house that has been boarded up for years on end might attract squatters. They can damage the place and be near impossible to evict. But in Morocco there is the threat of a far more turbulent force awaiting the unsuspecting. Leave your home empty for more than a moment, and it could fill from the floor to the rafters with an army of invisible spirits, called Jinns.

The Qur'an says that when God created Man from clay, he fashioned a second form of life from "smokeless fire." They are known by many names—Genies, Jnun, Jinns—and they live all around us in inanimate objects. Some Jinns are good-natured, but most are wicked, enraged by the discomfort they believe that humanity has caused them.

We spent many months renovating the house and cleansing it of the Jinns. The guardians insisted they were lurking in the water tanks, in the toilets, and under the floor. Living with Jinns or, worse still, around people who believed in them caused unimaginable stress.

Most of the time I was trapped in Casablanca. The days and nights were filled with builders, artisans, and an ever-expanding staff, all of them fearful of the paranormal forces they said encased our lives. From time to time I did manage to break free. I crisscrossed Morocco on the trail of building supplies, craftsmen, and exorcists capable of dispatching the wayward Jinns. It was easy to forget that out there, beyond the wilds of the shantytown, there was a land ablaze with vitality, history, and culture: a kingdom waiting to be discovered.

ONE MORNING I found Osman sitting on an upturned bucket staring out at the hibiscus hedge. It was early summer and already far too hot to work, too hot even to think. I had taken the guardian a cup of chilled orange juice, droplets of condensation running down the side. He smiled broadly, teeth glistening, thanked me, then God and, after a long pause, he said, "Monsieur Tahir, you have been here at Dar Khalifa for more than three years."

"It's gone fast," I said.

The guardian gulped down the juice and turned slowly until his watery brown eyes locked into mine. "And what have you learned?"

"What do you mean?"

"About our kingdom . . . what do you know?"

I thought for a moment, considering the journeys I had made in search of mosaics and exorcists, tortoises and cedarwood.

"I've seen a lot," I said. "I've traveled north to the Mediterranean, right down south to the Sahara, and all the way into the High Atlas."

Osman wiped a sleeve to his nose. He kept my gaze. "You don't know us," he said sharply. "You don't know Morocco."

A jab of disbelief pricked my stomach. What's he talking about? I thought. "I know Morocco as well as anyone who's lived here for as long as I have."

The guardian put his thumbs in his eyes and rubbed very hard. Then he looked at me again. "You have been blind," he said.

"What?"

"Blind."

I shrugged.

"Morocco may have passed under your feet, but you haven't seen it."

"I'm sure I have."

"No, Monsieur Tahir, believe me. I can see it in your face."

———

MANY OF MY earliest memories are of listening to stories. Our childhood home was filled with *A Thousand and One Nights* or, as they are more popularly known, the *Arabian Nights*. I would sit there enthralled hour after hour at the exploits of Aladdin and Ali Baba, of Sindbad, and the world of the Caliph Harun ar-Rashid. There was always talk of chests overflowing with treasure, of princesses, and handsome princes charging on stallions liveried in gold, of ghouls and *efrits,* dervishes, *divs,* and Jinns.

My father always had a tale at hand to divert our attention, or to use as a way of transmitting an idea or a thought. He used to say that the great collections of stories from the East were like encyclopedias, storehouses of wisdom and knowledge ready to be studied, to be appreciated and cherished. To him, stories represented much more than mere entertainment. He saw them as complex psychological documents, forming a body of knowledge that had been collected and refined since the dawn of humanity and, more often than not, passed down by word of mouth.

When my father died a decade ago, I inherited his library. There were five reinforced boxes of books labeled "STORIES: VALUABLE, HANDLE WITH CARE." Among them were Aesop's *Fables,* Hans Christian Andersen, and the Brothers Grimm. There were many others, too, the Arab collections and volumes of tales from every corner of the world—from Albania and China, Cambodia, India, Argentina, and Vietnam, from sub-Saharan Africa, Australia, Malaysia, from Papua New Guinea and Japan.

Once the Caliph's House was renovated I had more time to spare. So I sat down to read the five boxes of stories from my father's library. I would often come to penciled annotations in his small, neat hand. Many of the notes hinted at wisdom locked within a tale, or likened one story to another from an entirely different region of the world.

The only set of volumes missing was my father's copy of *A*

Thousand and One Nights, the rare edition translated by the Victorian scholar and explorer Richard Francis Burton. As a child I remember seeing the set in his study. It stood on a shelf at ankle height. My father prized the edition very highly, and would point out the quality of the workmanship, or tell of how he came upon the seventeen volumes as a young man. He said that he had saved for months to afford the books, and would go each afternoon to spend time admiring them in the shop. I realized later it was the prized first "Benares" edition of Burton's *Alf Layla wa Layla, A Thousand and One Nights.*

The volumes were bound in waxy black cloth, with bright gold lettering on the spines. I was young and inexperienced, but they were just about the most beautiful thing I had ever seen. They were so exquisite that I would caress my fingers over them, and stoop down to smell their scent.

They smelled like cloves.

One rainy winter afternoon a visitor arrived at my parents' home. He was overweight, flat-footed, and chain-smoked from the moment he stepped inside, until the moment he stepped out. I was too small to be told anything, but I remember my parents muttering before he came. I don't know who he was, but he was important enough to drink tea from our best china, and to have slices of lemon served on the side.

From behind the banisters, I watched him greet my father and move through the hall into the study. The door was closed and, when it was eventually opened, the visitor was struggling under the weight of the *Arabian Nights.* At dinner, I asked what had happened to the black and gold books. My father's face seemed to darken. He looked at me hard and said: "In our culture a guest is respected and honored very greatly, Tahir Jan. If he is under your roof, then he is under your protection. Your possessions are his for the asking. If he was to admire something, it is your duty to present him with it. Remember this, Tahir Jan, remember it for your entire life."

AT DAR KHALIFA, the guardians said they were too busy raking the leaves to waste time telling tales. I grilled them one at a time, but all they could tell me was that stories were not what they had once been.

"There used to be time to while away the hours, talking and listening," said Hamza, "but these days there's too much work. None of us have a moment to spare."

"There's no time to even scratch our heads," Osman chipped in. "Our traditions are disappearing, all because employers are working their employees like slaves."

The Bear appeared through the hibiscus hedge, and the three guardians fell into line, leering at me as menacingly as they could. Relations had been strained between us since I had implemented my brave new master plan. Unable to afford painters and gardeners, builders and handymen, any longer, I had initiated a fresh regime, which involved the radical idea of everyone on the payroll doing actual work. The scheme had been unpopular from the start. As long as any of them had been employed at the Caliph's House, the guardians were used to lazing about down at the stables, swapping stories and fanning the flames of their own supernatural belief. But with the exorcism and the banishment of the Jinns, a new era had been ushered in. They never said it, but I could sense that the guardians secretly longed for the old days, a time steeped in fear of the spirits, when they had had the upper hand.

EVERY FRIDAY AFTERNOON I would take a notebook and a newspaper and walk down through the shantytown to my local café. Sitting in a coffee shop is considered a waste of time in the West, like watching daytime TV—a pursuit for the man who has no life at all. But after a few months in Morocco I came to realize that café life is the gateway into the clandestine world of Moroccan men. No woman with any self-respect would ever venture to a male-only café, a point that provides the clientele with unprecedented pleasure, and with security from their dominating wives.

To be valued as a member of masculine Moroccan society, a man is expected to put in his time sitting, thinking, talking, or doing nothing at all.

My friends came to know that on Friday afternoons I could be found at the same table and at the same seat in Café Mabrook, a ramshackle haunt perched at the end of the Corniche. As soon as word spread that I frequented a male-only café, my standing in society was raised immeasurably. Everyone, from my bank manager to the guardians and the plumber, seemed to regard me with genuine respect.

Café Mabrook was like a down-at-the-heel gentlemen's club. The walls were gray-black, and the air so smoky that if it were anywhere else there would have been a health warning nailed to the door. The chairs were all wobbly and broken, and the floor permanently concealed by a thick layer of cigarette ends. The only waiter was called Abdul-Latif. He was middle-aged, hunched over, and missing both his thumbs. The deformity made counting out the change all the more difficult. He didn't take orders, but instead slapped down a glass of syrupy black coffee and an ashtray to anyone and everyone who walked through the door.

From the first time I poked my head inside Café Mabrook, I was hooked. There was an irresistible charm, a faded grandeur. But to glimpse it, you had to look beyond what the eyes or the other senses showed. You had to rely on your imagination. Take a seat, inhale the nicotine smog, swill a mouthful of the pungent café noir, and pause...Allow the atmosphere to seep inside, and you found yourself connected to generations of Moroccan men who had sought salvation within the gray-black walls.

Most of the clients were henpecked local men, all hiding from their wives. Their faces bore the same pained expression, the look of men hunted every waking hour. Their wives were all clones of the same alpha female, beefy and fearless, the kind of woman who preyed on the weak. But, thankfully, the henpecked husbands had come to learn that they were safe from persecution in the no-man's-land of Café Mabrook.

Each Friday afternoon an assortment of downtrodden characters would make their way to my table and balance on a broken chair—retired professors and medical men, librarians, police officers, and postal clerks. Anyone who enters a Moroccan café knows that there's no such thing as respecting privacy.

Your presence is a signal that you are ready and willing and available to chat.

Over the months, I came to meet a cross section of Casablanca's male society, most of them wrapped in fraying jelabas, feet pressed into tapered yellow slippers called *baboush*. There was a sense of fraternity, a common bond reached through their communal fear—fear of the women in their lives.

Friday afternoons are a time when most of Casablanca's men are cleansed, at ease, and are ready to relax. They have washed thoroughly, prayed at the mosque, and gorged themselves on platters of couscous in their homes. When the feasting is over they are tossed out of the house by their wives, and ordered not to return until the sun has dipped well below the Atlantic surf. With no more than a few dirhams to spend, and no courage to ask for more, they go in search of coffee and conversation.

The henpecked husbands and I discussed all manner of subjects on Friday afternoons—from Al-Qaeda and the state of the Middle East to the subtle flavor of argan oil and the ancient code of honor that bonds all Arab men.

Each week, I learned a little more about Moroccan culture, and each week it seemed as if I was welcomed a little deeper into their fold.

Of all those who patronized Café Mabrook, the best informed

was a calm retired surgeon named Dr. Mehdi. He was slim, dark-skinned, and had a sharp jawline that ended with a patch of trimmed beard on the tip of his chin. He was a man adrift on an ocean of self-confidence, and was regarded as a kind of champion by the other henpecked husbands. From time to time he would clap his hands and order them all to stand up against their ferocious wives at home.

Dr. Mehdi once told me he was eighty-two. His hands were flecked with liver spots but were as steady as they had been fifty years before. "A good pair of hands," he would say, "can kill a man or can save his life."

One afternoon I told him about the storytellers I had seen as a child, crouching outside the city walls at Fès. He stared into his glass of café noir, narrowed his eyes, and said: "They are the heart of Morocco."

"But hasn't the tradition been lost?" I asked. "After all, Morocco's becoming so modern."

Dr. Mehdi cracked his knuckles once, then again. "You have to dig," he said. "If you want to find buried treasure, you must buy a spade."

"Is the treasure still there, though, under the ground?"

The doctor put the glass to his lips and took a sip. "You may not see them," he said, "but the stories are all around us. They are in our bones."

I was surprised, as I assumed the tradition of storytelling had been replaced by the tidal wave of Egyptian soap operas that has deluged most Arab lives. I must have looked disbelieving, because the old surgeon jabbed his index finger toward me.

"The stories make us what we are," he said. "They make us Moroccan." Dr. Mehdi drained his café noir. "The storytellers keep the flame of our culture alive," he said. "They teach us about our ancestors, and give our children the values they will need—a sense of honor and chivalry, and they teach what is right and what is wrong."

It was as if my father was sitting before me again, preaching to his children. Dr. Mehdi touched his fingertips together in thought. He closed his eyes for a moment, sucked in a chest full of second-hand smoke, and said: "The stories of Morocco are like a mirror. They reflect society. You can live here a hundred years and not understand what this country is about. But if you really want to know us, then you have to root out the raconteurs and listen to them. You see, it's they who guard the treasure. They can teach you but only if you are ready. To hear them, you must close your eyes and open up your heart."

chapter three

An Arab horse speeds fast.
The camel plods slowly, but it goes by day and night.
Saadi of Shiraz

Five days later I found myself standing in Jemaa al Fna, the vast central square in Marrakech whose name means "Place of Execution." The medina's labyrinth of narrow covered alleys stretched out behind in an endless honeycomb of riches. Every inch of it bustled with brass lamps, silks, and rugs woven in kaleidoscopic colors, spices and perfumes, sweetmeats and dried chameleons for use in spells. The shade of the medina was contrasted by the searing light in the square. Only the brave or the mad endured it, crouching low on their haunches, whispering, waiting. I noticed a group of *gnaoua*, the famous Saharan musicians, dressed in indigo jelabas, their caps trimmed with cowry shells. Next to them was sitting a traveling dentist with his tin of secondhand teeth. Beside him was a knot of medicine men, touting snake oil, ostrich eggs, and rows of slim brown mice tethered on twine.

I crossed the square, dodging the pools of melted tarmac, wondering how a city could take root and thrive in such a furnace. I thought of Osman's comment—that I was blind to the real Morocco. At that moment I caught sight of an elderly donkey being led into the middle of the square. Its muzzle was gray, and there was an unusual white blotch on its rump.

A hooded figure had tucked the reins under the arm of his dusty brown jelaba. The animal was goaded forward until left standing in a puddle of melted tar. Its hooves were sticky and black, its head low and cautious. The figure pressed a palm to the donkey's brow, urged it to stop. He threaded his fingers together, seemed to flex them, then, bending down, he strained to lift the animal onto his back.

A chorus of wild frenzied braying followed, echoing to all corners of the square.

As someone who lives in the center of a shantytown, I am not unused to the sound of donkeys. But the clamor of that creature held astride a man's shoulders was shrill enough to wake the dead. Within an instant a crowd had gathered—tourists and mendicants, orange-sellers, pickpockets, and day-trippers from the Atlas. I staggered over and pushed my way to the front. The donkey's eyes were bulging, the back of the man's jelaba stained with sweat.

"What's going on?"

"He's about to start," said a man.

"Start what?"

"The tale."

EACH NIGHT BEFORE they sleep, I read a bedtime story to Ariane and Timur. As I read, I glance up from the page and look into their eyes. I see the twinkle of wonder, the sense that magic is at work. Some of the stories I read were left to my two sisters and me by our father when he died, in a manuscript he titled with my demand—"Tell Me a Story." He had read the same tales to us as children, and had composed them from ancient sources in Arabia and Afghanistan. Since his death many of the stories have been published as illustrated books.

"We are a family of storytellers," he would whisper before we slept. "Don't forget it. We have this gift. Protect it and it will protect you."

In the dozens of books he wrote, my father presented to the West many hundreds of traditional teaching stories, just like the ones I read to my children now. Such tales were developed by the Sufis, a fraternity of mystics found across the Muslim world and beyond. If asked about it, they say that their knowledge existed long before the rise of Islam, and that it can be received by anyone who is ready to absorb it. Sufis use teaching stories as a way to package ideas and information, making them palatable to the mind. Like a peach, they believe that the delicious flesh of the fruit is necessary to allow the seed to be passed on, to take root, and to be nurtured.

WHEN I RETURNED from Marrakech, I found the guardians and the maid huddled outside the front door of the Caliph's House. They were chattering away anxiously, but fell silent as soon as they saw my old Jeep rumbling down the lane. The Bear was standing with his back to the door, his arms out wide. It was as if he was trying to cover something so that I didn't see. I got out and asked what was going on.

Osman looked at the ground and shook his head from side to side.

"Nothing, Monsieur Tahir," he said. "It's nothing at all."

The maid, Zohra, slapped her hands together and tightened her headscarf. She was an intimidating woman, the kind who filled ordinary henpecked Moroccan men with terrible fear. We would have let her go long before, but neither Rachana nor I had the courage to ask her to leave.

"He's lying," said Zohra coldly. "He's lying because he's a coward."

"He's frightened," said Hamza. "We are all frightened."

"Frightened of what?"

The Bear moved slowly to one side, revealing a curious series of geometric shapes and numbers, etched on the door in chalk.

"The children have been playing again," I said. "The bad boys out there do that stuff all the time."

Hamza wiped the sweat from his scalp with his hand. "This isn't the work of mischievous boys," he said.

"This is work of…"

"Of who?"

The guardians and the maid shut their mouths and swallowed hard.

"Who has scrawled all this?"

"A *sehura*," said Osman, "a sorceress."

EACH WEEK I would visit the grave of Hicham Harass, which lay on a south-facing hillside at the edge of Casablanca. I would sit on the grass beside his tombstone and listen to the sound of the gulls swooping in the distance, and I would tell Hicham everything that had happened in the seven days before.

I have had many friends in Morocco, but none have matched Hicham Harass in their outright wisdom. He lived in a shack behind the small whitewashed mosque in the shantytown, and collected postage stamps for a hobby. Every few days I would take a handful of used stamps to his shack and we would talk. We had the kind of conversations that only great friends can ever share.

They were touched with magic.

Hicham had a heart attack and was suddenly gone. His wife and their three-legged dog moved away from Casablanca, and I was left feeling empty inside. I would think about the stories Hicham must have heard in his youth, and I pictured him on his grandmother's knee, listening. Nothing was quite so important to him as the telling of a tale. He was a natural raconteur, a man who delighted in polished delivery. Once he told me that he felt like a puppeteer, that the power to manipulate an audience was in subtle movements, the pulling of the strings. His life was rooted in firm values, all transferred, he said, through the tales his grandmother told. Hicham Harass was the kind of man who liked to be one-on-one, the kind of man who scoffed at Egyptian TV.

One Sunday afternoon in the summer, I took Timur with me to sit by the grave. It was so hot that we were both sticky with sweat as we climbed the steep cemetery slope. Timur was moaning about the heat, begging to be carried. I glanced up to see how much farther we had to go. A man was kneeling at Hicham's grave. He was dressed in a fine black jelaba, the hood pulled down over his head, his hands cupped upward in prayer. I was surprised because I had never seen anyone there before. Hicham used to tell me that he had no friends, and he didn't know his real family, for they had given him away to a traveling scrap dealer as a child.

When the man had finished praying, he washed his hands over his face, turned, and greeted us, *"As salam wa alaikum,"* he said in a careful voice. "Peace be upon you."

We sat down together at the foot of the grave and listened to the gulls. Timur pleaded for me to take him swimming, but I ignored him. After a few minutes, the other visitor asked how I had come to know Hicham. I told him that we would meet each week and share conversations paid for in postage stamps.

"He was a very wise man," he said.

I agreed, and I asked him how he had known Hicham Harass, as I did not recognize him from the shantytown. The man wove his fingers together and pressed them to his lips in thought.

"I owe everything I am to him," he said.

He fell silent, and I was just about to coax an explanation from him, when he said: "Twenty years ago I used to be a drug addict. My life was all about *kif.* I would smoke all day, and every night I used to roam the streets searching for an open window. When I found one, I would crawl inside and run off with whatever I could carry away. I robbed rich homes and poor homes, and sold the loot to buy more and more *kif*."

"But you don't look like a drug addict," I said.

"I am not, and it's all because of the man whose body lies in this grave."

"So what happened?"

"Well, one night," said the man, "I stole a car and drove to El Jadida. I had overheard one thief telling another that there were rich pickings there. Once night had fallen, I found a dark residential street, and started looking for an open window. It wasn't long before I found one. I chose it because a chair had been left underneath. Looking back, it was almost as if the owner was inviting me inside."

The man paused for a moment, pushed up the sleeves of his jelaba, and said: "I climbed up as quietly as I could. There wasn't a sound inside. I switched on my flashlight and looked for something to steal. I couldn't see much, except for a large leather-bound album open on the table. It was filled with postage stamps. Usually I went for silver and gold, but the album looked valuable, so I put it in my bag. At that moment, a figure moved across the room. He was little more than a shadow. I ran to the window, but the figure got there first. He slammed it shut. I shouted out, threatening to break his neck. Then the man did something very unexpected. He welcomed me to his home, introduced himself as Hicham the son of Hussein, and said he had been waiting for me.

"I sat down, half-expecting him to raise the alarm, and we began to talk. He asked my name, and I told it. I am known as Ottoman. I told him about my addiction to *kif*, my need for easy money, and apologized for causing him any trouble. Instead of scolding me, Hicham listened quietly, served me mint tea, and offered me a bed for the night."

Again, Ottoman broke off. He leaned over, touched Timur's cheek, and kissed his hand.

"The next morning Hicham made me a breakfast worthy of a

king," he said. "In my mind I was ready for the police to burst in. But I was so touched by his generosity, that I was unable to take flight. I stayed in his home all day, and he sketched out a plan."

"What kind of a plan?"

"A plan to change the course of my life."

Ottoman went on to explain how Hicham had sent him to live with a trusted friend, who had weaned him off *kif*, and how he loaned him the money to open a tailor's shop. Every week the two men would meet and talk.

"Hicham would urge me to set my goals high," he said. "He gave me confidence, and would say that I was as capable as anyone else. 'To succeed,' he said, 'you must reach for the stars, and let your imagination find its own path.'"

I wondered aloud why I had not seen Ottoman before, either in the shantytown where Hicham lived or at the grave.

"My tailor's shop was successful," he said, "because Hicham charged me with energy every week. I worked fifteen hours a day, and soon I had five shops in Casablanca, Marrakech, and Fès. Three years later, I set up my first factory, making garments. And two years after that, I opened up plants in Thailand, then in countries across the Far East. Before I knew it, I was living outside Morocco most of the time."

Ottoman stood to his feet. He seemed disconsolate.

"One day I lost touch with Hicham," he said. "He vanished from his El Jadida home. I searched everywhere for him, but no luck."

"He was living in the shantytown near where we live," I said.

"I know that now," said Ottoman. "It pains me to think of him living in poverty like that when he lost his home. After all, he helped me become rich."

"How did he lose his home in El Jadida?"

Ottoman glanced down at the grave and replied, "I heard he'd given all his money so that a man he hardly knew could have heart surgery."

"Hicham was selfless," I said.

"You are right," said Ottoman. "He didn't care for worldly goods. Nothing at all."

"Nothing except his postage stamps."

SETTLING INTO A new country is like getting used to a pair of shoes. At first they pinch a little, but you like the way they look, so you carry on. The longer you have them, the more comfortable they become. Until one day without realizing it you reach a glorious plateau. Wearing those shoes is like wearing no shoes at all. The more scuffed they get, the more you love them, and the more you can't imagine life without them.

Our lives at Casablanca went through the same cycle. At first, the discomforts of the house, the trouble with the Jinns, the headless cats we found in the garden, and the slaughter of exorcism all took a toll. I used to think Rachana might walk out. She didn't appreciate the hardship in the same way that it appealed to me. But the months of anxiety brought us closer together. We were united in a desire for a new life. There was something so intoxicating about the Caliph's House that I never imagined giving up.

Now, after so many months, the idea of living anywhere else seems outrageous. I am at ease. I am content. But I am still confused. Most of all I am confused by Moroccan society.

On the surface life seems quite understandable, a blend of culture and tradition. My family is from the East and I have grown up in the West. The equation helps me to decipher the riddles of the Arab world. Yet there is still so much to understand, like the business with the sieve.

During the summer Zohra, our maid, overheard me complaining of how I am eaten alive by salesmen as I walk through Casablanca's vegetable market. Like most Moroccan women she is an expert on life and in the art of controlling men. And she is always ready to advise.

"Tsk! Tsk! Tsk!" she snapped. "Of course the salesmen trouble you. It's because they think you are a tourist."

"But there aren't any tourists in Casablanca."

"Well, they don't know that!"

"So what am I supposed to do?"

Zohra motioned something with her hands. It was round, about the size of a dinner plate. "You have to carry a sieve."

"*What?*"

"No tourist would ever be carrying a sieve," she said.

The Friday after I had met Ottoman at Hicham's grave, I strolled down to Café Mabrook for a little coffee and conversation. Dr. Mehdi wasn't yet in his place, but his great friend Hakim was sitting at my usual table. He greeted me and grinned as I took my seat. Hakim the ancient plumber was one of the most sensitive men one would ever be likely to meet. He had a way of making you feel needed when he spoke, as if the future of the world depended on you. He was Dr. Mehdi's best friend, but was happiest of all when the surgeon wasn't there. It meant he could talk about his favorite subject. Hakim had a fascination for black magic, a subject of which Dr. Mehdi vehemently disapproved.

On the first occasion we met, he explained under his breath how he had been born a girl, how his gender had been altered by a sorceress from the Middle Atlas.

"When was that?" I had asked.

The plumber had pulled a tap from his pocket, and used it to scratch the top of his head.

"Long ago," he said.

"*When?*"

"When you were a glint in your mother's eye."

Since we were alone, I asked him about the chalk writing the guardians had found scrawled over our front door. Hakim asked for a second cup of coffee. Then he screwed up his face until his eyes were no more than slits. A thumbless hand slammed down the coffee, and Hakim said, "It sounds as if there's a Jinn."

"That's quite impossible," I replied. "You see, we did have Jinns but we held an exorcism and slaughtered a goat. The exorcists drenched every room in blood and in milk. They certified it squeaky clean."

"When did the exorcism take place?"

"Six months ago."

Hakim screwed up his face again. "You will have to do it all again," he said.

I thought of the upheaval the exorcists had caused. They had wrecked the house and terrified us all in a kind of Moroccan rendition of *Ghostbusters*. Cleaning up after them had taken weeks, and Rachana was still far from forgiving me.

"Another exorcism is out of the question," I said nervously.

The plumber raised a finger. "There is another way," he declared. "It's unusual, but it works, I promise you, it works."

"What do I have to do?"

"You must get a pot of honey from the forest of Bouskoura and paint it on all your doors, inside and out."

ARIANE CAME HOME from school and said she had learned the story of Robin Hood. She had drawn a picture of the folk hero in Sherwood Forest, with butterflies all around. She asked me if he was real.

"What do you mean 'real'?"

"Did Robin Hood have a mommy and a daddy?"

"I suppose that he did," I said.

"What were their names?"

"Ariane, that's not important," I said. "You see, stories are not like the real world, they aren't held back by what we know is false or true. What's important is how a story makes you feel inside."

"Baba, do you mean you can lie?"

"It's not lying, it's more like being fluid, fluid with the facts."

Ariane squinted hard, pushed back her hair. "Can I call them Henry and Isabelle then?"

"Who?"

"Robin Hood's mommy and daddy."

"Yes, of course you can."

"Can I pretend they lived here in Casablanca?"

"Yes, I suppose you could do that, too."

"Baba?"

"Yes, Ariane?"

"Can I marry Robin Hood when I grow up?"

THE NEXT WEEK I drove out toward Bouskoura in my battered old Korean-made Jeep. I had always heard stories of the forest there, perched on the southern edge of town. It spread out east from the highway in a great mantle of green. Zohra said the place was bewitched, that the trees had once been soldiers loyal to a malicious emperor from down in the Sahara. Fearing that Morocco was about to be conquered by his legions, a good-natured Jinn had transformed the army into trees, she said. When I asked her about the honey, Zohra agreed it was good for spells, that it was especially useful in keeping bad spirits in their place. The guardians were equally pleased by the prescription. The prospect of having a fresh influx of Jinns at Dar Khalifa had given them new energy. I suspected it was because it allowed them to spend all their time plotting against the forces of darkness.

Once at the forest, I drove down a long track framed in fir trees, and came to a school where attack dogs were being trained. The trees were tight together, like soldiers on the march. The farther I went, the more I found myself slipping into Zohra's fantasy, into what she claimed continually was the real world.

I hurried on until the track came to an abrupt end. Sitting there on a homemade bench was a wizened man wearing a thin cotton jelaba. It was fluorescent green. The color was reflected in his face. I climbed out, greeted him, and asked if he knew where I might buy some honey. He pointed to a hut encircled by a screen of conifers.

"Watch out for the bees," he said.

The path to the hut was sprinkled with pinecones and looked like the one in *Little Red Riding Hood*. On both sides of it were oversized white beehives arranged in clusters of six. The air was alive with their residents. I walked very slowly, as I had once been taught by a Shuar tribesman in the Amazon. Bees only attack when they sense death. They move at lightning speed, and so if you move in slow motion, they assume you are just another tree swaying in the wind.

Once at the hut, I knocked.

The door opened inward, and the same man in fluorescent green was standing in its frame. He grinned a big toothy grin and welcomed me inside, as I tried to work out how he had got there without me seeing.

On the table was an assortment of used mineral water bottles and secondhand jars. They were filled with tawny brown honey. The man looked at me without blinking, his eyes burning into mine.

"It's a little bitter," he said.

I kept his gaze.

"It's not for eating," I replied.

The man nodded, almost as if I had delivered the right password. He murmured a price, and I selected five bottles. Fifteen minutes later, I was on the highway again, the engine grinding its way back to Casablanca.

It was getting dark. The streetlights had died decades before. I was concentrating on the darkness and road when, quite suddenly, the engine stopped. As any owner of a Korean Jeep knows, they can be temperamental at the best of times. I pulled over to the shoulder and pledged my love for the spirit of the car. Nothing. So I tried every trick that had ever worked. Still nothing. There can be few situations more fearful than breaking down on the highway leading to Casablanca in darkness. I have rarely felt quite so vulnerable or alone. I abandoned the vehicle and, after considerable difficulty, managed to hitchhike home, the honey clutched in my arms.

THAT NIGHT WHEN I closed my eyes, the black faded to a warm yellowy red. We were at a camel market near Guelmine, on the edge of the Sahara. My father wanted us to see camels. He said that to understand the desert you had to understand camels, and to understand camels you had to understand the people who kept them. Camels, Sahrawis, and sand were all interlinked, he said.

I didn't like camels much because they stank, and I hated the sand because it got between my toes and into the food. My father told me a story about a little boy who ran away into the desert and dreamt of becoming a fish. It was a strange tale with an even stranger ending.

We all laughed at it.

"Did you like the story, Tahir Jan?"

"Yes, Baba."

"Do you understand it?"

"Yes, I think so."

"Keep it with you. As the years pass, you will feel it change inside you."

"How will it change, Baba?"

"It will be in there, growing quietly. One day you will realize that it has done something very wonderful."

"What will it do, Baba?"

"It will bear fruit."

THE NEXT MORNING I decided to drain our bank account dry, and buy a brand-new Land Cruiser. I had never bought a new car before. It had always seemed an extravagance way beyond my bank balance. But an evening marooned on the highway changed my outlook on priorities.

At breakfast, Zohra had noticed me all dressed up, and asked where I was going.

"To buy a new car," I said bashfully.

"Tsk! Tsk! Tsk!" she barked. "If you go in a suit, they will double the price. Believe me. I speak the truth."

I went back upstairs and changed into a moth-eaten sweater and a torn pair of jeans. Then I made my way through the shantytown on foot, toward the road. As I waited to hail a little red taxi, I heard someone yelling my name. I looked round. It was Zohra. She was waving a sieve, and was running as fast as her bedroom slippers could carry her.

"You must take this!" she crowed. "Don't forget it, I told you before!"

I put the sieve in my bag and took a taxi to the largest Toyota dealership I could find. The guardians had caught wind of my plan to buy a new car, and had insisted that it be a Toyota. Korean Jeeps were for the dim-witted, they said in agreement, but Toyotas were for bold, fearless men.

At the dealership, I pulled out the sieve and toyed with it threateningly. When the salesman was ready for me, I held it up, told him I was not a tourist, and demanded a large discount.

"Monsieur," he said, straightening his tie, "tourists do not usually buy our vehicles. They tend to rent."

I strained to look aloof, inquired what models of Land Cruiser they had available.

"You will of course be requiring all the usual extras, Monsieur?"

He scribbled a figure on the corner of the brochure.

"No, no," I said, "I just want the basic model. No need for all that expensive stuff."

The Toyota man seemed concerned.

"No leather seats, no cruise control, turbo engine, air bags, or alloy wheels?" he choked in disbelief.

"No. None of that stuff. I just want to get from A to B without breaking down."

"But, Monsieur..."

"But what?"

"But, Monsieur, if you take only the basic model..."

"Yes?"

"How will anyone be impressed?"

chapter four

Kings rule men, wise men rule kings.

Abu el-Aswad

Back at Dar Khalifa, the guardians were hard at work painting the doors with honey. They had cajoled me into buying them new brushes and toiled with a dedication that was rarely present in their work. Rachana had gone out to meet a friend. When she came back, the house smelled like a summer meadow. She commented on the pleasing aroma and went upstairs to change. There was a pause of thirty seconds and then a loud piercing shriek. Hamza came scurrying down the stairs with a honey-coated brush. Rachana was close on his heels.

"What on earth is going on?" she demanded.

"It's for the Jinns," I said limply.

My wife glared at me. "You had an exorcism, for God's sake! Harmless animals were cut down in their prime, all in the name of the damn Jinns. Don't you remember—the house was rinsed in blood?!"

"I'm just keeping everyone happy," I said. "Got to keep the status quo."

Rachana rolled her eyes. "You believe in all this stuff, don't you?" she said.

"I try not to," I replied. "But it gets into your head."

THERE MAY BE no tourists in Casablanca, but the sieve had worked its magic all the same. After much persuasion, I was given a sizeable discount for the car, while stressing again and again that I was in no need of impressing anyone. The salesman had gritted his teeth, and said that no one in the Toyota dealership's history had ever ordered the basic model before. It was such a rare commodity that he had to order it specially from Japan.

When the car eventually arrived, I returned to the dealership, took the key from the salesman, and clambered aboard. The Land Cruiser was shiny silver, and seemed to run very well. I was very pleased with it until I arrived at the shantytown.

The Korean Jeep had always offered a cloak of invisibility, just as the butcher's car had done before it. But the sleek lines of the gleaming new Land Cruiser stuck out terribly. As I descended onto the track that leads down toward the Caliph's House, I squirmed into the plastic-covered seat. A hundred eyes were on me. I was deeply embarrassed at such an open display of wealth.

When I pulled into the garage at home, the guardians lined up and saluted. Then they thanked me.

"Why are you thanking me?" I asked angrily.

They seemed confused.

"For making us proud," said Hamza.

In the days that followed I begged them not to wash the car, as I wanted it to obtain the lived-in look that went with the neighborhood. But they refused. Each morning before I got up, they cleaned every wheel-nut, polished every inch of bodywork, until the vehicle gleamed like a Roman chariot. It was Rachana who explained the guardians' obsession with the new car.

"It's raised their standing in society," she said.

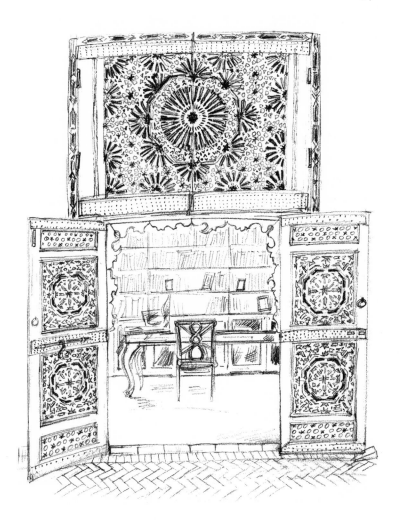

ONE MORNING I went into my library to find Ariane trying desperately to get a book from a shelf that was beyond her reach. She had placed a bucket on the floor and was using it as a step. But instead of turning the bucket over, and standing on its end, she had placed something across the mouth. It was a dull silver color, about an inch thick. It was my laptop. I rushed in, scooped her up, and reached the book she was hoping to get.

"If you had turned the bucket over," I said, "you wouldn't have needed to stand on my precious computer."

"But, Baba, it felt very strong," she said.

Ariane ran out into the garden with the book. I picked up my laptop, my eyes widening at my little daughter's inexperience. As I stood there, the laptop in my hands, I found myself remembering something my father had once said. We were sitting on the lawn, under the sprawling yew tree. I must have been eleven or twelve. It was summer. We were dressed in shirtsleeves. My father had said that a man had come to see him that morning from a long way away.

"Did he come from America, Baba?"

"No, farther than that."

"From Canada?"

"No, not from Canada. It doesn't really matter where he came from, Tahir Jan. What matters is that he wanted me to help him, but I couldn't."

"Why not?"

"Because he wasn't ready."

My father lay back on the grass. "In some ways the West is like a small child holding an encyclopedia," he said. "It has extraordinary potential in its hands, enormous energy, and the chance to learn from a thousand generations that came before. But it can't really benefit from the wisdom it holds until it's learned to read."

"Will the man who came to see you ever be ready?"

"I hope so."

"Did you talk to him, Baba?"

"A little bit. But he's not even ready for that."

"So what did you do?"

"I gave him a story, Tahir Jan," he said. "And I told him to study the story again and again until he didn't understand it anymore."

"Baba?"

"Yes, Tahir Jan?"

"Will you tell me the story you told the man who came today?"

My father sat forward, legs crossed. He cocked his head back for a moment, and said: "Once upon a time there was a Persian king. He spent all his time eating delicious things. As the years passed, he grew fatter and fatter, until he could hardly stand. He was forced to roll about on cushions. No one ever dared to speak out until, one morning, the king complained of bad circulation in his legs. The blood had drained away, leaving them blue.

"Doctor after doctor was called to the court. But the more doctors he saw, the more the monarch ate. And the more he ate, the fatter he became.

"One day, a very wise doctor arrived in the kingdom. He was immediately taken before the king and the royal condition was explained to him. The doctor said, 'Your Majesty, I can reduce your weight within forty days and then I can save your legs. If I do not, then you can execute me.' 'What special medicines do you require?' asked the king. The doctor held out a hand. 'Nothing, Your Majesty. I don't need anything at all.'

"The king suspected that the physician was going to have him for a fool. He asked his grand vizier what to do. 'Lock him up for forty days,' said the adviser. 'After that we will chop off his head.'

"A pair of royal guards stepped forward to haul the doctor to the dungeon. Before he was led away, the king asked him if there was anything he wished to say. 'Yes there is, Your Majesty.' '*Speak!*' shouted the king. 'I must tell you that I have seen the future, Your Magnificence. And I have seen that you will drop dead exactly forty days from now. And be assured that there is nothing you can do to prevent it.'

"The doctor was locked in the darkest, dampest cell. The days began to pass. As they did so, the king clambered off his cushions and walked up and down, fretting. He worried and worried, and worried and worried, until none of the courtiers could recognize him. He lost his appetite, didn't wash, and, through fretting, could hardly sleep.

"On the morning of the fortieth day, the doctor was dragged from the dungeon. He was taken before the king and ordered to explain himself.

" 'Your Majesty,' he said in a calm voice, 'forty days ago you were in danger of dropping dead from obesity. I could see your condition, but knew that an explanation would not lead to a cure. And so I caused you to endure forty days of anguish. Now that your weight has been so drastically reduced, we can administer the medicines that will restore your circulation and cure your illness.' "

PAINTING THE DOORS with honey may have protected us from dark forces, but it led to an infestation of biting flies. I have never seen anything like it. The flies swarmed in and coated the sticky surfaces so completely that they could be scraped off with the end of a spoon. Zohra forced the guardians to clean up the mess. She said that dealing with Jinns was men's work.

Rachana had stormed out of the house early, a stream of threats spewing behind her like a vapor trail. By the afternoon, I had been bitten from head to toe. Mustering all my strength, I ordered Osman to slay the flies and wipe away the honey.

He seemed disappointed.

"You cannot rush these things," he said.

Unable to stand it any longer, I went down to Café Mabrook, where I found Dr. Mehdi sitting in the sun reading *L'Economiste.* He was dressed in a thick maroon wool jelaba. It must have been eighty degrees in the shade. He shook my hand, pulled back the hood, and smirked.

The thumbless waiter, Abdul-Latif, dealt me an ashtray and a glass of café noir.

Dr. Mehdi removed his reading glasses and folded the newspaper neatly in half.

"I will tell you something," he said in a soft voice. "I am a Berber. You may not have noticed it, but we Berbers are very proud. This used to be our country before the Arabs invaded. We still laugh at them, and we say that they're lazy and weak. We are a much stronger race, you see. Why do you think that is?"

I shook my head. "I don't know."

"It's because of the Berber childhood," he said. "Until fifty years ago every newborn child in my village was left out on a hillside on the seventh night of its life. Those who survived were considered blessed, and were expected to live to maturity. Those who died were returned to God."

I sipped my coffee and asked myself what the surgeon was getting at. There was usually a point to any story he passed on. He stopped smirking and blinked.

"There's another thing we Berbers do in childhood," he said.

"Circumcision?"

"As well as circumcision."

The doctor combed a hand through his thin gray hair. "We search for the story in our heart," he said.

FOR SEVEN NIGHTS in a row I dreamed of the magic carpet.

In the late summer the evening air is still, punctuated by dogs barking at the shadows and the crazed braying of donkeys all around. Woken by the clamor outside, I would rise out of bed, and stroll down through the house and out onto the terrace. The gardens were filled with fruit bats and the sour fragrance of datura flowers, the trumpet of the devil.

The carpet would be waiting laid out on the lawn, its geometric designs highlighted by the moon. I would move over to it and

cautiously step aboard, my bare feet touching the silk. The carpet would ripple in anticipation, and gently rise heavenward.

We would fly out across the ocean into a realm of ink-black domes and minarets. The carpet would sense my wishes, swooping down through the narrow streets of the great sleeping city. There would be teahouses closing up for the night, thieves poised in the shadows, and soldiers from the royal guard patrolling the palace walls. The carpet would soar to the left, up over the parapets, until we were hovering outside the royal chambers. Beyond the apartments of the king was a tower, square walls of moss-covered stone. The door was bolted and locked, a pair of sentries standing guard. Inside sat the girl I had seen at the banquet, staring forlornly into the embers of a fire.

Zohra said the dream had a meaning, that her friend Sukayna

could interpret it for me. She lived behind a bakery in the nearby suburb of Hay Hassani, and had a skill, a knack at peering into the dark reaches of a troubled mind. After a week of insomnia, I should have gone for a reading, but all I could think of was Dr. Mehdi's comment, that Berbers search for the story in their heart.

ON THE FRIDAY morning, I came down to find the guardians scurrying about near the front door. A new crop of chalk symbols and numbers had appeared in the night. There were more than the first time. All of it was in white, except for a single word in pink chalk. It was Arabic, and read, *Mut,* "Death."

Osman, Hamza, and the Bear fell into line. They ordered me to buy more honey at once.

"That will not be happening," I said.

"But the Jinns have returned," Hamza insisted. "Do nothing about it, and there will be problems."

Zohra muscled in and echoed Hamza's words. "He is right," she said sternly. "Believe me. I speak the truth."

DR. MEHDI HAD the habit of rationing his conversation. He knew I would turn up the next Friday if he had left me with sufficient bait the week before. For seven days and nights I found myself thinking about his remark. There was something poetical about it, something irresistible. That afternoon I hurried through the shantytown and made my way to Café Mabrook. I nodded a greeting to the other regulars, took my usual place, and waited for a thumbless hand to slap down an ashtray and a glass of café noir.

After about an hour the surgeon entered. He was very calm, almost calculating. "You have been thinking about what I said, haven't you?"

"I can't help it," I said. "It's eating away at my mind."

A lengthy pause followed. Then the retired surgeon said: "The Berbers believe that when people are born, they are born with a story inside them, locked in their heart. It looks after them, protects them."

Dr. Mehdi flicked the hood of his jelaba down onto his neck and sipped his coffee. "Their task is to search for their story," he said, "to look for it in everything they do."

"But how do they know it's there?"

The doctor smiled. "You have never seen your lungs," he said, placing a hand on his chest, "but I am sure you will agree that they are in there."

The doctor broke off to greet his friend Hakim. As they exchanged salutations, I wondered what he was talking about. It sounded a little mad, but the more I thought of it, the more the idea grew on me. At the same time, it seemed like unbelievable luck— luck at ever hearing of such a secret Berber belief. It was as if I was being handed the idea on a plate, just like that, without having to dig away to find it.

"Some people find their story right away," Dr. Mehdi said, once Hakim had sat down. "Others search their entire lives and never find it."

"But how do you know when you have found it, your story, I mean?"

"It's a question of perception."

At that moment another regular of Friday afternoons came in, greeted us, and took his seat. He was an excitable giant named Hafad with a passion for clocks. We all enjoyed his company. The only problem was that he had often made clear his low opinion of anything Berber. No one dared mention the word in his presence. Eventually when he left, I coaxed the surgeon to continue.

"I've told you," he said, "you have to search and when you find the story it's as if your mind lights up. You know instantly when it's the right one. After that your whole life will be one of fulfillment."

"But there are so many stories in the world, what's the chance of finding the one connected to you?"

"That's the remarkable thing," said the surgeon. "If you search for it, the story will find you...by a kind of intuition."

"Have you found your story?" I asked.

The doctor glanced at the table. He seemed to blush. "Yes, when I was about ten years old," he said in little more than a whisper.

"Will you tell it to me?"

Dr. Mehdi scratched a fingernail to his ear. "There was once a group of three dervishes who decided to have a picnic," he said gently. "The weather was fine, and so they chose a place in the shade near the bank of a stream. As they laid out a tablecloth, with stones on the corners to keep it down should the breeze start up, a stray dog appeared. The animal sniffed around at the cloth. One of the dervishes said to the others, 'Should we tell it there is no food to spare?' 'No,' another said, 'because action is more powerful than words.' So they continued to weigh down the corners of the cloth. The dog suddenly ran off, yelping. The third dervish, who had learned the language of animals, interpreted the cries. 'He is saying, "If these humans have only stones for lunch, what hope is there of tasting real food?"'"

NOT LONG AFTER hearing Dr. Mehdi's story, I visited Marrakech once again. The heat was unbearable. There were almost no tourists, and the shopkeepers in the medina would flare into a rage at the slightest provocation. The combination of hot air and the drought in visitors was too much for them. I took advantage of their hard luck and bought a large framed mirror with silver octagons etched around the edge. Then, carrying the purchase on my head as a kind of sunshade, I wandered out to look for the storytellers.

Jemaa al Fna was all but deserted. The *gnaoua* musicians were sprawled in the shade, too hot to sing, their indigo robes drenched black with sweat. The traveling dentists with their tins of second-hand teeth had disappeared, as had the medicine men with their chameleons and their mice. Even the water-sellers in their wide-brimmed hats were too hot to work. I trudged into the middle of the square, the brown paper package on my head.

There wasn't a storyteller in sight.

As I made my way back toward the medina in search of refreshment, I noticed a tired old donkey standing outside a *fundouk,* a traditional caravanserai, the kind once used by traveling merchants. The donkey caught my eye because of the white blotch on its rump. It looked like the one the storyteller had lifted on his shoulders to draw a crowd. I went into the *fundouk* and asked who owned the animal. Someone pointed to a ladder. "Up there," he said. I put down the mirror and climbed the rungs until I was on the upper level, on a balcony overflowing with rotting bread and junk.

Again I asked about the donkey.

"It's mine," said a man wearing a cotton jelaba and a homemade turban. It was the storyteller. I introduced myself.

"And I am Khalil," he said, "the son of Khalilullah."

"May I sit for a moment?"

"*Marhaba,* welcome," he replied.

The storyteller's young son was sent scurrying down the ladder to buy a sprig of mint for tea. As I sat down on a cushion, I made out the sound of a hand rinsing a teapot behind, and caught the aroma of charcoal being fanned to life.

I told the master that I had heard one of his tales on my previous visit to Marrakech.

"My family have told stories here for nine generations, right on the same spot in Jemaa al Fna," he said. "Father, son, father, son. I continue the tradition because it is that—tradition. I promised my father that I would not let the tradition die. But I don't make enough money to live. So I teach history in a school each morning, and tell stories in the afternoons."

"What about the tourists? Don't they pay you?"

"No, no," said Khalil, "my tales are in Arabic and they don't understand. Anyway, tourists don't have time to listen. They just want to take photographs."

"Where are you from?"

"From the Atlas Mountains."

"Are you Berber?"

Khalil the storyteller untied his turban and rewound it tighter around his head. "Yes, we are Berber," he said.

I told him what Dr. Mehdi had said, that everyone is born with a story inside them, that it's their duty to discover what that story might be.

"That's the tradition," he replied. "But these days people are forgetting the traditions."

"I want to find my story," I said.

Khalil looked at me, his eyes mapping my face. He pursed his lips a fraction, revealing a row of sharp, square teeth. "You must take care," he said.

"Why?"

"Finding your story is harder than it sounds. It can be dangerous."

"Really?"

"Of course. To find your story you must trust. Trust the wrong person and the consequences could be bad."

I asked if he could tell me the tale that lived inside me. It would save me a lot of time and trouble, and he was a storyteller after all.

Khalil the son of Khalilullah smiled very softly. "I cannot do that," he said.

"Why not?"

"Because the search for your story will change you."

ZOHRA URGED ME night and day to have my dream interpreted by her friend Sukayna, who lived beyond the shantytown. She said there was probably poison inside me, a poison somehow connected to the chalk symbols on the door.

"How would I have been poisoned?"

"The Changed Ones."

"Jinns?"

"Tsk! Don't ever say that word!"

"It's a lot of old rubbish," I said.

The maid placed her right hand over her heart and spat out her favorite catchphrase: "Believe me, I speak the truth." Then, hoisting Timur onto her back, she climbed the stairs and was gone.

The mother to six daughters, Zohra longed for a son. She wouldn't admit it, but I used to get the feeling she felt the lack of male offspring to be a divine punishment. As soon as she arrived at the house each morning, she would scoop Timur up and feed him a packet of banana-flavored chewing gum. All day long she would carry him around, whispering stories into his ear, feeding him tid-bits, and boosting his ego with an endless stream of praise.

Zohra spent so much time doting on Timur that we were forced to hire a second maid to do the work she had been hired to do. Rachana and I were still far too fearful to fire her, and began to regard her wages as a kind of tax.

The new maid was young and innocent. She came recommended by Ariane's schoolteacher, and her name was Fatima. She smiled all the time, and was a whirlwind of activity. Unlike Zohra, who lived in the shantytown, Fatima moved in to Dar Khalifa. She rose before dawn and started with the windows, cleaning them until they shone like cut gems. After that, she would scrub the floors on her hands and knees, and then mop the ceilings and the doors.

From the first moment Fatima arrived, Zohra stalked her through the house, gripped with psychotic rage. She took to hiding behind the curtains and jumping out, and would sprinkle dirt from the garden on the sitting-room floor so that Fatima would have to start the mopping again.

The situation was not satisfactory, but it became far worse one morning in mid September. Fatima spent a few dirhams on buying Ariane and Timur candy floss. Their faces were lapping greedily at the spun sugar, when Zohra burst in. She looked at my son perched on Fatima's knee, scowled, and stormed out. Twenty minutes later she reemerged holding a huge bag of candy. She presented it to Timur and kissed him on the cheek.

The next day I found Timur playing with a miniature tinplate car. He said Fatima had given it to him. By lunchtime he had abandoned the car for a much larger die-cast vehicle from Zohra. By the afternoon he had discarded that, too, and was preoccupied with an expensive-looking spaceship with red and white stripes. When I approached him, he gloated, and lisped Fatima's name.

The next day, Timur was riding a brand-new tricycle through the house. On his arm was a silver-colored wristwatch, and over his shoulders there was a leather jacket, with his name embroidered across the back. I was going to stop the reckless overspending, but Rachana stopped me. She said that with time the pressure of economy would prevail.

AFTER MEETING KHALIL the storyteller, and talking it over with Dr. Mehdi, I decided to search for the story inside me. Both men assured me it was somewhere in there, deep in my heart, waiting to be heard. When I asked my Moroccan friends about searching for the tale inside, they all said it sounded crazy, that they had not heard of the tradition, that I was succumbing to the psychosis known to touch foreigners who live in Morocco too long.

The next Friday afternoon, I asked Dr. Mehdi if he had any tips.

"You want a shortcut, don't you?"

I nodded eagerly.

"Well, I will give you one. Although you are in Morocco," he said, "remember that you are in the East. That may be the Atlantic Ocean out there, but culturally it may as well be the South China Sea."

THE BATTLE BETWEEN Fatima and Zohra continued to rage. By the next week, Timur was drowning in gifts. Both the maids had blown their monthly salaries. As a way of protecting them, I forbade either of them from going near the little boy and took him out for a haircut.

In Morocco, henpecked husbands spend much of their time hiding from their wives in men-only cafés. The other place they go to escape are barbershops. In the West, if you turned up at a barber's and found the place full with unshaven men, it would likely mean you had a lengthy wait ahead. But in Morocco, a crowded barber's merely means its owner has a lot of friends. They come in and lounge about, watch TV, drink tea and smoke, flick through the grubby magazines, and, occasionally, they get their hair cut.

When I first moved to Casablanca, I began to frequent a small barbershop up the hill from the shantytown. I like to keep my hair very short, and nothing gives me more pleasure than getting it trimmed with the electric razor. The barber was a quiet man with pebble-gray eyes, strong hands, and an obsession for soccer. As he moved the scissors through a client's hair, or the cutthroat razor over a man's cheeks, he would be watching the game on TV from the corner of his eye.

On the day I took Timur for a haircut, the henpecked husbands were few and far between. So I chatted to the barber about razors and soccer, and asked him if he knew the story in his heart. He was about to say something, when a tall, suave man swept through the door, sat on the chair beside mine, and asked for a shave. He wore a pair of dark glasses across his slicked-back hair like a black plastic tiara.

While the barber sharpened the cutthroat razor on a worn-out leather strop, the man struck up a conversation. He asked me if I missed England.

"How do you know I've come from England?"

"Because you look too pale to be Moroccan and too content to be French," he said.

His cheeks were shaved once, then again, and were anointed with a home-brewed cologne that smelled of cherry blossom. He pressed a coin into the barber's hand, turned to the door, and said to me: "I will wait for you at the café opposite."

I had lived in Casablanca for three years, but was still unfamiliar with all the ins and outs of Moroccan society. I wondered if I should accept the invitation from a total stranger. Unable to resist, I crossed the street, holding Timur in my arms, and found the man, sipping a café noir topped up with milk. He said his name was Abdelmalik. We both sketched out the broad details of our lives—wives, children, hobbies, and work. He expressed his passion for Arab horses, and his lifelong dream of owning one.

It was a love we both shared.

We chatted about horses and life for an hour or more. Then Abdelmalik glanced at his watch.

"We will be friends," he said firmly, as he left.

From then on the suave, clean-shaven Moroccan swept into my life. He saw it as his duty to solve every one of my abundant problems, and stressed again and again that I could ask anything of him. As my friend, it was his duty to be there for me, he said. At first I found it strange that someone would make such a point about friendship, rather than just letting it develop naturally as we do.

We would meet every three or four days on the terrace of Café Lugano, near Casablanca's old ring road, where we always sat at the same table, just like I did on Fridays at Café Mabrook. At the other tables the same men were usually seated as well.

Abdelmalik, a man I hardly knew, became involved in all areas of my life. When I needed a lawyer, he found me a good one; when I wanted my watch repaired, he arranged it; and when I was in urgent need of a residency permit, he handled the paperwork. He never asked for money and always insisted that my friendship was ample payment for his efforts.

As the weeks passed, autumn arrived, and my suspicions grew that Abdelmalik was really out to line his pockets at my expense.

RACHANA'S CHILDHOOD IN India was framed in stories. Each night before she slept, her maid would reveal another installment from one of the great Hindu classics, the *Mahabharata,* the *Ramayana,* or the *Panchatantra.* The length and scope of those tales defies all imagination.

One evening in early October, Rachana heard me ranting on about the legacy of stories, about the responsibility, and the baton I felt so charged to pass on. She lit a candle and slumped down on the sofa beside me.

"You haven't got it, have you?" she said.

"Haven't got what?"

"You don't understand how it works."

"What?"

"The tradition of storytelling." Rachana stretched back. "Stories touch us even before we enter this world," she said, "and they continue until we go to the next world. They are in the dreams of an unborn baby, in the kindergarten and school, in news reports and movies, in novels, in conversations and nightmares. We tell each other stories all our waking hours, and when our mouths are silent, we are telling stories to ourselves in the secrecy of our minds. We can't help but tell stories, because they are a language in themselves."

"But, Rachu, things are changing," I said. "People are forgetting the tales they were weaned on as kids."

"How could you think that?" she replied sternly. "Look at Hollywood and Bollywood, they're the greatest storytelling machines of all time. The medium may be different, but the stories are the same. They're just being regurgitated in another form."

"But stories are dying out."

"They're not dying," Rachana said, "but morphing into something else. Look at them carefully. The essence is the same."

Just then, I remembered something my father once said to me. I think we were in Andalucia, rattling south toward Morocco. We had stopped to have a picnic in a field. It was the middle of nowhere. My sisters and I had found a clump of dandelions, and were blowing the fluff at each other. As we played, my father told us a story. We were only half-listening. When he had finished, I said to him: "Baba, what would happen if a country lost all its stories?"

My father became quite serious, touched a hand to his face. "That could never happen," he said.

"Why not?"

"Because stories are like a bath without a plug. You see, the bath has a tap that can never be turned off. So it will never empty. As the old water flows out, new water floods in. It's a balanced system. New stories are always pouring in, some come from near, others from far away."

I plucked the last dandelion and blew the seeds from the top.

"Do you understand what I mean?"

"Yes, Baba, I do."

"But there is something else, Tahir Jan, another kind of story. It's the most powerful of all."

"Is it like a bath, too?"

"No, it's not. You see, it's the kind of story that's lived in a place since the beginning of time. It's always there, buried in the culture, lying asleep. Most people don't even know it's there. But it is."

"When will it be told, Baba?"

"When the time is right."

"When?"

"When people are ready to understand it."

WINTER WAS STILL a long way off, but I didn't want to be caught out as we had been the year before. Our original architect had forgotten to put a chimney in the main sitting room, despite being begged time and again to do so. My dream was to spend the long winter evenings sitting in front of a crackling fire.

So I asked Hamza to find a mason.

He wandered out into the bidonville, and returned an hour later leading an old man. The man, who spoke no French, had a long graying beard and wire-rimmed spectacles, and was dressed in an indigo-blue laboratory coat.

Hamza pulled my ear to the side and whispered loudly, "Monsieur Tahir, he's a good man. He's *very* pious."

"Is that good?"

Hamza nodded. "Of course," he said. "In Morocco you can always trust a man with a long beard."

I asked the mason if he could construct the fireplace. He shot out a line of Arabic.

"What did he say?"

Hamza rocked back on his heels confidently. "He says that God has sent him the perfect plan."

"Oh?"

The old mason tapped his nose. "Two nostrils," he said.

"Nostrils?"

"God created us with two tubes instead of one. That's the key. We will use God's blueprint."

The next night, the mason arrived along with three bags of cement, a hammer, and his team of long-bearded Muslim brothers.

They tiptoed into the house and labored from dusk until dawn, only pausing to pray. The next night they toiled again, and then a third night. Hamza insisted their nocturnal shifts were because they studied the Qur'an during every hour of daylight.

After four nights the chimney was finished. I stacked up a pile of wood, interleaving it with newspaper and twigs. Then I touched a match to a corner of the paper. Within the blink of an eye, the fire was burning like a furnace in Hell. The mason moistened his upper lip.

"*Allahu Akbar!* God is great," he said.

THE NEXT NIGHT when I tucked Ariane in bed she asked me if the fairies would come while she was asleep.

"When your tooth has fallen out," I said. "That's when they'll come."

"Are you sure, Baba?"

I looked down, her chestnut eyes catching the light.

"Yes, I'm sure."

"Do you promise the fairies will come when my tooth has fallen out?"

"I promise," I said.

"How do you know?"

"Because . . ."

"Yes, Baba?"

"Because you believe in them."

"Is that what makes them real?"

"What?"

"Believing in them."

"Yes, Ariane, sometimes that's all it takes."

A POPULAR MOROCCAN proverb goes: "A man without friends is like a garden without flowers." It was told to me in the very first week

I arrived to live in Casablanca, by a plumber who had come to clean out the drains. He seemed distraught that I could have moved to a new home in a foreign land where I knew no one at all.

I told him that it felt liberating.

"I don't have to avoid people anymore," I said, jubilantly.

The plumber wiped a rag over the crown of his bald head. "But how will you live if you don't have friends?"

Looking back to that first week, I now understand what he meant. In our society friends are sometimes little more than people we go to the pub with so we aren't there alone. We have different expectations of them, or no expectations at all. If asked to do a favor, we usually inquire what it is before we accept. But in Morocco, friendship is still charged with codes of honor and loyalty, as it may once have been in the West. It is a bond between two people under which any favor, however great, may be asked.

After we had known each other for a month, Abdelmalik invited me to his apartment. It was small, cozy, and dominated by a low coffee table. On the table there were laid at least ten plates, each one piled with sticky cakes, biscuits, and buns. I asked how many other people had been invited.

"Just you," replied my host.

"But I can't eat this much," I said.

Abdelmalik grinned like a Cheshire cat. "You must try to eat it all," he replied.

A few days later, he called me and announced he had a surprise. An hour later, I found myself in the steam room of a hammam, a Turkish-style bath. For Moroccans, going to the hammam is a weekly ceremony, one of the communal pillars upon which the society is built. Abdelmalik taught me how to apply the aromatic *savon noir* and the ritual of *gommage*, scrubbing myself down until my body was as raw as meat on a butcher's block. In the scalding fog of the steam room, he presented me with an expensive wash-case packed with the items I would need. When I choked out thanks, embarrassed at the costly gift, he whispered: "No price is too great for a friend."

As time passed, I braced myself for Abdelmalik's ulterior motive. I felt sure he would eventually ask me for something big, some kind of payment for my side of our friendship. Then, one morning, after many coffee meetings, he leaned over the table at Café Lugano and said, "I have a favor to ask you."

I felt my stomach knot with selfishness. "Anything," I mumbled, bravely.

Abdelmalik edged closer and smiled very gently. "Would you allow me to buy you an Arab horse?" he said.

chapter five

A drowning man is not troubled by rain.

Persian proverb

From the first days we took up residence in the Caliph's House, I found myself in a world that lies parallel to our own. Morocco is a kingdom overlaid with a cloak of supernatural belief. A twilight zone, a fourth dimension, its spell touches every aspect of life, affecting everyone in the most unexpected ways.

At first you hardly realize it is there. But as you learn to observe, *really* observe, you see it—everywhere. The more you hear of it, the more you sense it all around. And the more you sense it, the more you begin to believe.

Believe, and what was impossible becomes possible, what at first was hidden becomes visible.

Like everyone else who has ever moved to Morocco, we were destined to brush with the supernatural, whether it be through the shantytown, the workforce, or through our new friends. But it was the purchase of Dar Khalifa itself that sucked us deep into the Moroccan underbelly. With its legions of supposed Jinns, the house was somehow directly connected to the kingdom's bedrock of supernatural belief.

The mere thought of spirits struck unimaginable fear into the hearts of the guardians, our maids, and all other believers who crossed the threshold. The Jinns may have plagued our lives through the belief and actions of those around us, but for me they became an almost tangible link to the world that created *A Thousand and One Nights.*

THAT COLLECTION OF stories is a byword for the exotic, the jackpot of cultural color. Even in our society, saturated by written information, the title is enough to raise the hairs on the back of our collective necks. It conjures emotion, a sense of treasure, opulence, magic, and the supernatural, a fantasy within the reach of mere mortals.

It is just over three centuries since the tales of the *Arabian Nights* arrived in western Europe. They appeared first in French, translated by Antoine Galland between 1704 and 1717, under the title *Les Mille et une nuits.* Galland had been cautious to censor passages he felt overly lewd for sensitive French tastes, as opposed to later translators, such as Burton, who delighted in the abounding obscenity. According to Robert Irwin, author of the remarkable *Arabian Nights: A Companion,* Galland's translation was based on a fourteenth- or fifteenth-century manuscript. There may have been an even earlier edition, perhaps dating to the tenth or even the ninth century. As Irwin suggests, Galland and subsequent translators added to the base manuscript, expanding it freely with as many new characters and tales as they could find.

Galland's translation was an overnight sensation. The salons of polite French society swooned with a richness in storytelling seldom seen on the Continent. The event can be compared to the blandness of European food prior to the sixteenth century, before spices arrived from the Orient. Granted the Latin and Greek classics were well-known, but they lacked the mystery, the dark layers and sublayers, of the East.

The public demand for the tales led to linguists, historians, and Orientalists struggling over translations of astonishing complexity and scope. During the eighteenth and nineteenth centuries, at least a dozen separate translations appeared in English, the most famous by Edward Lane, John Payne, Joseph Mardrus, and, of course, Richard Burton. They ranged from the concise to the encyclopedic, and were found in the libraries of royalty, of institutions, and of gentlemen.

From the moment they reached Europe, the *Arabian Nights* were surrounded by intrigue. The anonymity of the text led to incessant speculation. Some claimed that the stories were a kind of tonic that could boost flagging spirits. Others asserted that no man could ever read the entire collection without dropping dead from the feat. That of course was hyperbole. Translators, editors, and printers, as well as scores of readers, read them from cover to cover and lived to tell the tale.

The *Arabian Nights* are arranged with stories within stories. One character tells a tale about a character who recounts a tale, about another telling a third tale. The structure leads to multiple layers, extraordinary depth, and frequent confusion.

The premise for the collection is that a fictional king, called Shahriyar, discovers that his wife is having an affair with a servant. Enraged, he has her executed. So as not to be betrayed again, he marries a virgin each night and sleeps with her, before having her beheaded at sunrise. The arrangement goes on for some time, brides' heads rolling, until the daughter of the grand vizier, Sherherazade, begs her father to allow her to marry the king. With great reluctance, he agrees. Unlike the other victims, she has no intention of meeting the executioner or his sword.

She has a plan.

Sherherazade is wedded to King Shahriyar, and taken to his quarters. Before they sleep, she begins a tale that cannot be finished on a single night. The king allows her to live an extra day so that her tale may be completed. The next evening, she begins a tale inset, "framed," within the first. Each night that follows, the tale is left unfinished, or it links on to another. The king has no choice but to allow his bride to live another day, so that she might complete her story.

A thousand and one nights pass.

During that time, Sherherazade reveals the greatest single repertoire of tales ever told. And in the same span of time, she bears her husband three sons, calms his rage, and remains as his queen.

Throughout the eighteenth and nineteenth centuries, Western literature was influenced heavily by the *Arabian Nights*, as were the arts. Oriental themes were thrown into vogue. Paintings of scantily clad nymphs reclining in harems became popular, as were images of mysterious domed palaces and scenes of Arabian courts, bedecked in jewels and in gold. The effect of the stories was so profound that it touched everything from costume to furniture, from wallpaper to architecture.

The legacy continues to be seen to this day. Anyone unwilling to believe it need only travel to Brighton on the south coast of England and look upon the Prince Regent's Eastern aberration, the Royal Pavilion.

My friend Abdelmalik had seemed cheerless when I declined his offer of an Arab stallion. He said that by accepting, I would be honoring not only him but every male member of his family that had ever lived. The next week, when we were sitting together at Lugano's, the conversation turned from horses to stories once again.

Abdelmalik drew a horizontal line in the air with his finger. "Here in Morocco, we live on a tightrope," he said. "It's because of our belief. We know that God is there for us, and because He is there we hope He will send angels to catch us if we fall."

He slapped the table with his hand. "If the angels do not come," he said, "it's because He wants us to hit the ground."

The waiter distributed fresh glasses of café noir. When he had gone, Abdelmalik continued.

"The stories reflect our lives," he said. "The people in them walk a fine line between prosperity and disaster. That's the way it's always been, and that's what makes us who we are. In a single life a man can know wealth, poverty, thirst, and hunger, as well as satisfaction. You may describe our lives as being like a roller coaster, up and down. We would say that they are full, that they are rich even though we may be poor."

I asked him about Jinns.

"They're as real to me and every other man in this café as this glass of coffee," he said. "I may not be able to see them, but I know they are right here beside me."

"How do you know that, though?"

"Can you see clean air?"

"No."

"But, would you doubt its existence?"

I asked if he had ever searched for the story in his heart. He pushed his sunglasses up onto his head and grinned.

"You have been talking to a Berber," he said.

"Do you know the tradition?"

"Of course."

"If I wanted to find out my story, where would I look first?"

"You could search near a shrine," he said. "But you can't start just like that."

"Why not?"

"You must prepare yourself first."

"How would I do that?"

"By changing the way you see."

Abdelmalik explained that I would have to learn to observe with untainted senses again, like a child. "An athlete doesn't start running until he's warmed up," he said. "In the same way, you have to ready your mind if you want it to work for you. It's a point that has been known in the East for thousands of years, but something you're still ignorant of in the West."

"How do I ready my mind?"

"You must appreciate without prejudice," said Abdelmalik. "Only then will you be ready to receive."

THE NEXT DAY I was reading in the large garden courtyard, glancing from time to time at the tortoises meandering through the undergrowth. The sun was blazing gold against a cobalt sky, and I was thankful for the peace. Out of the corner of one eye I saw a shadow approaching fitfully, and heard feet shuffling over the rough terracotta path. I looked up and spotted Hamza edging toward me, his favored woolly hat stretched nervously between his hands.

"Monsieur Tahir, you must forgive me," he said.

"Forgive you for what, Hamza?"

The guardian didn't reply at first. He stood there, chewing his lower lip.

"Hamza, what is it?"

"I am going to leave you and find another work," he said.

"But, Hamza . . . you have worked here for twenty years."

"Yes, Monsieur Tahir, twenty years."

"What is the problem? I'm sure we can solve it."

Hamza lowered the lids over his eyes and swung his head from side to side in an arc. "It is the shame," he said.

FROM THE OUTSET, it seemed that the *Arabian Nights* had something for everyone. Early on, a shrewd publisher realized that if the language was simplified and the sexual innuendo toned down, the books would appeal to children. The attraction for younger readers was so widespread that our society tends to forget the collection has strong adult content and was designed very much as an entertainment to be kept far from children. Some translators, like Burton, high-lighted the mature content. During decades of Victorian repression, he relied on the surfeit of innuendo and the outright lewdness, contained within the collection, to reach a vast swathe of sophisticated society eager for such raunchy material.

One of the reasons Burton released his edition by private subscription was to avoid censorship laws that hammered books offered for public sale. The so-called Society for the Suppression of Vice hunted authors contravening the strict moral code, threatening them with hard labor. Publishers who released their work were fined or closed down, as were the printers who actually manufactured the books. While Burton toiled at the translation, word of its licentious nature reached the ears of the censorship squad. His wife, Isabel, wrote to the printer saying she thought their London apartment was being watched. The printing firm, Waterlow's, feared being hit with the Obscenity Publications Act, and pressured Burton to sign a contract assuming all responsibility for his text.

In a further safeguard at avoiding prosecution for pornography, Burton announced the arrival of his forthcoming series with a clarification, stressing that the volumes were reserved for academia alone: "It is printed by myself for the benefit of Orientalists and Anthropologists," he wrote, "and nothing could be more repugnant to me than the idea of a book of the kind being published or being put into the hands of any publisher."

AFTER HEARING ABDELMALIK'S words, I tried to do as I had been forced as a child, and look beyond what my senses revealed. I went down to Casablanca's old town, a place charged with a full spectrum of life. It was Friday morning, and the streets were packed with severe-looking housewives laden with shopping. There were street hawkers, too, touting the usual range of pressed flowers, puppies, and Shanghai bric-a-brac.

In the middle of the bustle I found an impressively dilapidated men-only café. I strode in, ordered a coffee, and sat down near the window. The room was curved like the shell of a snail, a counter running through it in an arch. Behind it, a man in maroon and black was steaming yesterday's croissants on a 1930s espresso machine. At each table sat the regulars cloaked in their jelabas, smoking black tobacco, staring into space.

When the waiter had deposited the café noir along with five sugar cubes in a twist of newspaper, I took out a wad of cotton wool. Then I shut my eyes, shoved the cotton in my ears and up my nostrils, and closed my mouth and hands. It was as if I had been transported back a generation.

I struggled to absorb the café through a kind of crude osmosis.

Close your senses and the imagination comes alive. It's inside us all, dulled by endless television reruns and by a society that reins in fantasy as something not to be trusted, something to be purged. But it's in there, deep inside, a spark waiting to set a touch-paper alight.

As I sat in the café, I felt my back well with energy. It was as if there were fireworks shooting down my spine. My eyes burst alive with brilliant colors—vibrant reds and shocking blues. My tongue tingled with zest, and my nose sensed the fragrance of a thousand jungle flowers.

It was raw imagination.

FOR THREE DAYS the guardians kept to themselves. Osman and the Bear climbed onto the roof and pretended they were sealing it with tar. I called up, pleading for them to come down and explain Hamza's decision to leave. Eventually, I cornered Osman behind the stables, where he was sprinkling grains of rat poison along a wall.

"Hamza has left and will not come back," he said. "There is nothing you can do to change his mind."

"But why? I don't understand. He's been here for decades."

"Monsieur Tahir," said Osman, straightening his back. "It is the shame...that is why."

THE NEXT DAY, I met Dr. Mehdi at our usual table at Café Mabrook. He was wearing his pajamas under a light gray raincoat. His brow was glistening with sweat and he looked much paler than usual.

I asked if he was all right.

"For three days and three nights I have had a terrible fever," he said. "Only this morning when I woke up, I felt a little better, although I'm rather weak. During the fever, I had dreadful frantic dreams—savage tribes slaughtering each other, monsters, ghouls, and Jinns. I didn't know how to get away from it all. And the harder I tried to escape, the deeper I became trapped in the nightmare."

Dr. Mehdi paused, and wiped his wrist across his face. "I should be in bed now," he said. "My wife was screaming at me to stay home, but I had to come to tell you..."

"To tell me what?"

The surgeon cracked his knuckles one at a time. "Well," he said softly, "when I was gripped by fever, I dreamed that I was a prisoner in a cage in a palace garden. Not far from my cage there was a magnificent fountain, and next to that a banquet table piled with platters of couscous, dates, and fruit. But the mirage was out of reach. I was bound in the cage, trapped like a wild animal. All over the floor were human bones, those of other prisoners who had met the fate I was hoping to avoid."

"Were you alone?"

Dr. Mehdi looked me in the eye. He was normally blasé almost to the point of irritation. But the fever had rattled him.

"I was alone, yes," he said. "All except for a tiny bird. It was a *hud-hud*, a hoopoe. Although it could fly in and out through the bars, it chose to stay with me. And it's because of the bird that I pulled myself out of bed and came to find you here."

I didn't understand. "What have I got to do with a bird you dreamed about?"

"The bird told me a story," said the doctor, "and it asked me to tell the story to *you*."

We sat in silence for the next minute or two. The old surgeon mopped the sweat from his head.

"What was the story?" I asked.

Again, Dr. Mehdi looked over at me hard. He only spoke when he saw my eyes locked in on his.

"It told me the story of the Indian bird," he said.

WHEN YOU HIRE a Moroccan maid, you imagine she will cook, clean, and generally help to run the house. You believe this because at the first meeting she paints a vision of tremendous comfort—the clothes washed and expertly ironed, the house spic-and-span, delicious meals bubbling away on the stove. If you're lucky, there's a honeymoon which lasts a week or ten days. After that she settles into her role, and the true character burgeons forth.

Every day I was savaged by Zohra's poisonous tongue. She barked at me for buying such cheap tea glasses. "How can you serve your guests in these?" she snarled. "You should be ashamed!" Then she roared at me for tiptoeing past Timur's room too loudly. And after that, I was castigated for pretending not to be at home when my bank manager telephoned.

At times, Zohra's behavior was so challenging that I found myself wondering how her husband coped. I asked her about him. She looked at me askance.

"He's a lazy man, my husband," she said. "I was senseless to have married him. But I was young and foolish."

"Does he have a job?"

"No. He's far too lazy for work. He leaves the house as soon as he wakes up and goes to a café near the Corniche. He sits there all day, drinking coffee, smoking, chatting to his friends. Believe me, I speak the truth."

"Which café is it he goes to?" I asked.

"I told you, it's near the Corniche."

"Is it called Café Mabrook?"

Zohra's face froze.

"That's it," she said.

DR. MEHDI HARDLY had to tell me the story of the Indian bird. It was one of my father's favorites, and was told and retold by him so often that I can close my eyes and picture him cupped in his great leather chair, poised to begin.

"Once upon a time, when camels had no hump, and when birds flew upside down, there was a merchant living in the great city of Samarkand. The merchant had no wife or children, but he had a small hoopoe, which he loved more than the sky and earth.

"One day he decided to go to India for business. Remembering that the hoopoe itself came from India, he went and asked it if there was anything it wanted him to bring. The bird asked for its freedom, but the merchant declined.

" 'I love you far too much to set you free,' the creature's master said.

" 'Well, then, please go to the forest for me,' said the hoopoe, 'and shout out to all the birds who live there that I am alive and well, but held captive in a cage.'

"The merchant did as the bird had asked. No sooner had he announced the bird's fate, than a wild hoopoe tumbled from its perch on a high-up branch, and fell dead at his feet.

"Distressed that he had indirectly caused the death of one of his hoopoe's relatives, the merchant returned home and related what had happened to his own bird. No sooner had he delivered the sad news, than his hoopoe collapsed on the floor of its cage.

"Fearing it was dead, the merchant opened the cage and placed the limp bird on the windowsill. As soon as his hand pulled away, the hoopoe flew out the window and was never seen again."

DESPITE MY VISITING his home in the shantytown to plead, Hamza refused to return to work at Dar Khalifa. I couldn't understand what had motivated him to leave. In a country of severe unemployment, quitting a job when you have a wife, six children, and an extended family network to support is tantamount to committing financial suicide.

Hamza's wife swept an arm across the low table in their two-room shack, pushing the tangle of knitting onto the floor. She flustered about preparing tea and making me feel welcome.

"Have I upset you in some way?" I asked.

The guardian glanced down at his hands. "No, no, Monsieur Tahir, it is nothing you have done."

"Then what is it?"

Again, Hamza looked down. His eyes seemed to well with tears. "I have cheated you," he said.

OTTOMAN, THE THIEF turned businessman, telephoned me the next week. He said there was an idea he needed to discuss very urgently indeed. I asked him if he knew Café Mabrook.

"I have spent half my life there," he said.

An hour later I was settled into my usual seat with a cup of café noir steaming before me. Ottoman had promised not to be late, but Moroccan society is not known for punctuality. At the next table was sitting an unshaven middle-aged man. He had no neck, thick fingers, and a long vertical scar running from his left eye down to his chin. The ashtray beside his glass of coffee was overflowing, suggesting he had been glued to the chair since early morning. I had seen the man there before. Now that I came to think of it, he was always in position. I leaned over and asked if he had heard of a woman called Zohra.

The man jolted backward, as if jabbed with a cattle prod. His face seemed to contort in pain.

"She works at our home," I said.

"Oh, Monsieur," said the man faintly, "I am so sorry. Believe me."

At that moment, Ottoman swept in. He was wearing a tweed business suit, and over it a gabardine raincoat, a neatly furled umbrella held like a cane in one hand.

Abdul-Latif, the thumbless waiter, presented him with an ashtray and a café noir. We exchanged pleasantries.

"*Alhamdullillah,* thanks be to God, I am well," he said.

I sipped my coffee and waited for him to explain his urgent need to meet.

Ottoman stared out at the Atlantic. He watched the waves rolling shoreward, tugged off his glasses, and rubbed the bridge of his nose.

"Since we met at Hicham's grave," he said, "I have been thinking about our old friend, and what was important to him."

"His postage stamps were important," I said.

"Of course they were," said Ottoman, smiling. "But there was something else as well."

"Conversation," I said.

"*Exactly!* Hicham Harass lived to talk. He was a raconteur."

"He was a storyteller," I said.

Hicham could have lounged in his favorite chair and told stories from dawn until dusk. He was consoled by the sound of words, by the idea that his conversation and his stories changed people, expunged immorality.

"I want people to remember Hicham's legacy," Ottoman said.

"And I want for them to absorb the values through stories just as Hicham did as a child on his grandmother's knee."

"But these days everyone's hooked on the Egyptian soaps," I said. "It's the only storyteller in their lives."

Ottoman leaned forward and touched my knee with his hand. "But we can change it, reverse it," he whispered. "We can shake up the system and get the storytellers talking again."

AT DAR KHALIFA, I found Osman pacing up and down anxiously. Beside him was a tall, rather slim man dressed in a memorable shade of pea green. He was wearing aviator sunglasses and looked as if he had stepped off a Bollywood set.

"This is my brother, Layachi," said Osman nervously. "He's thirty-one and he needs a job."

"Ah," I said.

"Hamza has gone, and so now there is a vacancy," said Osman.

"But I am still hoping that Hamza will come back."

"No, no, Monsieur Tahir," he replied fast. "He won't. It's because of his shame."

I had still not gotten to the bottom of Hamza's reasoning, and was still sure the matter could be settled.

"Why don't we use Layachi until Hamza comes back?"

It sounded like a good idea. I agreed, and Layachi was led out into the garden.

ZOHRA CRUSHED FATIMA in the battle for Timur's affection. My little son went around the house cuddled on her back. As soon as he saw Fatima he would hiss like a snake moving through long grass. When I told him it was not nice to hiss, he said that Zohra had taught him to do it. He pulled out a packet of chewing gum, tossed all the nuggets into his mouth, and swallowed hard.

In the afternoon, I found Zohra in the courtyard outside the kitchen. It had been there that the exorcists had slaughtered the goat. They had insisted it was the spiritual center of the house. I was just about to reprimand the maid for giving Timur chewing gum again, when she pointed to the floor.

Spread out in a crazed tapestry of lines was a pattern drawn in chalk.

"Did Ariane do that?" I asked.

The maid narrowed her eyes and frowned. "This is not the work of a child," she said, "it is the work of the..."

"The Jinns?"

The maid froze in fear. Then she spun round once, kissed her hand, touched the nearest wall, and mumbled a prayer. "Never say that word again," she hissed.

ONE NIGHT IN late October I dreamed of myself sitting in the shade of a fabulous courtyard, with peacocks all around. There was the sound of water issuing from an exquisite mosaic fountain, and the scent of azaleas perfuming the evening air. At one end of the *riad* was a pavilion and terrace on which a string quartet was about to perform. At the other, beyond peacocks and fountains, were chairs for the audience. Shielding my eyes from the sun, I looked up and realized that I was in fact in our home at Dar Khalifa, in a part of the house that did not yet exist.

Next day I could think of nothing but the dream. I played it back again and came to understand that the magical peacock-filled courtyard had been built at the far end of the house over the tennis court. As we didn't play tennis, I asked one of the guardians to hurry out and to bring me the mason who had built the chimney.

At ten o'clock that evening the mason arrived in his indigo laboratory coat. He stooped forward, took my right hand in his, and muttered a verse from the Qur'an.

"God has brought us back together," he said.

I told him about my dream, about the peacocks and the music pavilion. He pulled off his spectacles and combed a hand through his gray beard. His French was too limited to grasp the scope of my grand new courtyard.

So I called out into the darkness.

One of the guardians hurried in. It was Osman's brother, Layachi, wearing his pea-green suit. I asked him to translate my words into Arabic. As soon as Layachi caught sight of the mason, he seemed to bristle with rage.

I spat out the details—a large new courtyard with a single cavernous room at each end and gardens in the middle. Layachi began to translate, but in the middle he clammed up. There was something wrong. He began to tremble, the side of his face shaking. I asked him what the matter was. He didn't answer me. Before I knew it he was yelling at the mason, who had slunk into a chair, cowering as if a giant predator was bearing down on him. I shouted out that the mason was our friend, that he was a guest to be welcomed. The guardian began flailing his arms like scimitars, screaming every curse he knew.

Time proceeded in slow motion.

Layachi sucked his fingers into his mouth and jiggled them about. I shifted position to get a better view, squinting to make sense of it all. With some care the guardian removed an upper set of teeth, and then a bottom set. Then, as I watched in horror, he attacked the old mason with them, slicing and cutting, until he had drawn blood.

chapter six

A hand and a foot do not clap together.

Arab proverb

For a week after the episode with the mason and the teeth, Rachana, the children, and I slept in the same bed.

I propped a chair against our bedroom door and kept an Indian dagger under my pillow. I was a coward for not dismissing Layachi right away, as he was quite obviously deranged. I didn't know how to do it, and feared he would pull out his dentures and strike again—at us.

On the eighth day I plucked up courage and found Osman raking leaves. "I have to let your brother go," I said diplomatically. "He attacked the mason for no reason at all. And I just don't feel safe with him around. None of us do."

Osman leaned his weight on the rake, wiped a hand over his chin. "Since my brother Layachi was a small child," he said, "he's been crazy. He's a maniac. Everyone knows it. He should be locked up."

"But why didn't you tell me this at the start? You brought him to me, exclaiming how trustworthy he was!"

The guardian bit his top lip. "In our country," he said restlessly, "blood is thick, and where there is thick blood there is duty."

T HE DAYS WERE getting shorter, and I could smell winter approaching from the north. In Morocco, you know the cool months are drawing near because the streets fill with carts piled high with oranges. The fruit are slightly tart at first and each week they become a little sweeter.

Zohra began to spend her time hounding me through Dar Khalifa, ordering me to seek help from her sorceress friend. The last thing I wanted was to follow the maid's suggestion, as doing so would have increased the power she imagined she held over me. But at the same time, I felt I had to talk to someone about the cryptic chalk symbols on the doors, as well as about my recurring magic-carpet dream.

Then Ottoman called me again. Although I knew of his past, and a little of his business success, I had very little idea about his private life. I didn't even know if he was married. He was the kind of man whose personality gave off a scent, warding one away from asking certain questions.

We met at a café near his home in a fashionable suburb of Casablanca. There were the usual assortment of unshaven men in long, billowing jelabas. But the café was very different for two reasons. The first was that the coffee was delicious. I had grown used to slurping down the ubiquitous café noir, a beverage the taste buds can never quite accept. The second reason that made the café different was that there were women, plenty of them. And they were not the typical range of ruthless crones one found elsewhere, but skimpily dressed blondes, pouting mouths heavy with lipstick.

Even more unusual was that many of them were smoking.

Ottoman outlined his idea: "We start small," he said. "First we'll find a storyteller and bring him to the bidonville where Hicham Harass lived. I will pay his wages, and he will tell stories day and night, rekindling the culture that's in danger of being lost."

I nodded, made enthusiastic sounds.

"Gradually, we will hire other storytellers," Ottoman went on. "Before you know it, there will be dozens of them, in cafés all over Morocco. It'll be like the old times."

Ottoman's eyes lit up as if he was peering to make out the detail of a mirage. "We would not need to stop there," he said. "We could have storytellers in railway stations, at bus stops, in markets, and even in offices!"

By this point, Ottoman, who had until then struck me as a soft-spoken man, was ranting.

"Who will pay for all the storytellers?" I asked.

"Sponsorship," he replied. "Companies will sponsor them. On television you have commercial breaks, so our storytellers could promote products as well."

"So they would be traveling salesmen?"

Ottoman frowned. "No, no, not at all," he said. "Not salesmen, but representatives of the big brands. Coca-Cola, Pepsi, McDonald's... imagine it!"

My problem in life is that I'm a victim. I get dragged into schemes and find myself tangled up, unable ever to break free. I should have shaken Ottoman firmly by the hand, thanked him for the coffee, and fled. But instead, I flattered his ego and his creativity.

Then I offered to help.

SIX DAYS LATER I saw a man sitting in Jemaa al Fna, the vast central square of Marrakech. He was bald, with a long tatty beard and a single silver earring reflecting the light. I knew he wasn't a Moroccan because of the look in his eye.

He looked as if he had seen a miracle.

I had headed south to begin the search for the story in my heart, and to find the first storyteller for Ottoman's grand plan. Marrakech was the obvious place to start.

The foreigner struck up a conversation. He was a German called

Casper. He said that he had traveled for sixteen years, that almost every square inch of the world had passed beneath his feet. Sapphire eyes wide with wonder, hands out, fingers splayed, he explained that every minute until then had been preparation—the preparation for Jemaa al Fna, the "Place of Execution."

"This *is* the world," he said in a soft Bavarian voice.

I asked him what he meant. He smiled. "You don't feel it?"

I didn't reply.

"You don't feel it?" he said again.

"What? Feel what?"

"The humanity," he said.

Casper stood and staggered away, mumbling something about a drink of cold water. Then he was gone. I stood there, gazing out at the square's stew of human life—snake handlers and fortune-tellers, healers and madmen, door-to-door dentists, witches, water-sellers, and a single blind man waiting for a coin to be pressed onto his palm. Casper from Bavaria was right. There is perhaps no spot on earth so alive, so utterly human, as Jemaa al Fna.

Like almost everyone else who has ever been there, I have tried to understand Marrakech. I have sat in Café Agana, my favorite haunt overlooking the square, and I have watched, listened, and wondered. Is it Africa? Is it Morocco? Or is it a strange kind of paradise, a paradise for the senses?

The answer is that Marrakech is all of these things, and it is a great deal more.

I SCOURED THE square for Khalil the son of Khalilullah, the story-teller I had met a few weeks before. He was nowhere to be seen, nor were there any other storytellers.

When I quizzed the row of orange juice–sellers about this, they said most of them had part-time jobs because storytelling didn't pay.

"Why would you pay to listen to *them*," said one of the juice-

sellers, "when you could be at home or in a café watching television for free?"

With the light too bright for any but a Marrakchi's eyes, I slipped into the labyrinth of the medina, which spreads out behind the square in a vast cornucopia of life. Cool vaulted stone, courtyards latticed with bamboo staves, casting zebra stripes across the merchants and their stalls. Marrakech's medina is an emporium abundant with wares—mountains of turmeric, paprika, salted almonds and dates, yellow leather slippers laid out in rows, ostrich eggs and incense, chameleons in tattered wire cages, and beef tenderloins nestled on fragrant beds of mint.

Roam the narrow passages and you are cast back in time.

Marrakech may be prosperous these days, bolstered by tourist wealth, but the medina is still intact, vibrant, raging with life. There are Chinese plastic dolls on offer these days, and secondhand TVs stacked up by the dozen, and racks of mobile phones, but Marrakech moves to an ancient rhythm. The decoration comes and goes, as do the wares, but the soul stays firm.

Of all the stalls and shops, there was one I was hoping to find on my trail for a storyteller. Abdelmalik had said there was an unusual emporium to visit, called Maison de Mèknes; that stepping into it would change the way my eyes saw the world. He made me memorize the directions: Go to the Bab Laksour, take the third street to the left, and then fifth to the right, turn left again at the green mosque, and the second right at the butcher selling horse meat. When you see a hammam, turn your back to it, step two meters to the right, and slip down a passage filled with a sea of rotting bread.

For three hours I traipsed up and down, lost in lanes jammed with people and merchandise. Then, quite suddenly, the directions fell into place like clues on a treasure map. I found the mosque, the butcher, the hammam, and the rotting bread. At the far end was a low-fronted cavern, with a crude hand-painted sign. It read: *Maison de Mèknes.*

There were steps going down, rounded by generations of eager feet. Inside, the ceiling was low, cobwebbed, and the shelves beneath it cluttered with treasure. There were ancient Berber chests, silver teapots, ebony footstools, and swords once used by warring tribes, and cartons of postcards left by the French, Brownie Box cameras, candlesticks, silk wedding belts, and camel headdresses crafted from indigo wool.

The proprietor was a smug-faced man with tobacco-colored eyes, and dried coffee spilled down the front of his shirt. He said his name was Omar bin Mohammed. He was perched on a stool behind a pool of light just inside the door. I didn't see him at first, not until my eyes had become accustomed to the darkness. Omar seemed greedy for business. But, as I soon found out, there was one thing he enjoyed far more than loading tourists up with loot.

He loved to tell stories.

The first thing Omar explained when I crossed the threshold was that nothing—absolutely nothing—was for sale. However much I wanted one of the ancient Berber boxes, or the rough Saharan shields, or the amber necklaces, I was out of luck, he said.

"Is it a museum, then?" I asked.

Omar bin Mohammed clawed a hand through the scrub of gray beard on his cheek. "My shop isn't like the others in the medina," he said bitterly. "The others, they're frauds. They'll eat you up, sell you their mothers."

"Is your merchandise of higher quality, then?"

Omar blew his nose into a voluminous handkerchief, rubbed his thumbs in his eyes. "No, no," he said. "All this stuff I'm selling is worthless. It may look nice to you, because you don't know. The light's bad in here. I keep it like that specially. An empty tin can would look like treasure in here. Take something away and the first time you'd realize it's rubbish is when you are home."

"I really don't understand why you're telling me this," I said.

Omar held his right palm out in the air. "There's a problem," he said. "I have put up with it since I was a child."

I braced myself to be petitioned for charity. "We all have problems," I said icily.

"You are right, we all have problems," said Omar. "And mine is that I can't help but tell the truth."

"That doesn't sound like a problem. Quite the opposite, in fact."

Omar the shopkeeper blinked hard. "You have no idea. When you're a salesman here in the Marrakech medina, lying is the first thing you learn. Generation after generation, they pass it on. It's the secret ingredient, the foundation for a salesman's success. Lie well and you make a fortune every day. Your wife purrs like a kitten, and your children walk tall with pride."

"Can't you just pretend to lie?"

"That's it," said Omar. "The other shopkeepers say I'm a fool, that I should simply trick the tourists like everyone else. After all, most of them will never come back. And what are tourists for but for tricking?"

"So?"

"So in my shop nothing's for sale."

"Ah," I said.

Omar paused, flexed his neck, and smiled. "Nothing's for sale..." he repeated. "Instead, it's all free. Absolutely free!"

I looked at the shelves. One of the ancient Berber coffers had caught my eye. The thought of getting it for nothing was suddenly very pleasing.

"Can I have that, then?"

"Of course you can," said Omar.

"Without charge? Can I just take it?"

"I told you," he said, "I give the objects away."

"I'm so glad I came inside here."

"I'm glad you did, too," said the shopkeeper.

I stood up and moved over to the Berber chest. Omar encouraged me to pull back the lid, revealing a faded felt-lined interior.

"Oh, there's something I should tell you," he said gently.

"What?"

"That to every item in here there's something attached."

Again, I didn't quite understand. "What's that?"

"A story."

I glanced over at the shopkeeper and narrowed my eyes. "Huh?"

"If you want to take an item," he said, "then you have to buy the story attached to it."

Omar blinked. Then I blinked. He rubbed a hand to his face again, and I pondered the arrangement. In a city where competition for tourist cash had reached fever pitch, Omar bin Mohammed had come up with a ruse like none other. He grinned hard, then strained to look meek.

"What story is attached to that chest?"

The shopkeeper thought for a moment, pinched a hand to his mustache. "It's called 'The Horseman and the Snake.'"

"How much does it cost to hear it?"

"Six hundred dirhams."

"That's eighty bucks," I said. "The chest isn't worth that."

"I told you, the objects I'm giving away are not special at all. The chest looks nice but it's worthless."

"Then why should I fork out six hundred dirhams for something of such little value?"

Omar bin Mohammed wove his fingers together and bowed them toward the floor. "For the story," he said.

I pulled out three high-denomination bills. "Here's the money."

A moment later the bills had been tucked beneath layers of clothing, and the Berber chest had been wrapped in sheets of crumpled newspaper.

"It's a good choice," said Omar.

"But I thought you said you were dealing in rubbish."

"That chest may be rubbish," he said, "but 'The Horseman and the Snake' is worth three times the money I'm charging you for it."

Leaning back on his stool, Omar bin Mohammed stared into the pool of light just inside his door, and he began.

"Once upon a time," he said, "long ago and many days' travel from where we sit, there was a kingdom called the Land of Pots and Pans. Everyone there was happy, and everyone was prosperous, made so by their thriving business of selling pots and pans to the other kingdoms all around."

Omar the salesman paused to pass me a glass of sweet mint tea.

"Now," he said, "in the Land of Pots and Pans there were all sorts of animals. There were lions and tigers and crocodiles and even kangaroos. There was every imaginable kind of animal, everything except for snakes. No one had ever seen a snake, and no one had ever imagined such a creature.

"One day a woodcutter was asleep in the forest, when a long green serpent slithered up to him and slid into his open mouth and down his throat. The woodcutter woke up as the snake suffocated him. Panicking, he managed to stand up and flap his arms all around, moaning as loudly as he could.

"As luck would have it, a horseman was riding by at that precise moment. He saw the woodcutter waving his arms in distress. Having come from the neighboring land where snakes were plentiful, he realized immediately what had happened. Pulling out his whip, he leapt from his steed and began to whip the poor woodcutter's stomach with all his strength.

"The woodcutter tried to protest, but half-suffocated by the serpent and wounded from the horseman's seemingly unprovoked attack, he could do nothing except fall to his knees. Displeased at the discomfort of its hiding place, the snake reversed up out of the woodcutter's throat and slithered away. When he saw that the woodcutter was out of danger, the horseman jumped back onto his mount and rode off without a word. Hailing from a land where such attacks were frequent, he didn't give the matter a second thought.

"As he caught his breath, the woodcutter began to understand what had happened, and that the horseman had attacked him in silence because time was of the essence, before the reptile had injected venom into his bloodstream."

Omar bin Mohammed held up the Berber chest wrapped in newspaper and grinned.

"Don't forget the story," he said. "You may appreciate it all the more because you have paid to hear it. Allow it to move around your head; the more it does so, the more its real value will reveal itself to you."

AN HOUR LATER, I was sitting in the barber's shop across the street from Maison de Mèknes along with my Berber chest, waiting for a storyteller to arrive. The rendezvous had been brokered by Omar bin Mohammed, before he rushed out to splurge the prized income generated by "The Horseman and the Snake."

Omar had exclaimed that the storyteller, called Murad, was no ordinary raconteur, but a man whose ancestors had been telling tales for twelve centuries. His pedigree was so established, Omar had said, that the man's biology had been affected in some strange and unlikely way. I had asked him to elucidate. The shopkeeper had risen up to his full height of five foot five and punched his arms out above him like pistons, baring his wrists to God.

"His body doesn't have blood like you or me," he boomed, "but its veins flow instead with words!"

In true Moroccan style, the coiffeur thought nothing of me sitting on his threadbare couch, waiting for someone to arrive. While I was waiting, I asked if he had heard of a storyteller by the name of Murad. No sooner had he heard the name than his face lit up.

"The sound of his voice is like the singing of a thousand angels," he said. "Murad will hypnotize you with the stories that stream from his lips, in a waterfall of words."

"Is he well known?" I asked.

The barber brushed one palm over the other. "To every man, woman, and child in Marrakech," he said, gasping. "People cry his name from the balconies of their houses, and tear their hair out when he leaves their sight!"

The buildup was almost too much for me to take. I sat there, squirming into the barber's rotting couch, eager to meet the great Murad. Forty minutes passed. The barber opened a drawer below the mirror, fished about for an old CD, lathered it with shaving cream, rinsed it off. Then he blow-dried it with care, and loaded it into the stereo he kept in a box under the sink. The sound of Bob Dylan's "Tambourine Man" rang out through the streets of old Marrakech.

It was at that moment that Murad the storyteller swept in.

WHEN I WAS eight years old, my father arrived home from a journey to the East with a pair of tanned leather suitcases packed full of gifts, and a stout lisping redheaded figure following behind. My childhood was full of people coming and going. Most of the time I never quite knew who any of them were. As far as I could understand, they were a human stew, a jumble of all people, who came because my father was there.

The redheaded man with the lisp moved into an attic room, from where he would appear from time to time and tell stories. I don't remember his name now, or quite where he came from. I used to like to think my father had found him in some distant land, and coaxed him to return to our home near Tunbridge Wells.

Over the months he stayed, the redhead revealed to us some of the great characters of Arabian folklore. He lisped his way through dozens of tales from *A Thousand and One Nights,* then moved on to stories from other collections lesser known in the West—such as *Antar wa Abla* and the *Assemblies of Al Hariri.* A child's mind pieces things together in a way that makes perfect sense, creating kind of a story from fragments overheard. We assumed that the portly redheaded figure was there to entertain us. And he was. But as the years have passed, I have come to understand that the man had been brought as a sort of tutor as well.

Each one of his stories was chosen for the inner properties contained within it. Like the peach, the story was the delicious meat, which allows the nugget in the middle to be passed on and eventually be sowed. Every day, the redheaded man would sit in our playroom at the top of the house, with my sisters and me. Sometimes our friends would be there, too, clustered around. When we were all listening, the lisping voice would begin.

Of all the stories he told, the one that took root deepest was "The Water of Paradise."

Long ago, a Bedouin shepherd was crossing the vast expanse of the Southern Desert when he noticed one of his sheep licking at the sand. The shepherd staggered over and, to his great surprise, he found a spring. He bent down and tasted its water. No sooner had his tongue touched one drop, did he realize that this was no ordinary water. It was the most delicious liquid imaginable, even more perfect than any refreshment experienced in his dreams.

The shepherd drank a little more, before coming to understand the grave duty before him. As a humble subject of the great Harun ar-Rashid, it fell to him to take a gift of the water to the Caliph himself.

Filling his most reliable water skin with the Water of Paradise, the shepherd entrusted his flock to his brother, and set off across the dunes toward Baghdad. After many days of struggle and thirst, he arrived at the gates of the palace. The royal guards pushed him away at first, threatening to hack off his head for wasting their time. But he pleaded, held up the water bottle, and shouted, "I have a gift for the Caliph. It is the Water of Paradise."

The great gate of the palace opened a crack, and the Bedouin shepherd was pulled in. Before he knew it, he was crouching in the throne room at the feet of Harun ar-Rashid himself. While minions scurried about attending to their duties, the Caliph ordered to know why the shepherd had come.

Holding out the putrid water bottle, the Bedouin said, "Your Majesty, I am a simple man from the inner expanse of the Southern Desert. I have never known luxury, not until now. While herding my sheep, I came to understand that we had happened upon the most delicious liquid on the earth. Our fathers and forefathers have spoken of it, but none has ever tasted it. Not until now. Your Majesty, Your Magnificence, I present you this, the Water of Paradise."

Harun ar-Rashid clicked his fingers and a solid gold cup was borne forth on a jewel-encrusted tray. He gave a nod toward the water skin, and a finely dressed servant snatched the skin and poured a few drops into the royal cup. A bodyguard tasted the liquid first and, when he did not fall to the ground, the goblet was passed to the Caliph.

Harun pressed its rim to his lips, sniffed, and then tasted the Water of Paradise. The shepherd and all the courtiers leaned forward in anxious anticipation. Harun ar-Rashid, the Commander of Day and Night, said nothing. After several minutes of silence, the grand vizier bowed until his mouth was a fraction of an inch from the Caliph's ear.

"Shall we chop off his head, Your Magnificence?"

Harun stroked a hand over his chin.

He thanked the shepherd for the gift, and whispered a secret instruction to his vizier.

"Have him taken back to his flock under the cover of darkness," he said, "and on the way neither let him see the mighty Tigris River, nor taste the sweet water that we find so ordinary. Then present him with a thousand pieces of gold, and tell him that he and his progeny are appointed guardians of the Water of Paradise."

chapter seven

None learned the art of archery from me
Who did not make me, in the end, the target.

Saadi of Shiraz

M urad the storyteller was dressed like a dervish, in a patched
woollen jelaba and a strand of fraying calico wrapped around
his head. His eyes were frosted with cataracts, and his face was quite
flat, scarred, fatty on the cheeks. His fingers were so long and tapered
that I glanced down to inspect them more closely.

As soon as he entered the coiffeur, the barber dropped a razor he
was holding, and hunched down like a crow with a broken wing. The
two or three battered husbands taking refuge on filthy chairs ducked
their heads in subservience. Following their example, I bowed and
introduced myself.

The storyteller extended a bunch of tapered fingers, and waited
for me to shake his hand.

"*As salam wa alaikum*," he said in a low husky voice. He asked if
I had purchased anything at the Maison de Mèknes. I sensed he
wasn't interested in the Berber chest so much as the tale attached to
it. In any case, I found it a little odd that he hadn't spotted the box on
the floor.

"I bought the story of 'The Horseman and the Snake,'" I said.

Before I could bemoan its high price, Murad stepped forward and touched my arm.

"Some things in this world are beyond value," he said, "and that tale is such a thing. It is like a precious gem. Hold it to the light, turn it, and it shines like a ruby."

At that moment, a group of henpecked husbands slunk into the barber's, no doubt hiding from their wives. On seeing the storyteller, they cowered a little lower and wished him peace.

"We shall find privacy," Murad said darkly. I picked up the Berber chest, and the storyteller led me out into the narrow lanes toward the green mosque. I followed the patched hem of his jelaba as it jerked past stalls heaped with pink nylon sweaters, cows' hooves, and rice.

The passages of Marrakech are so packed with people, animals, and objects that you have to learn to move through them in a new way. I found myself watching local Marrakchis who have spent their lives roaming the medina. They don't walk so much as glide, ready at any instant to dodge to the right or the left to avoid a pile of oncoming hides, a blind beggar, or a charging pack mule.

Murad the storyteller wasn't as nimble as he might once have been. He ran a hand along the wall as he walked, steadying himself.

I followed the jelaba hem in silence, wondering where its owner was leading me. Suddenly, it slipped through a squat doorway, framed in peeling paint, and along a curved corridor. I hurried to keep up, weighed down with the Berber chest. At the far end of the corridor we climbed a ladder and found ourselves in a tall vaulted room. There was no furniture except for a mattress and a pile of rags, which seemed to be used as a kind of blanket.

Murad fluttered his fingers at the mattress, and we sat at either end. "This is where I live," he said. "Let it be your home."

We talked pleasantries a moment or two, before I launched into the reason I had come.

"My friend has a dream, and that's why I am here," I told him.

The storyteller touched the tips of his tapered fingers together and listened. "He wants you to come to Casablanca and tell stories. You see, he believes that Morocco is losing its cultural heart. He needs you to help in the war against television."

Murad didn't reply at first. He just sat there on the edge of his mattress, gently rocking back and forth, ruminating. Just as I was wondering if he would say anything at all, he opened his mouth a crack.

"Your friend is right," he said, "but he is also wrong."

"About what?"

"About stories, about what they mean."

The storyteller picked up a rag and fed it through his fingers. "To know about stories you must know about people," he said. "The listeners are the key. Understand how they listen and you will find you hold immense power in your grasp."

"But television—"

"Forget about television," Murad said, cutting in. "It's worthless because it enters through the eyes, and suffocates the imagination. Feed people something more tantalizing and they will close their eyes and open their ears."

Murad blinked. He sat still like a bronze Buddha, hands in his lap, frosted eyes staring to the front. I said something, I can't remember what. He didn't hear me anyway, for he was listening to the call of the fish-seller down on the street.

At that moment I realized Murad was blind.

ONE NIGHT, A few weeks after he had come to stay at our home, the redheaded man with the lisp gave me a matchbox. I slid the drawer open and found a pebble inside. It was blue-gray with a vein of brilliant white running down one edge. The redheaded man, who we had come to know as Slipper Feet, because he never wore ordinary shoes, tapped it onto my palm. I put it to my cheek and rubbed it up and down.

"It's so smooth," I said.

Slipper Feet smiled. "Of course it is," he said gently, "because it's from the end of the world."

I touched the pebble to my tongue. "It tastes salty," I said.

"That's because it's from the deepest depths of the greatest ocean."

I weighed it on my hand. "It's heavy."

"Yes, but when it's in the water it's light like a feather," said Slipper Feet.

"But it's just a pebble," I said.

The redheaded man smiled from the corner of his mouth. "To a fool it's a pebble," he said.

MURAD THE STORYTELLER told me he had never been able to see. He could tell light from dark and could make out vague shapes, but that was about all.

"I have never had eyesight to hold me back," he said when we met the next day at Café Agana on the main square.

I asked how he managed to get around without the power of vision. The storyteller let out a croak of laughter.

"How do *you* survive in a world so limited by one sense?" he replied. "Close your eyes, and your heart will open."

The waiter brought cups of milky hot chocolate. It made a change from the bitter café noir. We sat at the edge, me peering down at the hubbub of Jemaa al Fna, and Murad listening to it all.

I told him that I wanted to find the story in my heart, that I was searching but had no idea how to go about it. The storyteller sipped his hot chocolate and sat in silent concentration.

"You have to trust yourself," he said eventually. "It's in there, but you must believe that it really is . . ."

"Do you believe?"

Murad dabbed a finger to his eye. "Of course I believe," he said.

"Have you ever searched for the story in your heart?"

The storyteller gazed over at me, his cataracts reflecting the bright winter light. "I searched for it for years," he said, "like a madman hunting for a grain of salt in a bucket of sand. My neighbor's son agreed to act as my eyes, my fifth sense. We traveled from Marrakech up to the tip of Tangier, down the coast and inland, across the Atlas and into the Sahara. When we had reached dunes as high as mountains, we turned around and retraced our steps. On the journey, I asked every man, woman, and child we passed if they could tell me the story in my heart. They made fun of me, a stupid blind man led by a boy, looking for a part of him he couldn't see."

"Did you find the story?"

Murad paused. "I was walking down the beach near Assilah," he said. "A blustery winter day, damp and cold, with a scent of licorice in the wind. My discomfort was great. My hands had been burned in a fire, and were all bandaged up. Our feet sunk deep in the sand, and we staggered like shipwrecked sailors without a hope. I cursed myself for leaving the comfort of Marrakech when a great wave broke on the shore. I could smell it as it rolled in, and heard the tremendous force.

"The wave washed up an eel on the sand, near to where I was standing. I couldn't see it, of course, but the boy shouted loud when he saw it lying there."

"Was it alive?"

"Oh, yes, it was," said Murad. "And it spoke to me."

I sipped my hot chocolate.

"The eel raised itself as tall as it could and it laughed at me. It laughed and laughed until it choked." The storyteller bristled with anger. "Can you imagine how I felt?" he said. "A simple blind man being mocked by an eel."

"Why was it laughing?"

"The eel had seen me stumbling down the beach, bandaged and blind to the world, and it found humor in the sight.

" 'Look at you,' it said in a shrill voice, 'the grand race of mankind reduced to this!'

"I explained to the eel the circumstances in which it had found me were abnormal, that I was on a journey, searching for something invisible yet of great value.

"The sea creature cleared its throat and said, 'Why are you searching?'

" 'I told you, to find the story in my heart.'

"The eel sighed.

" 'Why are you *really* searching?'

" 'So that I might become whole,' I said.

" 'Well, this is a very auspicious day,' said the eel haughtily, 'because I am an electric eel and we electric eels have certain properties which are nothing special under the ocean, but are quite surprising to you humans. If you listen carefully I shall peer through the layers of your skin and flesh and look for the story in your chest.'

"At hearing this, I felt overcome with elation," said Murad. "I couldn't see the eel, but it was as if he had been sent to me, sent to me by God. I sat back on the sand, tucked my burned hands under my arms, and I waited.

"The eel cleared his throat once again and, penetrating my chest with his electric eyes, he whispered, 'Yours is the "Tale of Mushkil Gusha." ' "

THE STORYTELLER DRAINED his hot chocolate and wiped his mouth with his hand.

"Won't you tell me the story?" I said.

"What day of the week is it today?" he asked.

"It's Tuesday."

"Then you shall have to wait," said Murad, "for as everyone knows, the 'Tale of Mushkil Gusha' can only be told on a Thursday night."

We walked down the stairs of Café Agana, Murad running his long tapered fingers across the wall as he went. I offered to lead him back to his home, but the old storyteller scoffed.

"I am a spider and the medina is my web," he said. "I know every inch of it, and every inch of it knows me."

We arranged to meet at dusk on Thursday evening so I might hear the "Tale of Mushkil Gusha." It seemed somehow important, as if by learning Murad's own tale, I might be closer to finding my own.

The storyteller turned on his heel and pushed into the sea of bobbing heads. I followed him for a moment or two, the calico turban poking up out of the crowd like a flag.

Then he was gone.

IN MARRAKECH, NIGHT falls in the blink of an eye. I glanced up at the canvas of stars glinting above, mirroring the butane lamps on the food stands below. Sheep were roasting on a thousand homemade stalls, oily smoke rising heavenward, conical clay tagines sizzling like firestorms from Hell.

These days, tourists flock to Marrakech in the thousands. They find solace in the plush hotels out in the Palmeraie or in traditional riads set deep in the medina. Marrakech may not have lost its essence, but the people who venture to it have changed. A journey to the Red City used to be a rite of passage in itself, that is until the first passenger jets connected it to the world.

I believe that Marrakech ought to be earned as a destination. The journey is the preparation for the experience. Reaching it too fast derides it, makes it a little less easy to understand.

The narrow passages of the medina swell with tourists, except in the blazing summer months, when a searing drought blows in. I used to think the tourists were set to destroy the soul of the city. After all, there are towering hotels, guides, and restaurants wherever you look. The tourists have certainly brought wealth and have heralded change, but their effect doesn't penetrate.

Jemaa al Fna is the heart of Marrakech. By day it's a turbulent circus of life—teeming with astrologers, healers, storytellers, and acrobats. And when the curtain of dusk shrouds the city from the desert all around, the food stalls flare up, creating a banquet for the senses. A quick glance and you might think it's all been laid on for the sightseers. But the longer you spend there, the more you come to see the truth. The tourists take photographs but they don't connect.

With its outlandish customs, Jemaa al Fna is a focal point of folklore, a borehole that descends down through the layers and sub-layers of Morocco's underbelly. A lifetime of study couldn't teach you all it represents. To understand it, you must try not to think, but to allow the square's raw energy to be absorbed directly through the skin.

ON THURSDAY AFTERNOON, I waited as the sun arched over Marrakech. It was early November, and the Atlas Mountains were already charged with snow; a more glorious backdrop would be impossible to find. I sat at Café Agana and waited for Murad to feel his way up the stairs. Afternoon turned to dusk, and dusk turned to night. I was wondering if the old storyteller had forgotten the appointment, when I felt a hand on my shoulder.

"Mushkil Gusha is the remover of obstacles," said Murad in his soft husky voice. "If you have the patience to listen, you may see the world with new eyes. But a responsibility comes with this tale."

"What responsibility?"

The storyteller sat down and took a deep breath. "You must repeat the tale each Thursday night," he said.

I smiled, choked out some sharp retort.

"Take it lightly," he snapped, "and your obstacles will become all the greater."

"Do you tell the story every Thursday night?"

Murad agreed that he did.

"And do all the people who hear it go on and tell it, too?"

"Some do," he replied, "others sit in groups and listen. Whether you tell the tale or hear it, the effect is the same. For 'Mushkil Gusha' must enter your ears."

The storyteller pressed the tips of his fingers together, drew the lids over his blind eyes, and said: "Once upon a time, long ago, when Marrakech was no more than a hamlet, there were living in Arabia a widowed woodcutter and his daughter, named Jamia. Each morning, the woodcutter would leave his small cottage before the cockerel had crowed, to search for wood in the mountains to sell down in the valley.

"Now one night before she turned in for bed, young Jamia begged her father to buy for her one of the pies she had seen for sale in the town's market, and one of the frilly dresses hanging in the tailor's window. Her father promised to leave home well before dawn, and to cut twice as much firewood as he usually did, to make some extra money.

"So, long before the cockerel had woken, the woodcutter crept out of the house and made his way to the mountain. He cut double the normal amount of wood, prepared it well, put it on his back, and headed for home.

"Once back at the cottage, the woodcutter found the door was bolted shut. It was still early and his daughter was still sleeping. 'Daughter,' he called, 'I am hungry and thirsty after so much work. Please let me in.' Jamia was so sound asleep that she didn't wake from her slumber. The woodcutter went round to the barn and fell asleep on a pile of hay. A few hours later he awoke and knocked at the door again. 'Let me in, little Jamia,' he cried, 'for I shall have to set off for the market and I need to eat and drink.'

"But the door was bolted as before.

"Not realizing that his daughter had gone off to visit her friends, the woodcutter struggled to lift the firewood onto his back, and he set off toward the town, hoping to reach it before sunset. He was hungry and thirsty beyond words, but kept thinking about the delicious pie and the dress he would bring home to his beloved daughter.

"After an hour or so of walking, the woodcutter thought he heard a voice. It was the voice of a young woman, calling out to him. 'Drop your wood and follow me,' it said, 'and your mouth will be rewarded.' The woodcutter let the giant bundle fall to the ground, and he began to trudge in the direction of the voice. After some time, he realized he was lost. He called to the voice, but there was no answer. Night was approaching, and the poor old man fell to the ground and wept.

"After some time he regained his senses and tried to be more positive. To pass the time he decided to tell himself the day's events as a kind of tale, for it was far too cold to sleep. As he got to the end, he heard the voice again. 'What are you doing?' it said. 'I'm cold and hungry, and so I am passing the time by talking to myself,' said the woodcutter. The voice told him to stand up, and to raise one foot in the air. 'What do you mean?' he asked. The voice repeated the instructions a second time. 'Do exactly as I tell you,' it said, 'and your mouth will be rewarded.'

"The woodcutter lifted his right foot in the air and found it was standing on something, an invisible step of some kind. He fumbled with his hand and felt another step above the first. 'Walk up it,' said the voice. Following the orders, the woodcutter found he was suddenly transported to a deserted wasteland, covered in dark blue pebbles. 'Where is this?' the woodcutter asked. 'The place at the end of time,' the voice replied. 'Fill your pockets with the pebbles and make a promise that every Thursday night you will recount this, the "Tale of Mushkil Gusha," for it is he who has saved you.' The woodcutter did as he was told and, no sooner had he done so, than he found himself standing at the doorway of his own home. His daughter, Jamia, was waiting for him.

" 'Where have you been, Father?' she asked. Once they were inside, the woodcutter told her about the invisible staircase, and then emptied his pockets. 'But, Father, pebbles won't buy us food,' said Jamia. The old man put his head in his hands, but then he remembered the extra-large bundle of wood he had cut that morning. He put the pebbles near the fireplace and went off to bed, ready for an early start.

"Next day, he went out, found the wood easily, and hauled it down to market. The bundle sold without any trouble, for four times its usual price. The woodcutter bought as much food as he could carry, and a pink and blue dress from the tailor's shop.

"Now," said Murad, leaning back in his chair, "for a whole week, the woodcutter's fortune seemed to go from strength to strength. The wood was abundant in the forest, and his axe seemed sharper than usual. The path down the valley wasn't slippery as it tended to be, and in the town there was a great demand for well-chopped wood.

"A full week after his journey up the invisible staircase, it was time to recount the 'Tale of Mushkil Gusha.' But being a mortal, the old woodcutter forgot his duty and went to bed. The next evening, he noticed the cottage had filled with a strange red light. He soon realized that the light was shining from the pebbles he had scooped up the week before. 'We are rich beyond our wildest dreams!' he exclaimed to his daughter.

"Over the coming weeks, the woodcutter and Jamia sold the precious gems in towns all over the kingdom. Within a month or two, they were fabulously wealthy, so much so that they built a castle opposite the palace in which the king lived.

"When asked where he came from, the woodcutter put on a heavy accent and said he had journeyed from a country far to the east, where he had made a fortune selling silks from Bokhara. It wasn't long before the humble woodcutter was invited to the palace. He wore white satin gloves to hide the roughness of his hands, and presented the king with a large diamond pendant.

"Time passed, and Jamia became close friends with the king's own daughter, Princess Nabila. The two would go down to the royal stream and bathe. One day, before jumping into the water, the princess removed her golden necklace and hung it on a low branch of a nearby tree. She forgot about it and, that night, searched high and low for the necklace. Eventually she fell asleep, and dreamt that the woodcutter's daughter had stolen the necklace for herself.

"The next day she whispered to her father. Within an hour the woodcutter's daughter had been cast into an orphanage. And the old man was flung into the deepest dungeon in the kingdom. Weeks passed and he grew weaker and weaker. After six months, he was taken out in chains and tied to a pole. Every so often, people would throw rotten food at him or laugh at his miserable state.

"Then one afternoon, he heard a man telling his wife that it was Thursday evening. He suddenly remembered the story of Mushkil Gusha, the remover of obstacles. A moment later, a kindly passerby threw him a coin. He asked if the man might take the coin, cross the street, and buy a handful of dates for them both. The man did so, and the woodcutter recounted the 'Tale of Mushkil Gusha.'

"The next day," Murad went on, "the princess was bathing at the stream when she spied her gold necklace through the water. She looked up and saw that it was the reflection, and that the actual necklace was still hanging on the low branch where she had left it. Without wasting a minute, she ran to her father and explained her mistake. The king gave the woodcutter a royal pardon, compensated him handsomely, and released his daughter from the terrible orphanage."

Murad stopped talking. He blew very gently into his fist.

"The 'Tale of Mushkil Gusha' is very long," he said. "Some people say that it never really ends. But now that you know it, or some of it, it's your duty to retell it for yourself every Thursday after dusk."

I could hear the butane lamps roaring in the main square below, and smell the racks of skewers grilling over charcoal, sending a curtain of smoke up into the desert night. The way Murad had told his tale, the "Tale of Mushkil Gusha," touched me. It wasn't just another story recounted to earn a handful of coins, but something that had come from within him.

"The story in *your* heart," I said, staring into his frosted eyes, "if I remember it, and protect it well, perhaps it can help me to find my own story."

Murad tilted his head back and breathed in the scent of roasting mutton.

"I told you that if you believe," he said very gently, "if you *really* believe, a world of incredible possibility opens up, like the stairs in the 'Tale of Mushkil Gusha.' What was not invisible, will become visible." Murad bent forward and tapped my shoulder with his long, tapered hand. "But you must have the courage to climb," he said.

There was silence for a long time. Then I asked what had happened to the eel.

The storyteller adjusted his calico turban. "When he had finished telling the 'Tale of Mushkil Gusha,'" he said, "the great eel instructed me to value what was deep inside. 'The search for truth can lead a man around the world and back to the point from where he took the first step,' he told me in a squeaky voice. 'Always remember that the journey is nothing more than a path that leads to a destination.'

"And, without another word, the electric eel turned toward the ocean and slipped into the waves."

chapter eight

The destiny of a wolf cub is to become a wolf, even if it is reared among the sons of men.

Ibn el-Arabi

One frosty morning before I left for school, Slipper Feet was waiting for me down in the hallway. He said there was a story he had to pass on without delay. I reminded him of my prep school's policy on being late—six strikes with a cane. Slipper Feet ran his clawlike nails through his long red hair and said in a calculating voice: "I promise you, this morning you will not be late." I don't remember now which story he told me that dark winter morning, only that it was about a dragonfly and a Jinn. What I do remember is that by the time he finished, I was frozen to the bone. It was as if the story had sucked all the heat out of my blood. I went upstairs, took a steaming hot bath, and put my uniform back on.

By the time I got to school, it was late morning. I approached the main door in terror at the thought of being taken away and beaten. A prefect was standing there, holding up a sign. He told me to go home. I asked why.

"The headmaster is dead," he said.

From that day on, I never quite trusted Slipper Feet. At night he would come down from the attic and roam about the house. I have no proof, but I know he used to come into my room. I could smell him in my dreams. My mother didn't trust him, either. She started sitting with us when he recounted his tales. I asked her why, and she said it was because she hadn't been lucky enough to have a storyteller when she was young. Years later she admitted it was because the red-headed man had done something very bad.

Not long after that, Slipper Feet was gone. No one ever spoke about him again, although the stories he told stayed inside me, and they are still there.

A decade passed. Then, one morning, my father was opening his mail. An envelope came with an unusual stamp from a country in the East. He regarded the envelope for a long time, cut it open, and squinted at the lines of uneven black script. He looked quite pale.

It was a death threat from Slipper Feet.

THE CALIPH'S HOUSE has an agenda of its own. It's an agenda of self-sabotage. I've never quite understood it. As soon as I leave it for more than a moment, the building begins to destroy itself. The window frames rot through, the bougainvillea roots push up the courtyard tiles, and alarming patches of damp take hold on every wall.

When I wondered aloud why the house was so self-destructive, Zohra rushed over.

"Are you so foolish, so blind?" she cried. "How could you not understand?"

"Not understand what?"

"That Dar Khalifa is sick."

"That's nonsense."

Zohra stuck out her hands and waved them about her head. "Believe me," she yelled, "I speak the truth!"

In the days I had spent down in Marrakech, a wall had collapsed. Osman and the Bear were looking at the heap of rubble when I arrived home. They shook their heads and cursed.

"It's because of the ants," said Osman.

The Bear agreed. "The ants are bad," he said.

I couldn't believe what I was hearing. "The ants?"

The guardians nodded. "Yes, Monsieur Tahir, the ants."

"But how could such tiny insects do so much damage?"

"Do not be fooled," said Osman. "They look very small, so small you don't think of them at all. Weeks pass. Then years. Then one day you wake up, and your home has fallen down."

The Bear pointed at the rubble. "First a wall," he said. "Then the house."

RACHANA WAS BATHING the children upstairs. I burst in, babbling about Murad the storyteller and the "Tale of Mushkil Gusha." She looked at me blankly. Ariane kissed my ear and asked me to tell her about Mushkil Gusha.

"You will have to wait until Thursday," I said.

Rachana said that the two maids had been at each other's throats over Timur. "You go away, and this place is like a circus," she said.

"Don't worry, from now on everything will be much calmer."

My wife gave me a sideways look. "Why?"

"Because Murad the storyteller is coming to stay."

IT WASN'T MORE than a day or so before the guardians linked the broken wall to the business of the chalk symbols written on the door. I reminded them of their earlier deduction. They looked confused.

"The ants," I prompted.

"Yes, ants are strong," said the Bear, "but we see now this was not their work."

"It was a Jinn," mouthed Osman.

"What changed your mind?"

"When the wall fell down three days ago," said the Bear, "there was the bitter smell of sulphur in the garden. And after that came a ferocious storm and this morning we found a dead chameleon in the hedge over there."

"Who said sulphur, storms, and dead chameleons point to Jinn?"

The guardians looked at each other, then at me. "Sukayna did," they both said at once.

THE DAY AFTER I reached home, Murad arrived on the train from Marrakech. I went down to Casa Voyageurs, and found him sitting on the platform wrapped up in his patched jelaba, with a homemade sack at his feet. I had been anxious about bringing him when I discovered he was blind. But he seemed quite at ease at the idea of following me up to Casablanca. My other worry was how much Ottoman would have to pay him. I broached the subject of money an hour before I left Marrakech. The old storyteller said that hunger helped to keep his tongue moving well.

"Give your extra money to those who have use for it," he said, "and give me a soft pillow for my head."

As Murad was blind, I thought it best to put him in the guest room on the ground floor. Located at the far end of the large garden courtyard, it had been the room in which Qandisha the Jinn had supposedly resided. The exorcists had spent a full night at work in there, extracting her from the walls.

Since the exorcism, the room had maintained a dampness, as if it were on a different frequency of some kind. On the left side of the room there had been a short flight of steps leading down to a brick wall. We had blocked it off from the bedroom. The guardians had taken to storing the long ladders there.

Murad moved through the house and out into the garden courtyard, trailing his long fingers across the walls. Timur skipped up and kissed him on the cheek. Then Ariane stepped forward clutching her favorite doll in one hand and her pet tortoise in the other. She asked why the old man couldn't see. Murad the storyteller leaned down and patted his long fingers over her hair.

"My eyes have never worked," he said.

"Why not?"

"Because they were not meant to."

"Why were they not meant to?"

Murad touched her cheek with his hand. "Because God wanted me to be blind," he said.

"Why did God want you to be blind?"

"Because He wanted me to see."

Ariane wasn't listening. She ran ahead and pushed open the door to the storyteller's room. As soon as Murad entered, his face twitched on one side. Then he thanked me.

"You have given me a very special place to sleep," he said.

OSMAN AND THE Bear were not good at keeping secrets. When cross-questioned, they admitted that Zohra had brought her astrologer friend while I was away in Marrakech.

"She came in the night," said Osman in a soft voice.

"Who?"

"Sukayna."

"And she walked up and down," added the Bear.

"She burned incense and she killed a chicken."

"Where did she do that?" I asked.

"Out at the front door," said Osman.

"She dripped blood all over the step."

"What happened to the meat?"

The guardians looked sheepish. "We ate it," they said.

While we were talking in the shadow of the stables, Zohra strode up and tugged my sleeve. "You must go and see Sukayna right away," she said.

I resisted. "You know we had an exorcism," I said gruffly. "That's the end of it. We have to move on."

An expert in dominating men, the maid tugged my sleeve a second time. "There are two little children living under that roof," she said. "If you don't go and see Sukayna, you will live to regret it."

I cursed loudly. "Where does this woman, this astrologer, live?"

"You have to go to Afghanistan," said Zohra.

"*What?*"

"Afghanistan."

"I thought she lives up the hill."

"She does," said the maid.

"Well, then, what's she doing in Afghanistan?"

"That's where she works."

"In Afghanistan?"

"Tsk! Tsk! Tsk!" snapped Zohra. "Yes, I told you. Afghanistan."

My mind was reeling. "Am I missing something?" I asked.

Osman brushed a leaf from his shoulder. "Boulevard Afghanistan," he said.

THAT EVENING MURAD crept out of his room at ten o'clock and felt his way to the kitchen. Fatima had cooked him a colossal lamb tagine, which he promptly devoured. After sucking on lamb bones for a while, he ate three apples and a bowl of apricots. He thanked God, kissed his knuckle and touched it to his brow.

"I shall tell you a story," he said.

"But I'm going to bed now," I replied.

The storyteller's face sank. "It will help you sleep," he said.

As far as Murad was concerned, he was more than a humble raconteur, more than a teller of tales. He believed that his repertoire had an intrinsic power, an ability to change the way people feel and think, and even had the power to heal.

Before I joined Rachana and the children upstairs, he told me a tale that will stay with me until my last breath. It was about a little girl who learned to speak the language of fish. I put on my pajamas, crawled into bed, and slept more soundly than I had in years.

The next morning, Murad was waiting for me in the kitchen.

"How did you sleep?"

I told him.

"Of course you did." Murad the storyteller rearranged himself on the kitchen chair. "It was a sleeping story," he said.

OUT IN THE garden Osman and the Bear were polishing a pair of brass lamps I had bought in Marrakech. They didn't like polishing, and had always forced Hamza to do it. As far as they were concerned, polishing was woman's work, like doing the washing and opening the front door.

Osman said the polish made him sneeze.

"It makes us both sneeze," said the Bear.

"It didn't make Hamza sneeze, though," I said.

"Well, his nose was always blocked up, so he couldn't smell it," quipped Osman.

Since we were talking about Hamza, I probed again why he had felt it necessary to leave.

"We told you, it was because of the shame."

"What shame?"

"Hamza's shame."

"But why did he feel ashamed?"

"Because of his wife."

"What did she have to do with it?"

"Everything," said Osman.

"Can you explain?"

"Hamza's wife saw him looking at another woman. Then she made him quit," he said.

"Did he touch the other woman?"

"No! No!" said the Bear loudly. "Of course not. He just looked at her."

"His wife is very jealous," Osman prompted.

"Who was this other woman?"

"It was Fatima, the maid," said the Bear.

THAT AFTERNOON, I tracked down the address Zohra had given me on Boulevard Afghanistan. Up the hill from the coast, it wasn't far from Dar Khalifa, in an area called Hay Hassani. The place with a thousand uses—you went there if you needed a jelaba to be made, a tube of rat-catching glue, or a secondhand fridge.

Sukayna saw her clients one at a time in a small room at the back of a mattress maker's shop. I clambered over an assortment of half-finished mattresses and workmen sitting cross-legged on the floor, past a dozen bolts of bright purple cloth, until I arrived at a torn lace curtain. It was fixed to the ceiling with a length of barbed wire. Behind it, the astrologer was waiting for me.

Sukayna was not as I had imagined her. She was about twenty-five, with bottle-green eyes and a wavering smile. Her voice was deep, more like a man's, and when she spoke, she stretched her back straight, like a sergeant major on parade. Her jelaba was embroidered with a paisley motif, and her fingernails were painted bright red.

I sat down on a homemade plywood chair. We looked at each other for longer than was comfortable, and then the astrologer mumbled Zohra's name.

"She has urged me to come and see you," I said, "and that is why I am here."

"I have been to your home," Sukayna replied, "and I have seen the proof."

She blinked twice, as if to link the bottle-green eyes before me to her visit to the Caliph's House.

"There had been a problem with Jinns," I said. "But it's all been attended to well. We had twenty-five exorcists from Mèknes." I paused for a moment. "They made a terrible mess," I said.

The astrologer glanced up at the barbed wire, perhaps wondering if it would ever fall. "Zohra told me Dar Khalifa was locked up for years."

"For almost a decade," I said.

Sukayna touched a red-nailed finger to her chin. "When a house is left empty for a long time, Jinns can enter," she said slowly. "They live in the walls and below the surface of any water."

"I know. Believe me. I have firsthand experience."

"Something else can also happen," Sukayna mumbled.

"What?"

"The house can bleed," she said.

THAT AFTERNOON, I took Murad down to the stables to meet the guardians for the first time. He shuffled through the garden in his yellow baboush like a patient on forced exercise. "I have not walked on grass in a very long time," he said, as I led him firmly by the arm past the swimming pool and down to the guardians' bolt-hole.

News of the storyteller's arrival had spread through the house and grounds like wildfire. The Bear and Osman were waiting in the middle stable, which they had turned into a rough sort of social club. There were a row of colored lights nailed to the far wall, three half-broken chairs, and a low coffee table made from the giant wooden spool of an industrial cable. Osman had brewed a pot of extra-strong mint tea, and rinsed out the best glasses for the visitor. Murad fumbled his way into the stable's dim interior and shook hands with the guardians. He slumped on one of the chairs, thanked God, and began to recount a tale.

I went back to the house, where I found Zohra feeding Timur a packet of scarlet bubble gum. When she saw me, she grabbed my

little son, hugged him to her chest, and bared her teeth like a wolf
vixen protecting her young. I said I had been to see Sukayna the astrologer, that I was supposed to go back for a second consultation.

Zohra cupped her hand around Timur's head and kissed him on
the cheek. "Dar Khalifa is bleeding like an open wound," she said. "I
told you it's sick."

"That's what the astrologer said. But I don't quite know what it
means."

The maid flipped Timur onto her back and began to shuffle
away down the long corridor.

"I don't know what it means!" I called out.

Zohra didn't turn.

OTTOMAN WAS JUSTIFIABLY proud of his business achieve-
ments. He had created an empire with more than a dozen factories
across Africa and the Far East, and had more employees than he
could count. He wasn't so proud of his former addiction to *kif*, or of
his days as an underworld thief. But there was an element of the pro-
fession that did seem to touch him with pride.

He called it "The Art."

One afternoon, he invited me to take tea with him at a café
called Baba Cool, in the Art Deco quarter, down by the port. We
talked about all kinds of things that day, from a tailor's tricks of the
trade, to the rising cost of Chinese sweatshop labor. The conversation turned to theft. Ottoman tore the corner off a sachet of granu-
lated sugar and poured the contents carefully into his café noir.

"Thieves should pay for their ways," he said, "and they will, on
Judgment Day. I am ashamed of that life I lived, deeply ashamed. I
will be punished. I'm certain of it."

"Did that part of your life teach you anything at all?"

Ottoman glanced up, his face frozen. Very slowly, he smiled. "I
learned so many things," he said.

"What?"

"Dexterity, cunning, stealth, how to lie, and how to make you look over there when the action is right here."

"Did you learn anything from other thieves?"

"Yes, of course I did. We used to meet in places like this, and tip each other off about people to rob. I learned a few techniques, if you could call them that. And I learned about Latif."

"Who's Latif?"

"The patron of all thieves, a kind of hero, a mentor."

"Was he Moroccan?"

"I'm not sure. But that isn't important. You see, thieves are very proud of him."

Ottoman stirred his coffee, jerked out the teaspoon.

"Tell me about him," I said.

"It had been a long time since Latif the Thief had stolen from anyone at all," said Ottoman. "He had run out of cash and was so hungry he felt as if he was about to drop dead. The more he thought about eating, the hungrier and the fainter he became. Then, he had an idea. He looked around his den and found a sheet of paper, a pen, and a metal cup. Scooping them up into his robe, he ran out and was soon at the vast plaza in front of the palace. When no one was looking, he wrote a sign on the paper, placed the cup beside it, and lay down a few inches away. The sign read:

WHO WILL GIVE A COIN TO HELP
BURY A POOR BLIND BEGGAR?

"Latif kept as still as he could, and listened as coins fell into his cup from the hands of passing donors. All morning the charitable tossed in money, feeding Latif's greed. Then, just before noon, the king rode out of the palace. As his carriage passed the parade ground, he saw the supposed corpse, the sign, and the tin cup. He called the coachman to halt the horses. 'What low times we live in,' he thought, 'if a poor blind beggar cannot be given a decent burial!' He called for his imam and ordered him to take the body to his home, wash it, and ensure it was given a suitable send-off. 'Once you have done this,' said the king, 'you may come to the palace and collect a purse of gold from the treasurer for your services.'

"The imam dutifully removed the corpse as Latif struggled to stay limp. He took it through the town on a cart to his own home. Once there, he began to strip it and to prepare for the ritual washing. But after a few minutes he noticed there was no more soap in the house. 'I will have to go to the market and buy more soap,' he said to himself, putting on his coat and leaving the body alone. No sooner had he gone, than Latif the Thief ran to the imam's cupboard and helped himself to the grandest robe and the weightiest turban he could find. He put them on and went directly to the palace, where he sought out the royal treasurer. 'I am the imam to whom the king has promised a purse of gold,' he said.

"The treasurer counted out the money himself. 'Please sign here,' said the treasurer, 'to acknowledge you have received the funds.' 'Are times so desperate that you do not trust anyone, even a humble imam?' said Latif, putting on his most haughty voice. 'Forgive me, Your Reverence,' replied the treasurer, 'but there are so many thieves on the loose.' 'I quite understand your precautions,' said Latif, taking a gold coin from the purse and sliding it across the desk to the treasurer. 'You have been of great service,' he said. 'Don't mention it,' said the official, pulling his own purse out from layer upon layer of cloth, and slipping the tip inside. 'If only there were more honest men such as yourself in the kingdom,' he said, placing his gold-filled purse on his desk. 'Alas,' exclaimed Latif on his way out, as he snatched the treasurer's purse, 'but there are so many thieves about!' "

THE NEXT DAY I was back in the old Art Deco heart of Casablanca, near the café where I had met Ottoman. I was searching for a man who could resole my shoes in leather. Morocco still retains some of the greatest craftsmen working anywhere on earth but, these days, cobblers prefer to use heavy-duty rubber imported from Taiwan. It's cheap to buy and, as they kept telling me, it lasts ten times as long as leather.

After a great deal of walking up and down through the grand old arcades, where the French elite once strolled, I spotted a pair of lady's dancing shoes displayed in a grimy glass window. I peered in. An ancient man was huddled over a workbench, pulling stitches through the toe of a hobnail boot. The shop was not large, just about enough space for a client and his damaged shoes. I went in, wished the cobbler peace, and rummaged in my canvas satchel for my shoes.

The craftsman had the kind of face that could hold the attention of the most distracted mind. The forehead was a web of dark furrows, the eye sockets shadowy and deep, the neck and jaw emaciated as if all the fat had been sucked out with a straw. His hands were so calloused that the calluses had calluses. On his head was a seaman's navy blue woolly hat.

It was obvious he was the owner of the shop because of the way he sat at the bench. The world beyond the door may have been foreign to him, but this was his domain. It was a time capsule. I asked how long he had had the shop. He thought for a long time, pulled his hat off and played it through his fingers.

"I can't quite remember the year," he said. "It was just after the end of the war. There's been a lot of change. Change for the worse." The cobbler glanced at the boot he was holding. "It was all very different down here then."

"All clean and new?"

"Yes, like that," he said. "Casablanca was so clean, so sparkly, so filled with energy, with hope..." He broke off, stared out the window at the street. "It was like a new pair of shoes," he said.

I dug out the brogues I needed resoled. They were black with a small brass buckle at the side. I had bought them at Tricker's on

London's Jermyn Street long before, in a time when there was money in my pocket. The left shoe had a hole more than an inch across.

I placed the brogues on the counter. The cobbler took off his glasses, fumbled in a drawer, and fished for another pair. He put them on.

"These are very special shoes," he said. "Not like the rubbish people usually bring me."

I felt a twinge of pride run down my spine. "Can you resole them?"

The cobbler looked me in the eye. "You want rubber?"

"No, leather."

The old craftsman's eyes welled with tears. He turned round to the grimy wall behind his bench and tugged down a sheet of russet brown leather hanging on a makeshift hook.

"I have been keeping this since before my son was born," he said. "Every day I have looked at it, wondering if its time would ever come."

"How old is your son now?" I asked.

The cobbler scratched his hat. "About fifty," he said.

IN THE STABLES, Murad had finished one tale and moved on to the next. The guardians were lolling back on their chairs, smoking and listening hard. When I got home, they thanked me for hiring a storyteller for them.

"From tomorrow, he'll be working in the bidonville," I said.

"But where will he tell his stories?" asked Osman.

"In one of the houses," I said.

"Oh, no," said the Bear, "because the houses are very small and there won't be enough space for everyone."

"Well, out in the street, then."

"No, no, it's far too dirty and wet."

Murad lifted a hand from his lap and waved it outside. "We

walked through a pleasant garden out there," he said. "I will tell the stories there, and the people from outside will come in to listen."

The guardians said nothing. Like me, their memories were still fresh of the time their extended families had marched into Dar Khalifa and taken refuge within its walls. It had ended in catastrophe.

"The garden can be used until we find a better place," I said sternly.

That evening Ottoman arrived and met Murad, who was still holding court in the middle stable.

"We will hold the first storytelling session in our garden," I said.

Ottoman smiled. "Hicham would have liked that," he replied, "for a garden is a fragment of Paradise." Then he seemed a little uneasy. "Are you sure you want to hold it here?"

Just as I was about to reply, the doorbell rang.

Escorting visitors in had been Hamza's obsession. He would prowl up and down at the front door like a rottweiler waiting to be fed. He saw it as his responsibility to vet anyone who came to call, and would often turn people away, even invited guests, declaring that I was out, or that I was too busy to receive them. But now Hamza was gone, visitors had to wait until Rachana or I ran down. The other two guardians refused to go anywhere near the front door. They said it was beneath them.

Every afternoon a stream of people turned up, hoping their problems would be magically dispatched by the foreigner who had been foolish enough to take on the Caliph's House. There were electricians who had lost their jobs, former employees of ours whose wives had left them, and children who needed their school fees to be paid.

The doorbell rang again, longer and harder than before. Murad the storyteller began a third tale. The guardians looked at him adoringly. He was the answer to their prayers, their own personal entertainer. I walked across the lawn and opened the garden door.

A frail, squat figure was standing outside. He was carrying a claw hammer in one hand and a bundle of nails in the other, and seemed nervous. When he saw me, his jet-black eyes narrowed until they were no more than shiny specks. I greeted him. The man pressed a hand down to his wetted gray hair and introduced himself. It was then that I remembered him. His name was Marwan; he had done some carpentry work for us a few months before.

"I am sorry, but we don't need a carpenter any longer," I said.

Marwan stooped, ducked a little more, and pressed down his hair again. "Oh," he said.

"I am sorry."

"My son is ill and my wife's eyesight is almost gone," he said. "I am willing to do anything, anything at all."

I apologized again. "I wish I could help you," I said. "But I can't, unless..."

"Unless?"

"Unless you would like to work as a guardian. We had to let the last one go because he attacked a mason with his teeth."

Marwan's deep-set eyes glittered like shards of obsidian. "I promise to defend your house as if it were the Royal Palace," he said.

I thanked him.

The carpenter put down the claw hammer and the nails and held my hands in his. "You are a good man, Monsieur Tahir," he said under his breath.

A FEW DAYS later I went back to Sukayna the astrologer, at the mattress shop. I planned to ask her how a house could bleed. But the real reason I returned was because I had dreamed of the magic carpet again. This time, the princess was no longer locked in her tower. She was standing in the doorway, a sprinkling of snow covering the ground. A sackcloth hood had been thrown over her head. I couldn't see her face, but I knew it was the princess.

Nearby, a gallows had been erected. The girl was about to be led out. Her hands were tied with twine, her feet bare. Just as she started moving, staggering, I woke up with a start. I was drenched in sweat.

The astrologer welcomed me. She twisted the curtain so that it fell straight, hiding us from the mattress makers in the shop. She didn't say anything at first, but looked at me with concentration, her bottle-green eyes staring into mine.

"You did not come about the house," she said.

I sensed my mouth taste cold, as if in the presence of danger. "You said it was bleeding."

"I did, but that's not why you are here."

I sat down, cleared my throat. I told her about the dreams, about the flying carpet, the far-off kingdom, and the princess.

"She was being taken out to be hanged," I said. I wiped a hand over my face. I was sweating again.

The astrologer looked at me. I could feel her eyes scanning my face. "You have the answers," she said after a long pause.

I was going to deny it. But I knew the link between the princess and my life.

Sukayna seemed to read my thoughts. "Tell me about it," she said.

I stood up, pushed my hands onto the back wall of her room, leaned forward, my head down. I breathed in deeply, my ribs lifting, and my chest swelling with air.

"Last year while traveling through Pakistan," I said, "I was arrested by the secret police along with my film crew. They stripped me, blindfolded me, chained my hands high behind my back, and took me to a torture jail. They called it 'The Farm.'

"One morning I was taken out before dawn, blindfolded, manacled, and stripped to my underwear. The guard told me to pray. He led me onto a patch of gravel. I could feel it under my bare feet. He said that the end of my life had come."

Sukayna breathed in through her mouth. "How long were you kept prisoner?"

"For sixteen days. Most of it was spent chained up, all of it in a solitary cell. I was subjected to many hours of interrogation in a torture room."

"Have you ever been so scared?"

I shook my head. "The smell of my sweat changed," I said. "I was so frightened that my sweat smelled like cat pee. But the morning they took me out blindfolded to shoot me, I wasn't frightened any longer. I was just terribly sad—sad that I wouldn't see Ariane and Timur grow up. I knelt on the gravel as they ordered me, I held very still, waiting for the bullet.

"Keep still and they won't botch it, I thought.

"But the bullet never came."

chapter nine

You possess only what will not be lost in a shipwreck.

El Gazali

Word of Murad the storyteller spread from Dar Khalifa out into the shantytown. The imam approached me as I drove through on the way to Café Mabrook the next Friday afternoon. He was forever loitering outside the small whitewashed mosque, with a broom in one hand and a sharp-edged stone in the other, ready to hurl at the wicked boys.

He thanked me on behalf of the community.

"The television from Cairo is rotting their heads," he said forcefully. "It's time for them to remember their traditions, to remember the great tales we all heard in our youth."

He asked when the storyteller would begin his work.

"Tonight," I said. "He will start tonight."

The imam stooped forward and kissed my hand. "*Inshallah,* if God wills it," he said.

AT CAFÉ MABROOK, all the usual Friday afternoon characters were in position. Zohra's husband was sitting in the corner, lost in his own world. Hafad was telling Hakim about a grandfather clock he had bought from a junk shop in Der Omar, scoping out the shape with his arms. Dr. Mehdi was sitting at the same table, wearing an immaculate mustard-colored jelaba and a pair of matching baboush. He stood up to greet me, and kissed my cheeks.

Abdul-Latif's thumbless hand slid me an ashtray and a glass of café noir.

"We are together again," said the surgeon.

"Like old times," said Hafad.

"May we never be parted again," Hakim added.

I told them about my journey to Marrakech, about the shop where tales were for sale, and of my new acquaintance with Murad the storyteller.

Dr. Mehdi asked if I had discovered the story in my heart.

"Not yet," I said, "but Murad told me his . . . the 'Tale of Mushkil Gusha.'"

The doctor smiled broadly, the smile of a man whose face masked an elevated mind. "Now that you have heard the story," he said, "I hope you remembered to tell it last night."

"To my children," I said, "before they went to bed."

Hafad the clock-lover lit a cigarette and choked out a lungful of smoke. "That story's nonsense," he said. "Only an idiot would tell the same tale every week. Nothing but stupid superstition!"

We sat silently sipping our coffee, each of us pondering our own thoughts. Then, one of the henpecked husbands at another table stood up and came over. He was a regular, tall and nervous, with a thick crop of gray hair brushed down to the side. I had never spoken to him before, nor even heard his voice, for he was usually too henpecked to converse.

"Excuse me," he said in no more than a whisper. "I heard you speaking about Mushkil Gusha, the remover of difficulties."

Hafad stubbed out his cigarette and grunted.

"Yes, we were," I said. "Do you know the tale?"

The henpecked husband inched forward until he was standing at the edge of our table. "That story saved me from death," he said.

Hafad rolled his eyes. Dr. Mehdi pulled a chair from another table.

"Please sit with us," he said.

The fearful man sat down and wished us peace.

"Twenty years ago I was working at the port repairing fishing nets," he said. "I learned to do it as a child and got so good that everyone knew me. Whenever there was a tangled net or a complicated tear, the fishermen would come to me. They paid me well, and I was content. I used to sleep on a mattress in the shed where I worked. Sometimes they'd call for me in the middle of the night, when the boats were going out. I would turn on my gas lamp and pull out my twine.

"One evening I was sound asleep when one of the fishermen, the captain of a small boat, pounded at my door. He shouted that he needed me. I took out my box of needles and thread, pulled on my jelaba, and opened the door. The captain said three of his crew were sick, that he had to go and lay the nets right away, and he needed an extra pair of hands. I refused, for I get seasick easily. My place is on the land.

"The captain begged me in the name of his father and his grandfather. He said we would be back by dawn, that he would give me twice the usual pay. Reluctantly, I agreed, and we set off.

"It was so dark, the water looked like ink. The boat was unsound, and was taking in water from the start. I asked God to protect me. Right away I could feel the waves rolling under us, and hear the wooden frame creaking. I told the captain and the crew that I was frightened, but they laughed at me and called me bad names.

"Eventually we reached the fishing waters and cast the nets. I lay down and fell asleep, but was woken by a violent jolt. One of the fishermen started shouting. He said we had struck something, that the

he was picking them, he noticed a bright glowing light shining from a nearby hill. Wondering what was causing the strange light, he put the oranges down and approached cautiously.

"Shielding his eyes with his hand, he realized that the radiant light was beaming out from a cleft in the mountain. He tiptoed closer and peered through the crevice, only to be dazzled by the light. Assuming it was the lair of the Angel of Death, he turned and ran away as fast as he was able."

The storyteller broke off, and paused a moment until his audience could stand the anticipation no longer.

"The dervish ran and he ran," Murad went on, "until he saw three men standing under a tree. They were thieves, and they would have killed him, but they were curious why he was running for his life. Before they could ask him, the dervish cried out, 'The Angel of Death is in the mountain, and his face is shining like gold!' The thieves, who had heard of a fabulous lost hoard and were searching for it, guessed correctly that the dervish had stumbled across the treasure cave itself. They asked him to show them the cave's location so that they could be sure to stay away from it. The dervish agreed and led them to the entrance of the cave.

"Thanking God for leading them to the fortune, the thieves dispatched the dervish, and slipped through the crevice to lay their hands on the treasure. The cavern was filled with sacks of gold coins, emeralds, and rubies and even surpassed the men's greed.

"Realizing there was too much treasure to carry away on their backs, the thieves sent the youngest one to the town to find a horse and to bring back some food. When he arrived at the town, the youngest thief stole a horse, and then bought two kebabs, which he poisoned. He galloped back to the cave, where his two brother thieves were waiting to kill him, so that they could divide the treasure between the two of them.

"As soon as the youngest thief returned, his throat was cut by the other two. Searching through his bag, they found the kebabs, ate them, and fell down dead. Tethered outside, the horse managed to break free and run off.

"As for the treasure, it still lies in the cavern," said Murad, "protected by three skeletons and by the Angel of Death."

ON THE NIGHT the storyteller spoke in the garden of the Caliph's House, I felt myself connecting with Morocco's ancient core. It was as if I was peering into a well, and was able to glimpse down through stratas and substratas, through millennia, to the nucleus of the society.

The residents of the shantytown had been wrapped in blankets and woollen caps. They were frozen, but their numbness had melted away as soon as the story filtered into their ears. Just as in other public performances I have witnessed in North Africa, the audience stood up, wandered about, heckled, and chatted to their friends all the way through the tales.

In our society it's considered the height of rudeness to do anything but sit rigid during a performance, and then clap politely at the end. Such prim behavior is probably a vestige of Victorian etiquette, and is undoubtedly quite new to the West. The Moroccan audience echos how Europe must once have been, until the Elizabethan age and beyond. Spectators watching Shakespeare's plays at the old London Globe were expected to move around, heckle, and provide a constant flow of feedback. The European audience then must have been how the Moroccan audience is now: dynamic, overwhelming, and very much a part of the tale.

The residents of the bidonville were captivated by Murad's stories. Like my sisters and me sitting on the turquoise leather couch so long ago, they had been drawn into another world, into a realm without limits.

My father used to say that stories are part of the most precious heritage of mankind. As children, he would draw our attention to the inner meaning of tales, helping us to tease one layer apart from the next. "There are some areas of the mind," he would tell us, "which can only be reached with stories, because they penetrate deep into the subconscious, like ink dripped onto blotting paper."

The way stories were underappreciated in the West was something that preoccupied my father, and it sometimes dismayed him. He could not grasp why the West had marginalized such a powerful learning device for so long. After all, he said, the tool was in its hands, staring it in the face.

Every man, woman, and child had begged Murad to stay and talk all night. He did so, only ending when the first rays of dawn had chased the darkness from the shantytown. When the audience finally slipped away, back to their homes, the garden looked as if a herd of stampeding wildebeest had charged through.

But it didn't matter.

What mattered was that a traditional learning tool had been activated and had conjured a realm from pure imagination.

I HAD BEEN in solitary at The Farm for a week when one of the guards, a junior, whispered to me at dawn. He said my colleagues and I were not the usual prisoners, that there must have been some mistake. If I gave him a phone number, he said, he would make a call: tell the outside world we were being held. I asked him to get my cell phone from the colonel's office and look up my sister's new number.

"That's too dangerous."

"Then get me a scrap of paper and a pen and I'll write down a number."

"That's too dangerous as well," he replied. "You have to tell me a number now and I will remember it. It will be my duty."

These days with cell phones, we are used to getting through to family and friends by pressing a couple of keys selected from a menu. Like most people, I am hopeless at committing long numbers to heart. Heighten the pressure by the stress of solitary confinement, and the only number I could remember was my sister-in-law's. I had never bothered to save her home number and, somehow, had remembered it.

The guard memorized the number, and left a message on her home phone the next day. It said: "Tahir Shah and his friends are alive." When she received the message, she could not understand why someone would leave a message saying that we were okay, unless it meant we had been in danger. So she called Rachana, who had been wondering why I hadn't checked in. And Rachana called my sister Saira, who is known for her film about women under the Taliban.

Saira jumped on the next flight to Pakistan and applied pressure on the Pakistani government to reveal what they knew. The government admitted they had arrested us, but couldn't say which unit was holding us. It gives an idea how many torture prisons there must be in Pakistan.

After fifteen days, Saira was informed that we would be deported before dawn the next day. And we were. A guard cut our fingernails so short the fingers bled. He said the samples were for DNA. We were given our clothes, ordered to sign documents stating we had not been mistreated, and bustled aboard a flight to Abu Dhabi, with a connection to London. Our luggage was all sent to Oslo, the Norwegian capital, hinting at the Pakistani officials' faltering knowledge of European geography.

At Heathrow Airport we were taken aside by British Intelligence. They were in a huddle, gray-suited officers who spoke very quietly as if there were ears all around.

Once I got home, I tried to explain to Rachana what I had seen and felt in Pakistan. But it was as if spoken language was too weak a medium to pass on the depth of my sadness, my fear.

The day after being reunited, Ariane asked me where I had been and why Mommy was so worried while I was gone. I concocted a scaled-down version of events, because I thought Ariane had a right to an explanation, too. The next day she told her friends at school that her daddy had been in prison. The teacher never looked at me the same after that.

We let the dust settle and spoke very little about Pakistan. Too much emotion had already been spent on the episode, one which I wanted to forget. Then early one morning, when I was still bleary-eyed in bed, I felt Rachana's shadow over me. And I heard her voice: "An angel is watching you," she said.

I didn't know how to tell her that I had pledged to go back to Central Asia, to finish the film on Afghanistan.

A FEW DAYS after Murad's event, I dropped in on the cobbler to pick up my brogues. He was gluing a stiletto heel back into place. His eyes lit up when he saw me. I asked if the shoes were ready. The old man tugged off his woolly blue hat, clutched it to his chest, grabbed my hand, and shook it very hard.

"I have waited for years to work on such fine shoes as these," he said.

The cobbler turned to a wall of pigeonholes behind him and, with great care, removed a crumpled brown paper bag. He placed it on the counter and took out the brogues one at a time. They looked like new.

"These days no one challenges us," he said. "And because there is no challenge, there is no reason to work hard. And with no reason to work hard, we have all become lazy." The cobbler wrapped up the shoes and scratched a broken fingernail down his nose. "Lazy people are like cancer," he said. "They spread. Before you know it, the entire country is destroyed. But there is hope for us all when a man like you brings a pair of shoes like these to a small shop like this."

The cobbler put on his woolly hat and shook my hand a second time. "You have done me a great service," he said. "You have made me feel proud to be Moroccan again."

SUKAYNA SENT A message with Zohra the next day. It was written in red ink, and asked if I would visit her at the mattress shop once the sun had gone down. I spent the afternoon at the hammam with Abdelmalik, having the skin rasped from my body with a masseur's glove. The *gommage* process was so excruciatingly painful, I vowed aloud that I would never return. The masseur grinned through broken teeth. He knew as well as I that, however much you dislike it at the time, the hammam is an addiction hard to shed.

Once we were lounging in the dressing room, I told Abdelmalik about Murad. He said he had heard that in Iceland television was banned every Thursday night. It was a way of promoting reading and, better still, of encouraging families to tell their epic tales.

"We should do the same in Morocco," he said.

The astrologer was standing outside the mattress shop with a dead chicken in her hands. She furled the bird up in a sheet of nylon sacking, rinsed her hands clean. I didn't comment on the sacrifice. It was someone else's medicine. We clambered over a large double mattress being refilled with padding. Once behind the lace curtain, Sukayna lit a candle and tipped it so that three drops of wax splattered on the floor.

"I have been thinking about your dream," she said.

"The execution?"

"Yes."

"Do you think it has a meaning?"

"There's a beginning, a middle, but no end," she said.

"The execution's the end."

"No, no," Sukayna urged, "the end hasn't come yet."

"So?"

"So, you must let the dream slip into your head once again. It's telling you a story."

"What story?"

"The story of your own experience."

"But I've never flown on a magic carpet!"

Sukayna tipped the candle again, allowing a few more drops of wax to hit the cement. "Dreams are like fairy stories," she said, "and fairy stories are like dreams. They are reflections of each other, and they heal the sleeping mind."

Sukayna stopped because there was a commotion on the other side of the curtain. It sounded as if the owner of the double mattress was arguing about the price to repair it. When the noise had died down, I asked why Dar Khalifa was bleeding.

The astrologer looked over at me, her eyes an ocean of green. "You don't understand it, do you?"

"No, no, I *don't* understand."

"Your house is not like other houses," she said, "It's much more than the walls and the roof you see. There's a spirit, *baraka,* that touches the people inside from time to time."

"I don't follow."

"Dar Khalifa was once a long way from Casablanca," she said. "It was built where it is because it was so far from the town. And before the shantytown was there, you would have been able to see the ocean from the garden. It would have been tranquil."

"It *is* tranquil," I said defensively.

"It would have been much more tranquil." She smiled.

"I still don't understand what you are leading to."

Sukayna tightened her headscarf. "Dar Khalifa is not just a house," she said.

I looked at her, anxiously trying to work out what she meant. "What more can it be than that?" I asked, losing patience.

"It's a refuge," she said. "The refuge of a holy man."

MARWAN THE CARPENTER blended in well to life at the Caliph's House. He always arrived on time for work, made everyone laugh, and became great friends with Murad. The two men were so inseparable that Marwan pleaded with the blind storyteller to come and stay at his own home on the far side of the shantytown. His shack came with the added bonus that it had a small paddock beside it that could be used for nocturnal storytelling events.

I had been anxious that Osman and the Bear would turn on the newcomer. After all, they were related to each other through marriage and, unlike them, Marwan was a Berber. In Morocco, the bond of blood is as strong as tempered steel. But to my surprise and great relief, the existing guardians welcomed Marwan as if he were a long-lost brother.

There was something I found even more remarkable, Marwan's intelligence. On the surface he may have been an unassuming carpenter, and now a guardian, but he had a brilliant mind. He told me he had never received a formal education, had never even learned to read.

"My grandmother was my school," he said. "She taught me almost everything I know."

"Where?"

"At Azrou, in the cedar forest. My sisters were sent to class, but my grandmother refused to let me attend."

"Why?"

"Because she said they would teach me to read."

"That sounds like back-to-front thinking," I said.

"It does because you have been to school. But to her reading was a curse, a way of blocking real thinking."

Marwan broke off, leaned on his rake. "I'll tell you something," he said.

"What?"

"Everything I know has come in through my ears. I've never read a word."

"So?"

"So I see the world in a different way."

ORIENTAL CULTURE, OF which Morocco is certainly a part, has at its root a belief in selflessness. It's a subject rarely spoken of in the West, and even less frequently understood. To be selfless, you would give charity anonymously, walk softly on the earth, and look out for others—even total strangers—before you look out for yourself. For the Arab mind, the self is an obstacle, an impediment, in humanity's quest for real progress. Life in Morocco introduced me time and again to people who had achieved a form of everyday selflessness. It was a quality I respected beyond any other, a goal—perhaps unattainable—I hoped one day to touch. I found myself wondering if the search for the story in my heart might be a component, an element somehow linked to selflessness.

As always, my teachers were the people around me.

One morning I asked Zohra if she had seen a hundred dirhams which I remembered leaving in my trousers the night before. She looked worried, said she would search for the money, and ran off upstairs. When she came down, she was holding a crumpled hundred-dirham note.

"Here it is, Monsieur," she said, handing it over.

I thanked her.

That afternoon Rachana found the hundred-dirham note I had actually lost. It was on the nightstand beside my bed. Zohra had been prepared to forgo a hundred dirhams of her own money, a huge sum, more than ten dollars, to cloak my carelessness.

Nothing was really so important to my father as the achievement of selflessness. He rarely mentioned it directly, but tried to guide us to it in a roundabout way. It was sometimes like setting out for a specific destination without a map or the name of the place you are hoping to find. With their rock-solid culture of values, stories were a way of understanding the goal.

During one visit to Morocco, I remember traveling back up toward Tangier. I had been given a small coin for my pocket money. We stopped at a market to buy some fruit. Standing there, I saw a woman with no hands, begging at the side of the road. In front of her was a bowl. I felt very bad for the woman, went over, and dropped my pocket money in the bowl.

When we got back to the car, I told my parents what I had done. I expected praise, to be told how well I had done. But my father's face soured.

"Never give charity if the reason is to make yourself feel better," he said. "Real charity is not selfish, but selfless."

After his death, I began to learn of my father's own selflessness. Hearing that he had died, a number of people wrote to tell me how he had helped them anonymously; they only realized later that he had been the benefactor.

Perhaps his strangest act of charity involved the Queen of England.

On a state visit through the Middle East, Her Majesty Queen Elizabeth had presented an Arab head of state with her customary gift, a signed photograph of herself in a silver frame. Reading about the gift over his morning tea, my father must have balked at such a presentation. Through Arab eyes it would be regarded as a tasteless embodiment of ego. My father withdrew a large amount of money from his bank, purchased in cash a gift more appropriate to royal Arabian taste, and had it sent to the head of state on behalf of the Queen of England.

ONE AFTERNOON MARWAN saw me reading in the garden. Unlike Osman and the Bear, he was always keen to make conversation. He came over, shook my hand, and wished me peace.

"What is your book?" he asked.

"Folktales from Scandinavia."

"How does it feel?"

"Good, it feels good."

Marwan touched a fingertip to his eye. "There," he said. "How does it feel there?"

"To my eyes?"

"Yes."

"It feels good."

"But it's different."

"Different to what?"

"To a story that comes in through the ears."

Over the first weeks that Marwan worked for us, I found myself thinking about his situation. He was a product of a far more ancient and, in some ways, a far purer system than I. In our world we frown on the illiterate because we feel they are missing out on the wealth of information stored in books. In a way, it's true of course. The very word "illiterate" is heavy with negative connotation.

But at the same time we are who we are as a result of illiteracy throughout much of human history. If you have no written language, you have to commit information to memory. Instead of reading it, you rely on those with the information—the storytellers—to recount it.

By their nature, most tribal and nomadic societies have had no writing system. And they are blessed as a result. They depend on each other for entertainment, for stimulation. Huddled around the campfire, the storytellers pass on the collective wisdom of the tribe. Their oral tradition is perfected and sleek, like stones in a river, rounded by time. The information has an extra dimension because it enters the body through the ears and not through the eyes. Listen, stare into the flames, and imagination unfolds.

I have seen storytellers casting their magic in the depths of the Peruvian Amazon, and in teahouses in Turkey, in India and Afghanistan. I have found them, too, in Papua New Guinea and in Patagonia, in Kenya's Rift Valley, in Namibia and Kazakhstan. Their effect is always the same. They walk a tightrope, no wider than a hairsbreadth, suspended between fact and fantasy, singing to the most primitive part of our minds. We cannot help but let them in. With words they can enchant us, teach us, pass on knowledge and wisdom, as they had done to Marwan.

Stories are a communal currency of humanity. They follow the same patterns irrespective of where they are found. And, inexplicably, the same stories appear in cultures continents apart. How is it that similar tales can be found in Iceland and in pre-Columbian America? How come Cinderella is considered European, but is also a part of the folklore of the American Algonquins?

My father used to tell me that stories offer the listener a chance to escape but, more importantly, he said, they provide people with a chance at maximizing their minds. Suspend ordinary constraints, allow the imagination to be freed, and we are charged with the capability of heightened thought.

Learn to use your eyes as if they are your ears, he said, and you become connected with the ancient heritage of man, a dream world for the waking mind.

chapter ten

Work is not what people think it is.
It is not just something which, when it is operating,
you can see from outside.

Jalaluddin Rumi

The thought of our home being built over a holy man's grave was unsettling at first. I didn't want to tell Rachana about it, in case it proved to be the straw that broke the camel's back. During the time we had lived in Morocco, we had crossed an ocean of difficulties, ranging from locusts to overweight rats, from police raids to Jinns and dismembered cats. At long last Rachana was getting used to life at the Caliph's House. Deep down I knew she regretted ever leaving the imagined tranquillity of London, and wished we were living in a sleepy corner of suburbia. But, as I kept reminding her, a life without steep learning curves is no life at all. I didn't want to tip the balance with another unwelcome revelation.

So I bit my lip.

As so often happened, I found myself trapped by Casablanca, or rather by Dar Khalifa. The maids, the guardians, and the surfeit of workers, who drifted in and out like the Atlantic tide, ensnared us with demands. I longed to take to the road and go in search of the story in my heart but, each time I tried to break free, a giant wave washed me back to shore.

Then, one morning, I received a telephone call from a stranger in Tangier. He spoke in a frail Italian voice and said he would explain who he was.

A month before, I had been accosted by a door-to-door salesman. Somehow he had made his way through the protective barrier of the shantytown and happened upon our house. He rapped hard on the door. I went out to see who was there. The salesman had a battered vinyl case, a scruffy mauve-colored suit, and dark circles round his eyes. I guessed he was in sales before he even opened his mouth. There was something about his fingers that gave it away. They fidgeted about, as if hoping to tantalize me with a range of manufactured goods.

The salesman lunged forward and pressed a business card onto my palm. "What do you need?" he asked.

I looked at him, wondered how I could get away without being too impolite. "I need to go back to my work," I said.

The man, whose card advertised his name as Abdul Hafiz, flipped open his shabby attaché case and snatched a handful of brochures.

"Whatever your need, I have a product," he said confidently. "If you have rats, blocked drains, dandruff, or boils, I can solve your problem."

"We did have rats," I said, "but they seem to have been chased away, because we rent a cat twice a week from a neighbor in the bidonville. As for blocked drains, the guardians clear those. And, dandruff and boils, well..." I said, "I think we have them both covered."

I thanked the salesman, stepped back into the house, and shut the front door.

Another member of society might have felt disheartened at having a door shut in his face. But to a salesman it's the dropping of a gauntlet.

I turned to go back to my library and my book. There was another loud thump at the door. I am a believer that everyone deserves a certain amount of attention, even salesmen with goods no one wants.

So I opened the door a second time.

Abdul Hafiz jabbed a fidgety finger across the threshold. "I know," he said menacingly, "I have guessed it."

"Guessed what?"

"What you need."

I took a deep breath.

"You need an electric razor," he said.

"No, I don't."

I was about to close the door again, when the salesman slipped a pad of paper from his case.

"Write on this what you do need," he said.

"But I don't need anything."

Abdul Hafiz brushed a hair off the lapel of his mauve jacket. "Everyone needs something," he said.

It was then I remembered. There was one thing I wanted very much to find, an original edition of Richard Burton's *Arabian Nights*, like the one my father had given to the guest. I wrote the title of the book and the details of the edition on the paper. Abdul Hafiz squinted at the words, took my telephone number, clicked the catches of his attaché case closed.

He shook my hand, turned about, and trudged back down the muddy track through the shantytown. I never expected to hear of him again. The chance of there being a first edition of Burton's great work in Morocco was slim; the chance of it being for sale was one in a million.

So when the call came from Tangier, it was all the more of a surprise.

"Monsieur Shah?" said the Italian voice on the phone.

"Yes, I am Tahir Shah."

"Monsieur Shah, I have the books."

"Which books?"

"The books you asked Abdul Hafiz to find."

BEFORE CATCHING THE train to Tangier, I stopped in at the cobbler's shop with another pair of worn-out shoes. The ancient craftsman was huddled up against the cold, the navy wool hat pulled down low on his creased brow. He greeted me, the lengthy greeting of old friends. He asked me my name. I told him.

"I will call you Tahir," he said, "and you must call me Noureddine."

"I am honored to do so."

The cobbler licked his top lip. "Have you brought me another treasure?" he asked.

I fumbled in my satchel and dug out a pair of suede brogues. The soles were completely worn through. I apologized for not having taken more care of the shoes. The old cobbler's eyes seemed to glow. He picked them up one at a time and ran a thumbnail down the stitching.

"Your feet have known luxury," he said.

"I'm going to Tangier to buy some books," I explained, "and I'll be back in three or four days."

"They will be ready by then, if God wills it," said the cobbler, nudging the shoes into one of the pigeonholes behind him.

I was about to leave, when the old man touched a finger to my cuff. "Would you bring the books to show me?" he asked.

TANGIER HOLDS A special place in my heart. It was there that my grandfather lived, then died, knocked down outside his villa on the steep rue de la Plage by a reversing Coca-Cola truck. He was an Afghan named Ikbal Ali Shah. Much of his life was spent traveling the Middle East and Central Asia, writing books on the worlds he encountered. When his wife died of cancer before she reached sixty, he was distraught beyond words. He set sail to Morocco with a sea-trunk full of books, because it was the one place he could think of where they had never been together.

Whenever I visit Tangier, I can feel my grandfather's presence. I imagine that I spot him walking up the hill to take his usual seat at Café France, or strolling down near Cecil's Hotel on the palm-fringed Corniche. His air of quiet sophistication, a bridge between East and West, matched the city in which he spent the last decade of his life.

My grandfather had passed the baton of storytelling to my father, a baton which he had received from his own father, the Nawab Amjed Ali Shah, a century ago.

I was only three when he was struck down and killed, but I just remember him, an elderly figure in the yellow light of afternoon, sitting on his terrace holding court. The more time I have spent in Morocco, the more I have come to appreciate his own love of the kingdom, and have understood the way it must have reminded him of home.

He had been raised at Sardhana, our family's principality in northern India, as well as at our ancestral lands in Afghanistan's mountain fortress, the Hindu Kush. His childhood had been tinted in the rich colors of Eastern folklore, an immersion in the tales of great heroes and archvillains, a backdrop woven from the *Arabian Nights*.

Like his father before him, he had been taught to think and learn through the matrix of stories. He regarded them as a repository of information, a tool for higher thought, a baton to be passed on and on.

THE TRAIN PULLED into Tangier's new terminal, a mile or two from the town. It was a damp winter day, a chilling wind ripping in from across the strait from Spain. I followed the other passengers' example, shunned the underground passage, and scurried over the railway tracks despite the oncoming trains.

No sane Moroccan would ever forgo a good shortcut.

I dialed the number of the salesman's contact, a man called Señor Benito, who was supposedly selling a first edition of Burton's *A Thousand and One Nights*. No reply. I tried a second time, and a recorded voice revealed in French and then Arabic that the number had been disconnected. I hailed a taxi.

"To the Continental," I said.

THERE CAN BE no twentieth-century travel writer who has not been at least a little affected by the life of Richard Francis Burton. He was a polymath, a man of astonishing ability, who pushed his body and his mind to the limits of their capacity. In modern terms he was racist, sexist, politically incorrect beyond all measure, but at the same time he was a man propelled by the devil's drive.

Despite his personality flaws, I regard Burton as a champion, a kind of role model. After reading his *First Footsteps in East Africa* in my teens, I traveled to Africa and lived there for three years. Then I journeyed to the port of Santos, in Brazil, where Burton had been based as a diplomat. After that I went to Iceland, to Trieste and Salt Lake City, each one a destination on the Burtonian map. I took up fencing because it had been his passion, joined London's Athenaeum Club because he had been a member and, when we were first married, I spent all our savings on a secret report in his own hand, detailing the wealth of the Sultan of Zanzibar.

THE TAXI ROLLED down the Corniche, past the port, and up the hill through narrowing streets lined with random life, to the Continental. I knew of the hotel because Richard Burton had stayed there waiting for his long-suffering wife, Isabel, while translating the *Arabian Nights*. A grand, square colossus of a building, it leers out across the strait toward Spain, as it has done for a century and more.

The hotel was sprinkled with the usual array of tourist kitsch, meek-looking porters, and imposing wear and tear. It couldn't have changed much since Burton had arrived in December 1885, laden with trunks filled with papers and with books.

I asked for a single room. A key was slid across the mahogany counter and a finger pointed to the stairs.

"Fifth floor," said the clerk.

"Is there a lift?"

"Certainly not, Monsieur."

There was a sense that only the hardiest of travelers would ever put up at Hotel Continental. The staircase was like a shearing mountain path, the treads between each step extra deep, hinting at the Victorian hardiness that built them. Once at the top, I found my room, little more than an alcove hidden between two others, smothered in blood-orange paint. I turned on the tap to wash my face. The water supply had run dry.

I retraced my steps down to the reception, and dialed the salesman's contact once again. The number was still out of order. The clerk demanded to know whom I was calling.

"There's a man selling some books," I said.

"Books?"

"Yes, by Richard Burton."

"You are an actor, Monsieur?" the clerk inquired.

"No, not by the actor," I said. "There's another Richard Burton. He was a traveler. In fact, he stayed here a long time ago."

"Last year?"

"No, not last year. Before that."

"The year before?"

I replied in the negative. "No, more than a hundred years ago," I said.

The clerk combed his lower teeth through his mustache. "How do you hope to ever find him now?" he asked.

It was one of those inane conversations, the kind which gets trapped in your head, and you find yourself replaying mentally again and again on long-distance bus journeys. I showed the manager the telephone number and the name.

"Ah, Señor Benito," he said knowingly. He tapped a hand to the reception's bell.

A submissive bellboy with large feet appeared.

"Ibrahim will show you," he said.

As I plodded in Ibrahim's oversized footsteps, up the steep slope toward the top of Tangier's medina, I cautioned myself to remember how the Arab world is arranged. In Europe we bluster about demanding answers to direct questions. Whereas in the East a far more circuitous and ancient system is at work, where a little inane conversation can open gilded doors.

ALMOST A MILE from the Continental, Ibrahim the bellboy froze in his tracks. He turned ninety degrees to the left, to face an ordinary door painted gloss white. He stuck out a hand. I rewarded it appropriately.

"Señor Benito does not appreciate women," he said.

I thanked him for the tip, tapped at the door. A dog growled through the letterbox, and its din mingled with the scent of figs. A firm hand struck the dog, and the animal yelped away. Then came the grinding sound of tired old feet approaching slowly, a key turning, and rusting hinges pressing back on themselves.

The smell of figs became all the stronger when the door was fully open. Señor Benito stepped through the frame and out into the sunlight. His movements were made in slow motion, allowing ample time for observation. He was a relic of old Tangier, dressed head to toe in pressed cream linen, with a fuchsia handkerchief overflowing from his top pocket. His slender form dazzled all who saw it. There was not an ounce of fat. His face and all visible skin were as pale as his suit, almost dove gray. I offered my hand. Señor Benito held the ends of my fingers for a moment and squinted.

"*Bonjour,*" he said.

"I have come about the *Arabian Nights.*"

"Please come inside."

Moving in slow motion, I followed the lines of cream linen through the doorway, past a miniature sharp-toothed dog, into a rambling villa, painted in off-white inside and out. The building was less of a house and more like a temple, dedicated to flamboyant indulgence and to phallic art. Every inch of space was adorned with paintings, sketches, and sculptures, each one a study on manhood.

The elderly Italian led the way into the salon, a well-proportioned room adorned with phalluses great and small. There were phalluses torn from Greek marbles, phalluses portrayed in oils, sketched in charcoal, and, on an elaborate mantelpiece, was a phallus crafted from wire mesh and parrot feathers.

"We spoke on the telephone," I said, when we were seated in the salon. It was a sentence designed to break the silence, and to cure my unease at the phallic decor. Señor Benito smoothed a crease from his cream linen shirt. He sauntered over toward the window, filled with the winter blur of Gibraltar in the distance, and he turned.

"I have a nice bottle of port," he said, "a Sandeman sixty-three."

He rolled back the northern hemisphere of an ornamental globe, revealing a concealed drinks cabinet. His ashen fingers fished out the bottle, poured two glasses.

Benito touched the port to his lips. "Thank God for the Iberian Peninsula," he said softly.

"Could I see the books?"

The old Italian jerked his chin toward a built-in set of shelves at the far end of the room. "Help yourself," he said.

I scanned the bookcase. There must have been five hundred books, half on phallic interests in every language of the world, the other half dedicated to works of African exploration. At ankle level, I found the set of ten volumes, the black cloth spines bejeweled in gold, *Alf Layla wa Layla,* "A Thousand Nights and a Night."

"Go on, take them out," said the Italian.

I leaned forward and pulled out the books on either side. Then, carefully excavating them from the shelf, I pushed my fingers behind the set, and urged them out one by one. The bindings were exquisite, the condition near perfect. I opened the first book. It began with the name of the Indian city, Benares, the date in Roman numerals, MDCCCLXXXV, 1885. After that, the words "Printed by the Kamashastra Society for Private Subscribers Only."

"Two thousand copies were printed," said Benito, topping up our glasses. "After the first ten volumes, Burton published six more, *The Supplements*."

"They were really printed in London, in Stoke Newington," I said.

The Italian put a hand to his heart. "The censorship police," he said dimly. "They have hounded good men before and since."

"I don't understand how Abdul Hafiz the salesman found you."

Benito meandered over to the bookcase, stroking a hand over an oversized Roman phallus as he went. He only stopped when he was standing a foot away from me, his face three inches from mine.

"The Network," he said.

I stepped back and he stepped forward, like a tango partner following the lead. I was pinned to the bookcase.

"Are you a salesman as well, then?"

Benito blinked. "A collector," he said. "And as such I am connected to the Network."

"What is the Network?"

"A group of people who link other people together," he said. "A man with a want, and another with a need."

"Where is it, the Network?"

The Italian turned his palms upward and stuck his arms out to the side. "It's all around us," he said.

"But your need... to sell such a fine set of books as these?"

Benito glanced down at his white canvas shoes. "It's a need

inspired by a certain standard of living," he said. "Ask any collector and he will tell you."

"Tell me what?"

"Tell you that there's no good having all this if you can't afford a nice glass of port from time to time."

AFTER AN HOUR of conversation I plucked up courage to inquire the price of the books. I sensed Benito had lived in Tangier since the old days, when Paul Bowles's salon attracted the great writers of the Beat generation. As an adoptive Moroccan, he knew the protocol. Unlike the West, where the price is the first thing you demand, in the East a transaction is far more subtle. You first establish that you want to buy an object. You inspect it and, only then, do you ask how much it might be.

The Italian didn't say the price at first.

He strolled back to the window, taking in two millennia of phallic art, and took a good hard look at the rain.

"I've lived in this house since before you were born," he said. "Tangier is sleeping now. But back then it was wide-awake. It raged with life, with vitality like a circus of the bizarre." He put out a hand and weighed his words. "I heard from the Network that a young man, a writer, was searching for one thing in life," he said. "When asked to write it down on a piece of paper, he wrote its name. Imagine how I felt...for that object you dream of is sitting in my own home, gathering dust."

Benito mumbled a price, a quarter of the market rate. I thanked him, wrote out a check. He stepped slowly across the room to a fine bureau with tooled cabriole legs, opened one of the miniature drawers, removed a scrap of crumpled paper, shuffled back over, and passed it to me. Written on it in my hand were the words "Richard Burton's *Arabian Nights,* Benares Edition, 1885."

The Italian collector looked out at the rain. "Perhaps we could have lunch tomorrow," he said in a whisper. "I know a nice little place for fish."

OPENING THE CURTAINS next morning at the Continental, I was dazzled by a flood of canary-yellow light. I held a hand to my brow

and spied the ferries straddling the strait. Tangier is a hybrid of Europe, Africa, and the Arab world. It is a city of such charm and sophistication that the people who reside there sometimes forget their astonishing good fortune.

Eager to explore, I descended the steep steps and found the desk clerk eating his breakfast on the counter. He grunted a greeting, leaned down to open a cabinet below, and pulled out a pair of scratched sunglasses.

"We keep these for special guests," he said with loathing.

I thanked him, bolstered at the thought of extra privilege, and ambled out to the street. For thirty minutes I roved up and down and up again until, after endless twists, turns, and dead ends, I came to the Grand Socco, Tangier's great square.

Poised at the edge of the old medina, the Grand Socco is a cross-section of East and West. There are market stalls erupting with produce, cafés packed with gritty no-nonsense men, fountains, benches, and a great mosque. There is a gate, too, leading into the shadowed passages of the medina.

Burton had passed through it into the square during the winter of 1885. He had come to seek fresh air, while working on his epic translation. Part of the reason for his visit to Morocco was to scope the country out. It had long been his dream to become the British ambassador, and the signs were good that his appointment was imminent. With twenty-five years of experience in the Consular Service, Burton had never been promoted, despite regarding the Prime Minister himself as a personal friend. He put his stalled diplomatic career down to a report he had written four decades earlier while in the employ of Sir Charles Napier, on a Karachi male brothel, touting a wide range of eunuchs and young boys.

The first volume of *Arabian Nights* had appeared with much media attention in the second week of September, three months before Burton docked at Tangier. Each month or two another volume was completed, then printed and mailed directly to subscribers. The early reviews had been mostly encouraging, and no subscribers had demanded their money back. Despite the good reception, Burton must have been seething from an article in the well-respected *Edinburgh Review*. Its correspondent, Harry Reeve, had written: "Probably no European has ever gathered such an appalling collection of degrading customs and statistics of vice. It is a work which no decent gentleman will long permit to stand upon his shelves… Galland is for the nursery, Lane for the study, and Burton for the sewers."

Tangier's damp winter climate had brought on Burton's gout. He didn't much appreciate the town, so it was perhaps just as well that he was passed over for the position of ambassador. He wrote to John Payne, a fellow translator of the *Arabian Nights:* "Tangier is beastly, but not bad for work." His description of the Grand Socco is recorded in the tenth volume. He said that the coffeehouses were all closed after a murder had occurred in one of them. The usual clientele had been forced to drink their refreshments and take their *kif* out on the street, despite the miserable conditions.

It was there he found a storyteller plying his trade. Characteristically harsh in his judgment, Burton was scathing about the square, just as he was of the town in which it was found. He wrote: "It is a foul slope; now slippery with viscous mud, then powdery with fetid dust, dotted with graves and decaying tombs, unclean booths, gargotes and tattered tents, and frequented by women, mere bundles of unclean rags..."

Of the storyteller, he was a little more approving: "...he speaks slowly with emphasis, varying the diction with breaks of animation, abundant action and the most comical grimace: he advances, retires and wheels about, illustrating every point with pantomime; and his features, voice and gestures are so expressive that even Europeans who cannot understand a word of Arabic divine the meaning of his tale. The audience stands breathless and motionless surprising strangers by the ingeniousness and freshness of feeling under their hard and savage exterior."

Alas, there were no storytellers in evidence any longer. I scanned the square, taking in the detail, wondering how the atmosphere had changed in the century and more since Burton had stood there. One significant alteration was the fabulous Cinema Rif.

Now restored to its former glory, the Rif is an Art Deco jewel, a reminder of the years when the kingdom was a French protectorate. I sat on a bench opposite, closed my eyes, and let my mind slip into the past. I could see the high society limousines rolling up, mink coats and lip gloss, greased-back hair, and flashbulbs popping on opening night.

The sound of young voices stirred me back to the present.

Five boys were sitting at the far end of the bench. They were dressed in weatherworn clothes, all caked in mud. Their leader said something fast. The others groped through their pockets and pooled their funds: six marbles, four bottle tops, a painted twig, a blunt penknife, and a few coins. The money was separated out. Three of the boys started arguing, shouting at one another. Their argument broke into a scrap. One of the older boys suddenly turned on the smallest. They fell into the dirt, punches flying. The leader pulled them apart. He handed all the coins to the youngest boy, whose shirt had been ripped in the fight, and sent him off toward the cinema.

The others began playing marbles.

I asked why only one of them was going to the cinema. The leader glanced up, his sienna eyes catching the light.

"We only have the money for one to see the matinee, Monsieur," he said. "So we send Ahmed. We always send Ahmed."

"Why him?"

The leader flicked a marble into the dirt. "Because Ahmed has the best memory," he said.

chapter eleven

The alchemist dies in pain, and frustration,
While the fool finds treasure in a ruin.

Saadi of Shiraz

Señor Benito raised a fork of sautéed swordfish to his lips and rolled his eyes with shame. We were seated on an expansive terrace overlooking the strait, taking lunch at a restaurant known for its fish. The other tables were empty, almost as if the old collector had booked the entire place so that we would be left undisturbed.

"The parties were decadent in the extreme," he said. "We would dance through the night until the sun was high, and we would bathe in chilled champagne."

"What brought you to Tangier in the first place?"

Benito sipped his Muscadet. "A love affair," he said.

The waiter approached, poured water, then wine, hovered like a black and white butterfly, flitted away.

"Tangier is a city built on scandal," he said, when the waiter was out of earshot. "Whatever anyone tells you to the contrary is wrong. Everyone you see from the waiter there to the men selling crabs down in the port . . . they are all involved."

"Involved in what?"

"In the scandal, of course."

I asked about the love affair.

The Italian hunched forward a little, tightening the cream linen across his back.

"True love can touch the heart once in a lifetime," he said. "And it touched mine a long time ago in Milano. I met a young sailor, tall, fair, perfect in every imaginable way, and in ways that you would never imagine. He was posted to Tangier. I followed him. We were like two halves of the same fruit. We spent every moment together, never apart. We lived in a dream world. But all dreams must come to an end."

Señor Benito took a swig of white wine and rinsed it around his mouth.

"What happened to the sailor?"

"He drowned."

"Where?"

"Out there near the rocks."

We both fell silent, ate our fish, and strained to think of happier times. I asked Benito why he had stayed in Morocco. He thought carefully before answering.

"Because of the life," he said, "and because when I walk through the streets it is as if I am strolling back in time, into the world of Harun ar-Rashid."

"The *Arabian Nights*?"

"Yes, those books, but in living form."

Again, the waiter flitted over, cleared the plates, and was gone.

Señor Benito shut his eyes for a moment, breathed in. "After you have penetrated deep into a labyrinth," he said, "it's hard to leave it, even when at last you know how to find the door."

"Do you miss Europe?"

The Italian grinned. "If I do, it's waiting across the strait, just over there." He waved a hand to the far end of the terrace. "But Europe has nothing to offer me now," he said. "It's lost its traditions, its values, its freedom. Why would I want that when I have this feast for the senses, this *Arabian Nights*?"

Señor Benito ordered espressos for us both. When they came, he crushed a sugar cube with the end of a teaspoon, and sprinkled half the powder into his cup. I asked about his interest in Richard Burton.

He downed the coffee in one gulp.

"When I was a child I longed to be an explorer," he said. "From morning to night that was all I thought about. I drew little maps and plans in notebooks that I made myself. I used to pretend my sisters were from a dangerous cannibal tribe, and I would charge at them with a homemade sword. My mother said I was the devil, but my father gave me a picture book about African explorers. When I was a little older, he presented me with *First Footsteps in East Africa*. I fell in love."

"Why didn't you become an explorer?"

The collector stroked his hands over each other. "All the great exploring had been done," he said, "and, besides, I think I am a little too soft inside." He looked at me gently, blushing. "I am a romantic," he said. "And when I need a touch of romance, I slip into Burton's world."

"Have you read all seventeen volumes of the *Arabian Nights*?"

Benito's eyes widened. "Of course I have," he said. "It was an education in itself."

"Do you have a favorite story?"

"They are *all* my favorites," he replied. "But a favorite passage? It would have to be the 'Terminal Essay.' Make sure you read it."

The call to prayer rang out over the flat white roofs of Tangier, the muezzin's voice sharp, before blurring into the background. Señor Benito asked why I prized the *Arabian Nights* so highly. I told him my father had once owned a copy, that it was the most exquisite thing I had ever seen, that it smelled of cloves.

"One day a guest arrived at our home," I said, "and he left clutching the volumes to his chest."

"Did your father sell the books?"

"No, he presented them to the guest, for the man had admired them."

Señor Benito raised his gray eyebrows. "What do the books mean to you?" he asked.

"They are a maze, a labyrinth...part of a dream."

I told him about my fondness of stories, about the baton passed down through our family, father to son. "I am searching for the story in my heart," I said.

Benito stood up in slow motion, and led me to the edge of the terrace. We watched the passenger ferries bridging Europe to Africa. The Italian collector fastened the buttons of his cream linen suit with care, pushed up the knot of his tie.

"I think you ought to go and meet Mrabet," he said.

THAT EVENING RACHANA telephoned me from Dar Khalifa. Her voice sounded worn, as if in my absence the house was collapsing around her. I asked if everything was all right.

"The chalk's come back," she said. "There are symbols all over the front wall. This time they're in red."

"Did the guardians wash it away?"

My wife took a deep breath. "They are out there with Zohra," she said, "all of them chatting very fast. They're begging for you to come back."

"Is that the only problem?"

Rachana groaned. "No, there's another thing," she said.

"The guardians?"

"No, Murad."

"What about him?"

"He's run away," she said.

MOHAMMED MRABET WAS a friend and confidant of the American writer Paul Bowles. They shared a passion for life, a love of poetry, painting, and music, and the same orientation. Together they were the heart of the Tangier literary scene. Bowles transcribed and then translated Mrabet's works and found them publishers in the West. Mrabet gradually became famous and is regarded as a Moroccan icon, an important literary figure in his own right. The curious thing is that Mohammed Mrabet never learned to read or write. He was illiterate, a man who had begun as a simple fisherman but whose life was powered by the need to tell a tale. As an illiterate, he had depended on his ears and his memory, facets that shaped him in the mold of the great storytellers of the Moroccan past.

Like just about everyone else I met, I assumed Mrabet was dead. His name is attached to another time, and to the Tangier salons in which Tennessee Williams, Truman Capote, Allen Ginsberg, and William S. Burroughs fraternized. So the news he was still alive and living in a Tangier suburb filled me with great interest.

Señor Benito had given me the name of a small bookshop, Le Colombe d'Or, and suggested I go and meet a young Frenchman, Simon-Pierre, who worked there. I telephoned him in advance. We met in the café next door to the bookshop, the dense smoke of burning black tobacco heavy in the air. Simon-Pierre pulled up a chair, ordered a café noir, and lit a Gitanes. His face had rugged features but was gentle, his skin flushed with a touch of pink. He bore a striking resemblance to a painting I had seen of the explorer Wilfred Thesiger as a young man.

I asked him about Mrabet. He sighed.

"His health is up and down," he said. "He smokes too much."

"Gauloises?"

"No, *kif.*"

"Is he still working?"

Simon-Pierre looked across the room, out toward the street. "He's painting," he said.

An hour later we were sitting in Mrabet's modest apartment at the far end of Tangier. The walls were hung with abstract art, conjured in many colors from the deepest reaches of the icon's mind. Half of the main salon was given over to a kind of platform, on which the work was done. There were paints everywhere—gouache and watercolors, pigments packed in bottles and cubes the size of dice. The brushes were scattered about, some ready for use, others clogged with dry paint. On the other side of the room, a long thin table ran along the wall. It was heaped with papers and photographs, with children's toys and boxes, with broken candles and bottles of ink.

There were no windows, but the room was not dark. The lack of ventilation trapped the smoke from Mrabet's pipe, causing all visitors to be overcome by mild delirium. Mrabet himself was perched at the narrow end of the platform, his back pressed against the wall, knees tucked up under his chin. The long angular shaft of the pipe ran from between his bare toes up to his lips. From time to time he poked the end in his mouth and sucked.

On the far wall was pinned a large black-and-white photograph of the storyteller as a young man. He was naked to the waist, standing half-profile on the beach, his chest and shoulders a mass of muscle, his mouth roaring with self-confidence. My eyes left the picture and panned through the room, down to where Mrabet was sitting, the pipe's fire crackling between his feet. Time had been harsh. The great idol of Tangier had lost his physique, and his faculties were dimmed by decades of *kif*. He sat, crouched, contemplating. I said I was an admirer of his stories, and of the tradition of oral folklore, that my grandfather had lived and then died in Tangier.

Mrabet asked his name. I told him. He closed his eyes in an extended blink.

"I remember him," he said. "Ikbal the Afghan. He lived on . . ."

"On rue de la Plage," I said.

"Yes, I remember. He had brought a bodyguard from Afghanistan. He had a huge white turban and a very old gun. He never moved from the door. Not even when it was pouring with rain."

The storyteller blinked again, swallowed hard and opened his mouth just a crack. "We were friends," he said in a somber voice. "It's because we were both from the mountains. He was from the Hindu Kush, the roof of the world, and I come from the Rif."

I asked Mrabet about stories.

"In the Rif, stories are the blood which runs through our veins," he said, "they are the air we breathe, the food we eat."

He paused to draw at the pipe.

"Why did you leave the mountains for the sea?"

The old storyteller stared at his toes. "To swim with the fish," he said.

SIMON-PIERRE COAXED HIM to tell me a story, to perform. We sat in awkward silence, Mrabet gazing at his feet. I felt like a devotee waiting at his guru's deathbed, a little excited and a little ashamed. I was desperate for a few words of wisdom, or a clue of how to proceed. The storyteller filled the pipe again, lit it, and took a long contemplative drag. He coughed and spewed a mouthful of blood onto his painting rag. Like a tired old lion in a circus ring, he was content to just sit motionless. He was quite rightly ready to endure punishment rather than perform one last time.

I explained I was following the Berber tradition, searching for the story inside me, in my heart. Mrabet peered up. He put the pipe on the floor. I noticed his eyes for the first time. We looked at each other, pupils locking on. I thought I saw a sparkle in there, a touch of magic. The old storyteller sat up tall. He touched a thumb to his own chest.

"It's in there waiting," he said.

"What is?"

"Your story."

"Waiting for what?"

Mrabet closed his eyes. "It's waiting for you to close your eyes and wake up."

THE NEXT EVENING I arrived back at the Caliph's House. As usual, Rachana had a long report, detailing the trials and tribulations that had occurred in my absence.

"The chalk came again in the night," she said. "It's green now, wilder than before, scrawled the entire length of the outside wall. Zohra cut her hand this morning and claims it's because the house is bleeding."

"What about Murad?"

"I told you, he's run off."

"To Marrakech?"

"No one knows. But that's not all." She sighed deeply. "Osman's wife has left him for another man."

"Poor Osman," I said, remembering his wife, who was regarded by all as the prettiest woman in the bidonville. Zohra never stopped ranting on jealously about her fine looks.

I strolled into the garden where I found Osman stooped over a rake, his head hung so low that I couldn't see his neck. His private life was none of my business, for in Morocco family matters are kept well behind sealed doors. I put a hand on his shoulder blade and wished him well.

"She has brought shame on us," he said.

I tried to mumble something supportive.

Osman looked upward until our eyes were level. He blinked, and a single tear rolled from the corner of his eye, down his cheek to his chin.

"I still love her," he said.

EVERYONE IN THE bidonville had the same question: Where was Murad and why had he gone? I ferreted out Marwan at his shack on the north side of the shantytown, hoping he could shed light on the storyteller's disappearance. He was helping his wife hang out the washing. As soon as he saw me he dropped the damp shirt he was holding into the mud, embarrassed to be doing women's work. His wife slapped the back of his head for being so clumsy. Then, when she saw me, she spun round in a frenzy, furling a scarf over her hair, making flustered preparations for the guest.

Marwan ushered me into the lean-to and then corralled me into the most comfortable chair. His son was sent to buy a two-liter bottle of Coca-Cola, the ultimate indulgence. I apologized for arriving without notice, and expressed my concern about Murad.

The carpenter's face froze.

"Is there something wrong?" I asked.

Marwan put a hand to his mouth. "He left," he said.

"Where's he gone?"

"Back to Marrakech."

"Why?"

"He…"

"Yes?"

"He…"

"Yes, Marwan, what is it?"

"He's gone back to Marrakech and…"

"And?"

"And taken Osman's wife with him."

BURTON USED THE *Arabian Nights* as a kind of repository of oddities, scraps of information, and obscure lines of thought. He was getting on in age when the books appeared, and you get the feeling that he was keen to lay down the gems of a lifetime's scholarship before it was too late. The vast scope and length of the collection—which runs to over six and a half thousand pages—allowed him to embed all sorts of annotations.

The text itself is peppered with hundreds, perhaps thousands, of footnotes. Understanding them in their entirety calls for a working knowledge of Latin, Greek, German, French, and classical Arabic. They cover an edifying spectrum of material, and frequently border on the sacrilegious, the illegal, or more usually the obscene.

The more pedestrian notes address areas such as breeds of Arab horse, camels' names, door hinges, carrier pigeons, and cannibal tribes. A great number of others stray into territory that would have been regarded with outright horror by gentle Victorian sensibilities. They dote in dazzling detail on matters such as syphilis, incest, penile size and dismemberment, flatulence, menstrual discharges and hymeneal blood, castration, eunuchs, aphrodisiacs, and bestiality. Indeed, a long note on that subject explains a safe and foolproof method of enjoying "congress" with a female crocodile.

Whereas the footnotes provide entertaining relief from Burton's tremendously old-fashioned use of English (it was even regarded outmoded at the time), his masterpiece of even greater irrelevance is the "Terminal Essay."

Running to almost two hundred fifty pages, the essay has very little to do with the stories in *A Thousand and One Nights*. Agreed, it begins with a reflection on the origin of the stories, and their introduction into Europe. There is, too, a study of the "matter and the manner of the Nights," as well as an academic commentary on the use of poetry in the collection. But the nucleus of the "Terminal Essay" is an extraordinary dissection on what Burton describes as "Pederasty." We would call it homosexuality.

At a time when anthropology was in its infancy, and moral decency was at the fore, the essay developed and made public Burton's own theory on homosexual practice throughout what he called the "Sotadic Zone." He considered that pederasty was motivated by geography and climate rather than by race or genetic configuration. The zone in which Burton had isolated homosexual tendencies as "endemic" encompassed the Americas, North Africa and southern Europe, the Holy Land, Central Asia, and much of the Far East. Over many pages, he relayed aspects of the history, literary association, sociology, and spread of, and the pleasure derived from, homosexual activity.

Reading it in today's liberal climate, one's eyes widen, and you can only wonder what effect it had on puritanical Victorian society. It is no surprise that Burton did everything in his power to avoid the long arm of the censorship police.

The section is awash with the peculiar. Toward the end of the essay, Burton notes: "A favorite Persian punishment for strangers caught in the harem is to strip and throw them and expose them to the embraces of the grooms and slaves. I once asked Shirazi how penetration was possible if the patient resisted with all the force of the sphincter muscle: he smiled and said, 'Ah, we Persians know a trick to get over that; we apply a sharpened tent-peg to the crupper-bone (os coccyges) and knock till he opens.'"

To deflect the censor's attention, Burton frequently broke into Old English, French, Latin, or Greek when describing the sensitive or the indescribable. Another touch, found throughout his collection, is the use of idiomatic language. It tends to hinder easy comprehension, but adds to the general poetry. Burtonian language includes phrases such as "his prickle stood at point," "a stiff-standing tool," "wee of waist and heavy of hip," "he abated her maidenhead," and "thrust boldly in vitals with lion-like stroke!"

Some of the material was so explicit that it is no great wonder the "Terminal Essay" was excised from any edition but the first. It fell to Lady Burton to edit a version of her husband's work fit for the parlor as well as the nursery. But you get the feeling Burton himself didn't give a damn for that, or for the moral limitations of his time.

Pushing even his own absent boundaries of acceptability, Burton's pièce de résistance must surely be this: "The Jesuits brought home from Manilla a tailed man whose moveable prolongation of the os coccygis measured 7 to 10 inches: he had placed himself between two women, enjoying one naturally while the other used his tail as a penis succedaneous."

AT CAFÉ MABROOK, Dr. Mehdi was sitting at a different table from where he was usually to be found, on account of a drip, leaking from a pipe on the floor above. The thumbless waiter Abdul-Latif was extremely agitated, and was throttling a plumber in a back room, albeit with great difficulty. The surgeon seemed uneasy at the change in position, and kept scratching his back, as if the new seat had brought on an allergy.

When he saw me slope through the door, he stood up.

"I have been here an hour waiting for you," he cried.

I said I had been in Tangier, that I had met Mohammed Mrabet.

"Is he still alive?" Dr. Mehdi asked in disbelief.

"Barely," I said. "He's smoking rather a lot of *kif*."

"What did he tell you?"

"That if I want to find the story in my heart I must close my eyes and then wake up."

The doctor touched a fingertip to my knee. "You must listen to me," he said.

There was urgency in his voice.

"Okay, I'm listening."

"We are friends," he said.

"Yes."

"Then as a friend I must ask a favor of you."

I picked up my glass of coffee and pretended to sip it. In the West one might inquire what the favor was before agreeing to carry it out.

But in the East a sense of honor is attached to the asking of a favor. Demanding to know the nature of the favor before accepting it would call into question the trust on which the friendship is built.

The doctor touched my knee again, emphasizing the grave importance of the duty being asked. "My family has encountered a problem," he said.

I nodded. "What kind of problem?"

"A delicate one."

I nodded again. "How can I help?"

"I need you to take a message to my nephew, Ibrahim."

"I would be happy to," I said.

"Very good."

"What's the message?"

"You are to tell him that Hasif Mehdi of Casablanca has asked you to bring some rock salt. I have written him a letter," he said, pulling out an envelope.

"What's the salt for?"

"It's special to our family, from a particular place," he said. "We must use it at weddings for good luck, for purifying the wedding garden. It's a tradition for us. My granddaughter has just become engaged, and so we will need some soon. But this time there's no one to go and get some. Without it there can be no marriage."

Dr. Mehdi widened his eyes. "Do you see the problem?" he said.

I accepted the favor willingly, and felt my friendship with the doctor strengthen as a result. But I didn't quite understand why he didn't go and fetch salt himself.

"Do you promise you will do it, as one friend to another?"

I promised. "Is your nephew living in Casablanca?" I asked.

"No, not in Casa."

"In Rabat?"

"No, not there, either."

I paused, and looked into the surgeon's rock-steady eyes.

"He lives in the south," he said.

"Where exactly?"

"In the Sahara."

THE LENGTH OF the *Arabian Nights* has always been a matter of contention. Even though the eighteenth- and nineteenth-century compilers and translators expanded the collection many times, its length has never reached much more than five hundred stories (Burton's translation has four hundred and sixty-eight tales). But then the title of the collection refers to the length of nights rather than to the number of stories recounted. In its original form, the treasury of tales may have been far longer, but it's very unlikely. I expect this is due partly to the limit of oral recitations.

A storyteller would surely find his audience satisfied with a few hundred tales at most, and those spread over weeks or even months. The endless repetition and frequent summaries suggest a time when the tales were recounted verbally, a time when the audience would need refreshing on what events had come before.

Before the collection was arranged in a more rigid written structure, oral recitation must have allowed extreme fluidity. It is a point that modern academics sometimes find baffling: how a large body of work, an encyclopedia in itself, could be so free from boundaries. Tales would have come and gone depending on the storyteller, the geographic setting, fashion, and the audience waiting to be entertained.

A Thousand and One Nights in its written form allowed the work engine of Victorian scholarship to outdo itself. As with other triumphs, like Hastings's *Encyclopaedia of Religion and Ethics* and, of course, *Encyclopaedia Britannica,* the translations—and especially Burton's translation—pulled out all the stops. Although his edition copied liberally from earlier versions—especially that of his colleague

John Payne—it was its own entity and in many ways is the most expansive.

For more than a century, scholars and laymen have railed against Burton at every available opportunity. They have attacked his prejudice, his snobbery, and his loathing for the establishment. It's a fact that Burton was no saint. But his translation of the *Arabian Nights* is a work of titanic achievement. It is so because the translator was a polymath, a man versed in literature and history, expert in multiple sciences, languages, and skills. His translation drew upon a lifetime of knowledge to create a magnum opus that has rarely, if ever, been equaled.

THE WEEK AFTER my arrival back from Tangier, I remembered my promise to the cobbler, the promise to take the *Arabian Nights* to show him. I had spent days and nights reading the volumes, absorbed by the sheer peculiarity and detail of the footnotes. The morning I went to meet the cobbler, I had read over breakfast a firsthand account of a eunuch's dismemberment.

It was the kind of passage that causes tears to well in any man's eyes:

> *There-upon she called out to the slave women and bade them bind my feet with cords and then said to them, "Take seat on him!" They did her bidding, upon which she arose and fetched a pan of copper and hung it over the brazier and poured into it oil of sesame, in which she fried cheese. Then she came up to me and, unfastening my bag-trousers, tied a cord round my testicles and, giving it to two of her women, bade them hawl at it. They did so, and I swooned away and was for excess of pain in a world other than this. Then she came with a razor of steel and cut off my member masculine, so that I remained like a woman: after which she seared the wound with burning oil and rubbed it with a powder, and I the while unconscious.*

*Now when I came to myself, the blood had stopped; so she bade
the slave-girls unbind me and made me drink a cup of wine.*

The cobbler was standing outside the shop, as if waiting for
someone or something to arrive. We greeted, and he kissed my
knuckles. I asked what he was waiting for. The old man jerked off his
navy blue hat and held it to his heart.

"I spend my life in that shop," he said. "It's full of dirt and noise.
Sometimes I feel that I am going mad in there."

"But it's noisy and polluted out here on the street," I said. "The
traffic's terrible."

Noureddine the cobbler grinned and put his hand on my shoulder. "Well, it *was* very bad here," he said. "I used to run from the
street into my shop and slam the door closed behind me. But then
suddenly this morning everything changed."

"What changed?"

The cobbler stretched out an arm and pointed to the tree outside
his shop. Winter had robbed it of most of the leaves, and the trunk
was adorned with a mass of carved graffiti.

"Do you see it?"

"The tree?" I said.

"No, what is *in* the tree..."

I looked up and peered into the naked branches. Noureddine's
finger jabbed.

"Up there, up at the top." The old man guided my gaze. "Do you
see it...? The nest."

He was right. At the very top of the tree was a frail twig nest,
and sitting on the nest was a miniature brown bird. It looked very
ordinary.

"Can you hear it?" he said.

I listened hard. The traffic was so loud that it drowned out anything natural. I strained, angled my left ear toward the tree. Then,
suddenly, the bird opened its tiny beak, and went: "Tweet, tweet!"

Then Noureddine kissed his hat, praised God, and led me into the shop. Once in position behind his counter, he swiveled round and rummaged in the pigeonholes. He brought down my suede brogues, soled in the fifty-year-old leather. They looked brand-new. I thanked him effusively.

"It is you whom I should thank," he said. "Because you know the value of fine shoes."

I opened my satchel and pulled out the first volume of the *Arabian Nights*. The gold on the jet-black cloth caught the light. The cobbler touched one of the books and kissed his hand. He praised God again.

"This is one of the books I bought in Tangier last week," I said.

The cobbler looked out the window at the tree and up at the nest. Then he gazed down at the book.

"This day has been full of wonder," he said.

He asked if he might open the book.

"Of course you may."

His calloused fingers prized the covers apart, and he scanned a page. "This is *Alf Layla wa Layla*," he said in a whisper.

"Yes, *Alf Layla wa Layla, A Thousand and One Nights*."

Noureddine slumped on his stool. He seemed overcome with emotion. "My grandmother told me these tales," he said softly. "I remember them all."

"Did you read them to your sons?"

"Of course! It's a tradition. Stories are our culture."

"Did your sons read them to their sons?"

At first the cobbler didn't answer. He looked out at the nest again, his enthusiasm gone.

"No, no," he said despondently. "They didn't read the stories. The old ways are disappearing. My sons are too busy with their foolish friends. Too busy to ever see their father, and too busy to read a word to their children." The cobbler wiped a finger to his eye. "My grandchildren spend their time watching television," he said.

Rachana and the children were waiting for me nearby. Apologizing, I put the book away and opened the door. Just before I pushed out into the traffic and fumes, the old man called me back.

"Come here any day," he said, "and I will tell my favorite story from *Alf Layla wa Layla*."

"Which story is it?"

Noureddine grinned again. "The 'Tale of Maruf the Cobbler,'" he said.

ON MY FIFTH birthday my father gave me an exquisite box. It was crafted from turquoise micro-mosaic, with ivory beading along the edges, and was about twelve inches long and half as wide. My father said it came from Paghman, the ancestral home of our family in Afghanistan, and it had been passed down through generations. I was used to being given wooden blocks and plastic toys, and so the box caught my attention. It was the sort of thing that is sometimes kept away from children because of its delicateness and value. I laid it on my bed and carefully removed the lid.

Inside were three sheets of paper, all folded up.

I pulled out the paper, looked at the lines of type, and asked what all the writing meant. My father sat on the edge of my bed and said that the writing was a story, a story as old as the world. He said it was very important and that I would learn to love it like one of my friends. I asked him about the box. I was so small, but I remember his exact words.

"This box is very lovely," he said. "You can see the colors, and the work on the sides. But don't be fooled, Tahir Jan, this box is only the container. What's held inside is far, far more precious. One day you will understand."

I *didn't* understand. I didn't know what he was talking about. To my eyes, the box was the box, and the story on the paper was a story, and just that. The gift was put on a high shelf in my bedroom, and brought down from time to time to be admired. The pages inside stayed protected by the box, but yellowed with time. They are still in there, in the very same box, which now sits in my library on my desk.

Sometimes when I feel the need, I open the box, take out the story, and read it.

It is the "Tale of Melon City."

chapter twelve

Sleep with the remembrance of death,
And rise with the thought that you will not live long.

Uwais el-Qarni

O nce upon a time the ruler of a distant land decided to build a magnificent triumphal arch, so that he could ride under it endlessly with great pomp and ceremony. He gave instructions for the arch's design, and its construction began. The masons toiled day and night until the great arch was at last ready.

The king had a fabulous procession assembled of courtiers and royal guards, all dressed in their finest costumes. He took his position at the head, and the procession moved off. But as the king went through the great arch, his royal crown was knocked off.

Infuriated, he ordered for the master builder to be hanged at once. A gallows was constructed in the main square, and the chief builder was led toward it. But as he climbed the steps of the scaffold, he called out that the fault lay not with him, but with the men who heaved the blocks into place. They, in turn, put the blame on the masons who cut the blocks of stone. The king had the masons brought to the palace. He ordered them to explain themselves on pain of death. The masons insisted the fault lay at the hands of the architect whose plans they had followed.

The architect was summoned. He revealed to the court that it was not he who was to blame, for he was only following the plans drawn out by the order of the king. Unsure who to execute, the king summoned the wisest of his advisers, who was very ancient indeed. The situation was explained to him. Just before he was about to give his solution, he expired.

The chief judge was called. He decreed that the arch itself should be hanged. But because the upper portion had touched the royal head, it was exempted. So a hangman's noose was brought to the lower portion, for it to be punished on behalf of the entire arch. The executioner tried to attach his noose to the arch, but realized it was far too short. The judge called the rope-maker, but he stated it was the fault of the scaffold, for being too short.

Presiding over the confusion, the king saw the impatience of the crowd. "They want to hang someone," he said weakly. "We must find someone who will fit the gallows."

Every man, woman, and child in the kingdom was measured by a special panel of experts. Even the king's height was measured. By strange coincidence, the monarch himself was found to be the perfect height for the scaffold. At finding a victim, the crowd calmed down. The king was led up the steps, had the noose slipped round his neck, and was hanged.

According to the kingdom's custom, the next stranger who ventured through the city gate could decide who would be the new monarch. The courtiers ran to the city gate and waited for a stranger to arrive. They waited and waited, and waited and waited. Then they saw a man in the distance. He was riding a donkey backward. As soon as his animal stepped through the great city gate, the prime minister ran up, and asked him to choose the next king. The man, who was a traveling idiot, said, "A melon." He said this because he always said "A melon" to anything that was asked of him, for he liked to eat melons very much.

And so it came about that a melon was crowned the king.

These events happened long, long ago. A melon is still king of the country and, when strangers visit and ask anyone there why a melon is the ruler, they say it's because of tradition, that the king prefers to be a melon, and that they as humble subjects have no power to change his mind.

As ARIANE'S FIFTH birthday was approaching, I decided to have a special box made for her, a container for the "Tale of Melon City." The next time I met Abdelmalik at Café Lugano, I asked if he knew a carpenter skilled in the art of box-making. He leaned back and flipped his sunglasses from his face up onto his hair.

"What do you need to have made?" he asked.

I told him about the "Tale of Melon City," and my wish to pass its gift on to my little daughter. Abdelmalik said that Casablanca's carpenters were mostly thieves. It was something I already knew. During the renovation process at Dar Khalifa, we had employed dozens of them. If they didn't steal from us, they had lied, and if they hadn't lied, they had cheated us. Most of them had stolen, lied, and cheated. We sat in silence for a while, reflecting on the sad situation of carpentry.

Abdelmalik clapped his hands.

"I will send you to Reda," he said.

SINCE MY PREVIOUS visit to the astrologer, I had tried to put out of my mind her conclusion, that Dar Khalifa had been a refuge of a holy man. In more usual circumstances, I might have embraced the idea, but after dragging Rachana and the children to live in Casablanca, I felt I had too much to lose. For months I had tried my best to steer our lives away from talk of the supernatural, and follow Rachana's dream...the dream of living in an ordinary house, stripped clean of surprises.

Seeking answers, I stopped in at the mattress shop in search of Sukayna. The place was awash with daffodil-yellow cushions, an order from a restaurant. The mattress maker said the astrologer was attending to a purification rite at someone's home.

"Casablanca is filled with evil," he said, darkly.

"Not all of it, surely?"

The mattress maker threaded a needle. "Every inch of this city is wicked," he said. "Why do you think Sukayna has so many clients?"

"If it's so wicked," I asked, "why do you live in Casablanca?"

The tailor pulled a stitch through a square of yellow cloth. "Because we have Sukayna," he said.

THE MOOD AT Dar Khalifa depended greatly on the weather. At the end of December it rained for five days and five nights. It wasn't the usual light rain, but the kind of squall you get on the high seas. We stayed cooped up indoors, all of us depressed beyond words. The children caught the flu, the maids spent their time fighting for the pole position at Timur's bedside, and the guardians shut themselves up in the stables and refused to come out. Struggling against the lashing rain, I made my way down to their retreat.

Marwan, Osman, and the Bear were clustered around their makeshift table playing cards and drinking watery mint tea. They sat upright when they saw me and looked uncomfortable. My presence tended to conclude in a demand, and demands were always unwelcome, especially in the rain. For once though, I had nothing to ask of them. I had come to check how Osman was bearing up. I hadn't seen him for days. He was sitting in a shadow, his shoulders rounded forward with melancholy, his mouth turned down at the corners like a cartoon. A steady stream of water was dripping onto his back, soaking him.

But he was too sad to care.

I took Marwan outside. We stood in the rain, sheltering under the foliage of a banana plant. I asked whether there was any news from Osman's wife. Marwan shook his head.

"Osman is miserable," he said.

"Do you think he will ever be happy again?"

"Perhaps," said Marwan. "Perhaps, many years from now."

"Maybe his wife will come back," I said.

Marwan the carpenter scowled. "He will never take her back," he said.

"Why not?"

"She has brought shame, terrible shame. As far as Osman is concerned, his wife is dead."

OPPOSITE THE SMALL railway station of Oasis, I found the address Abdelmalik had written down. There was a newsagent on one side and a pharmacy on the other. Between them was a narrow furniture shop. It went back very far, like a bowling alley. There was no sign, no name. I must have passed it thirty times before and never noticed it. Most of our furniture had been shipped to us from India, or was made from cane, bought cheap from a stall on the highway to Rabat. We had never bought anything in a Casablanca furniture shop.

In Moroccan homes there tend to be two types of furnishings. The first are everyday items for use by the family. Such pieces are usually simple, lacking expensive detail, but solidly made. The second type of furniture is generally reserved for guests. Those pieces are far more elaborate. They are beautified with attractive upholstery and gilt, carved with pleasing geometric designs. In Arab culture a visitor is held in very high esteem. No amount of expense is ever too great to make sure he is more comfortable than he would be in his own home.

As soon as I stepped up to the shop, I saw that it specialized in the second type of furniture, the kind reserved for guests. There were finely tooled sofas, exquisite tables, cabinets, and chairs, all of them with inlaid fragments of mother-of-pearl. At the front of the shop sat a large wooden chest. Its top was arched, its surfaces carved with the most intricate geometric design. Like everything else on sale, it was a work of art. But I was confused, for none of the furniture was in the Moroccan style. It was all Damascene, from Syria.

I touched my hand to the wooden chest and caressed the tooled surface. Then I bent down and smelled the wood. It was cedar. My nose was pressed down onto the relief when I heard a voice.

"The nose is a far worthier judge than the eye," it said.

I jolted upright. A man was standing beside me. He welcomed me. I took a step backward. He was about sixty, a square head on squared shoulders and glazed-over eyes. There was a gap between his two front teeth, a gray bristle pencil-line mustache, and a carrot-colored blotch of nicotine between the first two fingers on his right hand.

"I am looking for Monsieur Reda," I said.

"At your service, sir."

Reda lit a cigarette and led the way back through the shop, shuffling in his tattered bedroom slippers, until we arrived at a small office. As we progressed deeper into the heart of the building, the fine decor and furnishings melted away, replaced by a line of trestle tables. Standing over each was a craftsman chiseling away at a great slab of beech.

The office was dark and functional, the walls hung with sheets of geometric design, and with samples of wood. Monsieur Reda stubbed out his cigarette and lit another straightaway.

"Do you mind if I smoke?" he said in a gravelly voice.

I said I did not.

"It helps me to think," he said.

I told the carpenter about the box. "I need it to be exceptional, for it will hold something very precious indeed."

"Jewelry?"

"No, no, something far more valuable than jewelry," I said.

Monsieur Reda coughed, thumped a fist to his chest, and coughed again. "Gold?"

I shook my head. "No, no," I exclaimed. "Much more valuable than jewelry or gold."

Reda thumped his chest again.

"The box will hold a story, for my little daughter."

The carpenter stubbed out his cigarette and shook my hand. His palm was soft, a little sticky, and smelled of Gauloises. "I will create a masterpiece," he said.

DURING THE FIRST year we lived in Casablanca, I employed an assistant called Kamal. He had spent time in the United States, spoke good English, and had a genius for fixing unfixable problems. Over the months he worked with me, his life became intertwined with my own. We spent almost every day together, from early morning until late at night. We became friends, but I always harbored a deep seated fear of Kamal. It was something about the way he looked at me, especially late at night, when I caught him off guard.

There was hatred in his eyes.

While in the United States, Kamal had been married to an American girl, a secret he kept from his family at home in Casablanca. He had been interrogated by the FBI, and claimed to have been acquainted with Mohammed Atta, the leader of the 9/11 suicide squads. After the Twin Towers fell, his American wife left him and joined the U.S. Army. He claimed she had been brainwashed against Arabs, turned against her own husband by the Feds.

Late one night Kamal drove me out to the rocks near the lighthouse. He turned off the engine, told me to get out. He was very drunk, stumbling all over the place.

"Where are we going?"

"I'll show you," he said.

He led me up onto the rocks, until we were staring out at the black Atlantic waters. There was no sign of human life, not a light, nothing. I half-wondered if Kamal had brought me there to kill me. It may sound dramatic, but he was the kind of man who was completely unbothered by right and wrong. We sat on the rocks for a few minutes in silence. Then I asked Kamal what he wanted to show me.

"If someone betrayed me," he said, "I would react."

There was anger in his voice, a kind of cold rage.

"Has someone betrayed you?" I asked.

Kamal stared out at the crests of white on black. "They are just about to," he said.

I wasn't quite sure what he meant, but I knew it was time for our paths to separate. I stood to my feet and, keeping my weight low, moved over the rocks, back to the shore. Kamal was waiting for me at the car. I don't know how he got there so fast.

We clambered in, slammed the doors shut. He was about to turn on the engine, when he swiveled around very slowly, the whites of his eyes leering at me. I could smell the drink on his breath.

"I never forget," he said calmly. "Remember that, I never forget."

A week passed and I didn't see Kamal. I tried calling him, but as usual he didn't answer. Rachana begged me to draw the line, to step over it.

"You must fire him," she said.

"But he'll kill me."

"Do you *really* believe that?"

I looked at her, my face taut with fear. "Yes, I do."

The next morning Kamal arrived. He was dressed in a suit, charcoal gray with maroon trim around the cuffs. As ever, he was silent on why he hadn't answered my calls, or where he had been. We drove to Café Napoleon near the suburb of Oasis, where Reda the carpenter worked. We both ordered orange juice and scrambled eggs with toast. Kamal was in a good mood. He said his ex-wife had called him out of the blue.

"Does she miss you?" I asked.

Kamal gulped a mouthful of eggs. "More than she knows," he said.

A hawker was going from table to table selling lottery tickets and fake Gucci belts. When he came over to us Kamal bought five tickets.

"Are you feeling lucky?"

"I am on top of the world," he said.

I went to the toilet, splashed water on my face, and vowed not to leave the café until I had severed our lives. Back at the table, we ordered more coffee. Kamal lit a Marlboro. I pushed up my sleeves.

"I am ashamed," I said. "My cash hasn't come through. We have hardly enough money to eat. I feel terrible about this, but I think you'd better look for another job."

Kamal stared into space, the cigarette hanging from his top lip. He didn't say anything. Not a word. After breakfast, he hailed a taxi and drove away toward the coast.

I took a deep breath and exhaled. Kamal was out of my life.

THE NEXT FRIDAY afternoon, I went to Café Mabrook for my weekly session with Dr. Mehdi and the other regulars. Abdul-Latif the waiter said the leak had been repaired, but no thanks to the plumber.

"That man is the son of the devil," he spat. "He has no skill. I would strangle him if I could!"

The waiter glanced down at his thumbless hands and licked his lips. "God is merciful," he said.

I took my usual seat, exchanged pleasantries, and asked the surgeon when I ought to leave for the desert, to fulfill his favor. He clicked his fingers.

"When I am ready," he said.

"But isn't the wedding very soon?"

Dr. Mehdi rubbed his hands, as if he were trying to get warm. "Some things cannot be rushed," he muttered in a low voice.

"But you had said it was urgent."

"It is."

We sat in silence, drinking our café noir, staring out toward the ocean. In the Arab world silence is golden, something precious, something to be relished. As one who has come from the West, I found it fearsome. I tapped my foot uneasily, hoping the doctor would speak. I struggled to start a new conversation. But like a seedling without water, it failed to take root.

"Are you nervous?" Dr. Mehdi asked after a long pause.

"No."

"Then what's the matter?"

"The silence," I said. "I can't stand silence."

He narrowed his eyes. "Have you never known sadness?" he said.

THAT EVENING I met Osman down at the end of the garden. He was raking leaves near the ornamental well, which he and Hamza had made. They never admitted it, but we all knew it was designed as a dwelling for the Jinns. I asked if he was coping at home. He touched a hand to his heart.

"I am not a bad man, Monsieur Tahir," he said.

"I know, Osman."

"But, Monsieur Tahir, I do not want you to think badly of me now."

"I respect you greatly, Osman. Believe me."

The guardian clicked his tongue to the roof of his mouth. "Tongues move," he said.

"Where?"

"In the bidonville."

"What do they say?"

"Bad things."

"What?"

"That my wife is not like the rest of us." He paused, lifted his head. "You see, she is very beautiful."

"And?"

"And they are jealous."

"Don't listen to them."

Osman sniffed. He wiped his nose with the side of his hand. "They say she is a bad woman," he said again.

"So don't listen."

"But they say she is a whore."

TEN DAYS AFTER meeting Reda the carpenter, I went back to his shop. He was sitting in the sunlight near the front, reading *Le Matin*, stroking a hand over the back of a large tabby cat. He eased himself from the chair when he saw me, stubbed out a cigarette, and praised God.

"May you always walk on rose petals," he said.

I thanked him and asked if business was good. He shook his head, fumbled through his pockets for the Gauloises.

"No one wants this work," he said dolefully. "Morocco has been flooded with cheap furniture from China. There are mountains of it everywhere. The shopkeepers almost give it away."

"But the rich can afford your work," I said.

Reda gritted his teeth. "Of course they can," he replied. "But they are misers. The only time they buy from me is when their friends are watching. And even then they don't pay."

The carpenter poured a saucer of milk for his cat.

"I will close this place down and make a nice little restaurant," he said, leading me away from the sunlight, into the body of the shop.

I followed him to the left, down steps into a kind of grotto. As I descended, I made out the sound of mallets striking chisels, and the scent of freshly carved wood.

"This is the workshop," he said.

There must have been half a dozen chambers down there, each one hollowed out from the yellow stone, filled with benches at which armies of carpenters were at work. The ceilings were so low that they toiled sitting down, or on their knees. Each one had a chisel in one hand, a small rounded mallet in the other.

Monsieur Reda struck a match on the wall and lit a Gauloises.

"But if you shut down, they would all be out of work," I said.

"They are adaptable," he replied. "I am sure they will learn to cook."

We edged sideways through a narrow passage and up to a small cavity, in which a lone carpenter knelt. A bare lightbulb was suspended above him, throwing a shadow over the lower part of his face. The room looked like a confessional. We squeezed inside. In front of the carpenter was a special workbench, much narrower than the others. On it was a box. It was inlaid with marquetry, crafted from rare woods, and quite the most beautiful box. Along the top, excised in beige veneer, ran the words "The Tale of Melon City."

Monsieur Reda led me back through the grotto, up the stairs, and back into the sunlight. He wrapped the box carefully in his copy of *Le Matin,* and inhaled on his cigarette.

"Do you have five minutes?" he said.

"Yes, of course."

"Then I shall like to offer you some Syrian hospitality."

He shuffled past the tabby cat to a kitchen area, where he brewed up a single glass of Arab coffee flavored with cardamom. He placed it before me, and urged me to lean back and kick off my shoes.

"Close your eyes," he whispered.

I did as he asked.

"Now I will tell you a tale," he said. "It was told to me on the day of my birth, and given to me as an amulet, just like you are giving the story to your daughter."

"What is it called?"

The carpenter exhaled. "It is the 'Tale of the Sands,' " he said.

I felt myself drift off into another world, and Reda the carpenter began:

"Once there was a stream," he said, "a lovely, cool, clear stream. It was created from melted snow in the high mountains, and it flowed down through all kinds of rock, until one bright morning it reached the desert.

"The stream was worried, but it knew that its destiny was to cross the sand. So it called out, 'What am I to do?' And the desert answered, 'Listen, O stream! The wind crosses my sands, and you can, too.'

"The stream didn't listen. He let his water roll forward. The first drops disappeared without trace.

" 'Desert! Desert!' he called. 'You are sucking me up!' The desert was old and wise, and grew angry at the foolish young stream. 'Of course I am sucking you up,' replied the desert, 'because that is what deserts do. I can't change. Please listen to me, and allow yourself to be absorbed into the wind.'

"The stream was far too hotheaded to listen. He had his pride, and was happy being who he was. 'I am a stream,' he shouted, 'and I want to stay a stream!' The sand, growing in impatience, replied again: 'O foolish stream! You must throw yourself into the wind, and you will fall as rain. Your droplets will cross mountains and oceans, and you will be far greater than you are now. Please listen to my words!'

"The stream did not believe the sand, and cried, 'Desert, desert, how can I be sure you speak the truth?' The desert rose up in a sandstorm and called, 'Trust me, O young stream, and think back, surely you can recall being in another form.' The stream thought hard, its waters swirling as its memory worked. Then, gradually, it did remember . . . it remembered a time when it was something else.

" 'Let yourself rise up!' cried the desert, 'up and up into the wind!' The stream did as the sands ordered, and let himself rise in a curtain of mist, until he was absorbed in the wind. It felt wonderful, and right, as if it was meant to be."

Monsieur Reda thumped his chest and coughed.

"And that is how the stream which is life continues," he said, "and why the tale of its great journey is written in the sands."

chapter thirteen

Knowledge is better than wealth. You have to look after wealth, but knowledge looks after you.

Hazrat Ali

The day before Ariane's fifth birthday, I met an Englishman called Ralph. He had found me through the friend of a friend, and was eager for me to come in on his business venture. Ralph had one of those round pink faces, with a single wispy curl combed across his shiny head, a pair of fragile tortoiseshell glasses pushed back close to his eyes, and a double-barreled name. He burped a great deal and, when he thought I wasn't looking, he shoved a finger up his nose and rooted about, as if digging for buried treasure.

I am not good at business, and steer clear of anyone trying to rope me into their fantastical schemes. The only time I gave in was when I handed over a whole book advance to an old school friend. He promised to double the money "in a week, two weeks tops," in a scheme selling rubber boots to Swaziland. He lost the money immediately and ran off to the Arctic, or the Antarctic. I can't remember which.

So when Ralph asked me to stake everything I owned on a crazed plan to search for diamonds in the Congo, I politely declined.

"Are you sure I can't talk you into it, old boy?" he said.

"Sorry, can't," I said. "Overstretched, you see."

Ralph brushed down his curl. "The stakes are high," he said. "You could be a millionaire by this time next year."

"I moved to Morocco to live a quiet life."

The Englishman sneered.

"Where's your sense of adventure?"

"It's all used up," I said.

Ralph unbuckled his briefcase and slid out a slim dossier, bound in crimson covers. "I wasn't going to mention this," he said.

I looked at the dossier. It was labeled "Secret" in small blue type. "What is it?"

"A gold mine," he said.

"Where is it this time?"

Ralph gave me a sideways glance. "In Haiti."

"I'm broke, completely broke," I said.

I sensed that Ralph was not listening. I looked at his face. He had started sweating alarmingly, liquid pouring out of him, soaking his shirt. He tugged off his glasses and ran to the toilet. He was gone twenty minutes. When he came back, he apologized.

"Sorry about that, old boy," he said. "It's something I picked up in West Africa. I was on the loo half the night. This morning at the hotel I went down for breakfast. Felt a movement coming on. Couldn't get to the bog in time."

Ralph coughed, then blushed. "Terrible mess," he said.

The Englishman stood up and stuck out his hand. It was still wet.

"Why don't you sleep on it?" he said.

"I've already decided, though," I replied. "I told you, I'm flat broke."

Ralph spat on his hand and pressed down his curl. "You don't make it easy, do you?"

———

AT DAR KHALIFA, Rachana was in the kitchen cooking an enormous pink cake. Ariane had insisted that it have a real Barbie doll poking out of the top, because her friend at school had had one like that. I arrived just in time to give Barbie a double amputation. Her torso was stabbed through the inch-thick pink frosting. Ariane then led me to the playroom, where Fatima the maid was standing with her bag. She was wearing her jelaba. I asked if everything was all right.

"I am leaving, Monsieur," said the maid.

"Has Zohra offended you again?"

Fatima kissed Ariane on the cheek. "No, it is not Zohra," she said.

"Then what?"

"I am leaving because the room you give me is not good."

"Is it too cold?"

"No."

"Then what's the problem?"

"The washbasin."

"Doesn't it work?"

"Yes, it works, Monsieur."

"Well?"

"That is the problem."

I paused to digest the facts. "The washbasin works and that's why you are leaving?"

The maid said that was right.

"Am I missing something?" I asked.

"She lives in the basin," said Fatima.

"Who does?"

The maid shuffled her hands. "You know..."

I looked at her hard. "No, I don't," I said.

Fatima picked up one of Ariane's crayons, and wrote a name. She handed it to me. "Aisha Qandisha," I said, reading the words.

Fatima covered her ears. "You mustn't say that name aloud."

"Why not?"

"Because the Jinn will be summoned," she said.

———————

ARIANE'S BIRTHDAY WAS bright pink from beginning to end. An army of little girls trooped into the house, all dressed in pink tutus, waving pink magic wands. They gorged themselves on pink jelly, pink Barbie cake, and fluorescent pink meringue.

When the little girls had raced away, I took Ariane up for her bath. She put on her pink pajamas, climbed into bed, and asked me to read her a story.

"Shall I get a book from the shelf, Baba?" she asked.

"As it's your birthday, we will have a special tale tonight," I said.

Ariane beamed up at me, her eyes shimmering like stars. I pulled out a package from under her bed. She tore away the pink wrapping paper, and stared at the wooden box. The marquetry letters caught the light.

"Baba, it's so beautiful," she said. "It's a princess's box."

"Yes, it is beautiful," I replied, "but always remember that it is a box, and a box is just a box. It has one job, to keep something very special very safe."

"Can I open it?"

I nodded. "Of course, it's yours."

Ariane's miniature fingers pulled back the lid. She fished out the papers. "What is this, Baba?" she asked.

"It's a piece of treasure," I explained, "something so precious, so valuable that it must always be kept safe. One day you will understand the value, but now you can lie back and let it enter your dreams."

I read the "Tale of Melon City."

Ariane kissed me on the cheek, and put the story back in its box. "I will keep it very safe," she said.

I turned off the light. As I did so, I felt a tinge of great satisfaction.

The baton was at last being passed on.

———————

A FEW DAYS later, *The Caliph's House* was published. The book charted the trials and tribulations of our first year in Casablanca. The reviewers were kind and, very soon, e-mails started to arrive from readers. Some of them had questions, others had praise, or their own reminiscences of Casablanca long ago. A few of them wrote for another reason—to ask directions to Dar Khalifa.

I reply to almost everyone who writes to me, and believe there's nothing worse than an author who avoids his readers. I never imagined the day would come, though, when people would start tracking down our home.

Dar Khalifa is so difficult to find that everyone gets lost the first half-dozen times. There are no landmarks nearby, and a labyrinthine shantytown stands between us and the outside world.

One bright morning in the last week of January, I received a long e-mail from a Californian called Burt. He had liked my book very much, he said, and had bought copies for his mother, his aunt, and all his friends. But his enthusiasm for *The Caliph's House* didn't end with recommending the book to others. As his e-mail explained, he had printed out pictures of me from my website, had them framed and hung all over his home. Then he had located the house on Google Earth, had bought a one-way ticket to Casablanca, and made the journey across eight time zones. Burt had landed and was staying at a small hotel near the port.

I broke the news to Rachana that a rogue Californian fan was out there, not far away, hunting us.

"He'll never get through the bidonville," she said confidently.

"You don't think so?"

"Of course not, because—"

My wife's words were cut short by the doorbell. It was a long, persistent ring with three buzzes at the end.

I opened the door. Before I saw the person standing there, my eyes focused on the makeshift map he was holding, a printout of Google Earth.

"Hello," said a frail voice. "I am Burt."

THE BEAR SPENT all afternoon removing the washbasin in Fatima's room. After flooding the place in the process, he plugged up the pipes with wax seals, and took the basin down to the stables. The maid looked around her room and put her bag on the bed. She was still perturbed, as if the idea of the Aisha Qandisha was at the front of her mind.

"Fatima, tell me, who said a Jinn was living in your basin?" I asked.

She locked her eyes on one of the floor tiles, held rigid. "No one," she said.

"Are you sure, Fatima?"

She forced her lips tight shut, and nodded. I asked her again. Her eyes widened, and her mouth burst open.

"Zohra told me," she said.

OTTOMAN RETURNED FROM a long business trip and invited me to lunch at his home. He lived in a large villa, all painted white, down near the Art Deco Vélodrome.

A servant in white gloves, and wearing a maroon tarboush, served us an assortment of Chinese dishes, from matching silver salvers.

Right at the start I broached the subject of Murad, and filled Ottoman in on the sordid events. He winced.

"That's not good," he said in a deep voice. "Not good at all."

"It's amazing to me that such a young and attractive woman would fall for an old man like that," I said.

"And she loves him even though he is blind," said Ottoman, motioning to his servant to clear our empty plates. "Murad is a storyteller," he said. "You may not realize it, but that means he has a kind of power over us mortals." He stood up and led the way through to the salon, a grand room hung with abstract art. "I have seen it with my own eyes," he said.

"Seen what?"

"An audience hypnotized. A few words from a master raconteur and they are overcome. You can't fight magic like that," he said. "That's what has happened to your guardian's wife."

"Can the spell be broken?"

Ottoman tapped his watch. "With time all magic ends," he said.

THE SERVANT RETURNED with a silver tray balanced between his hands, a pot of coffee balanced on the tray. He served us both. When he was gone, Ottoman added sugar and stirred a silver teaspoon around his cup.

"You must think very carefully," he said.

"About what?"

"Whether Murad did any favors for you while he was here."

I scrolled back in my mind, to the time when I had first met Murad at the Marrakech barber's shop.

"No, he never did any favors for me, nor for any of us," I said.

"Thank God," said Ottoman.

I asked why it mattered.

"The favor network," he replied.

I frowned.

"If Murad had done you a favor," he said, "then you would be responsible for repaying the favor, even though he had done something as wicked as taking away another man's wife."

You can't live in Morocco for long and not brush into the favor network. It's always there, a blurred backdrop to life. If you want to get something done or to climb socially, you pay into the system, and wait for your return.

I am always being asked for favors by people who must expect me to ask them for favors. I try to help if I can, but ask for nothing in return. My father drummed his motto into me: "Never owe anyone anything."

Ottoman was equally scathing about people who played the favor game. He said it was like the abuse of credit cards in the West.

"You start off borrowing a little, then a little more than you can afford," he said. "Before you know it, your life is collapsing, with a line of favor creditors hammering at the door. It can get wildly out of control."

"But what happens if you have to ask someone a favor?"

"Then make sure you give a gift first. Pay into the system before you make a withdrawal."

"What do you give?"

"It depends on whom you're giving it to. Chocolates, aftershave, or jewelry go down well. But the best kind of gift is something with sentimental value."

"Why?"

"Because it touches the receiver's heart."

"What if they refuse the gift?"

Ottoman looked shocked. "In Arab society refusing a gift is like a declaration of war," he said. "It almost never happens. You can be certain that once a payment has been made into the favor system, no one will ever forget. It's as if it's chalked up on an invisible board in the sky."

"So I give a gift of chocolates, a huge box of them, and ask a favor . . . some help with my paperwork."

"That's right."

"But won't that person see my ulterior motive straightaway?"

"Yes, of course," he said, "but the system tangles them up. They can't refuse the gift and, when they've accepted it, they're bound to reciprocate."

I thought of Dr. Mehdi, and the favor he had asked—for me to fetch some special salt from the Sahara. I told Ottoman about it. He smiled, broke into a laugh.

"Do you think he will abuse my trust?" I asked.

Ottoman stopped laughing. "I am sure you can trust him," he said.

"How do you know?"

"I think you'll find out."

BURT WAS WEARING a gold plastic raincoat and a matching hat. He moved very slowly and seemed extraordinarily fragile, almost like a porcelain figure. His skin was so pale it looked as if he had spent the last fifty years underground. His hair was white as talc, his voice shrill, and his mannerisms decidedly strange. When he talked, he twitched his eyes; when he had nothing to say, he hummed the tune to "Yankee Doodle Dandy."

"I found it," he squeaked, pushing his way through the door. "Bet you didn't expect me."

"No, we didn't," I said.

Burt shook my hand, then tugged off his coat and his matching hat, and threw them over a chair.

"I can't wait to get the full tour," he said.

"Tour?"

The Californian opened a daypack and removed a large camera. He tested the flash twice, blinding me. The sound of the equipment recharging filled the sitting room.

"Yup, ready," he said. "Where do we begin?"

"Welcome to Morocco and to Dar Khalifa," I said feebly. "Thank you for coming, and for buying my book. But there's something I ought to explain..."

Burt's eyes twitched once, then again. "I know what it is," he said.

"Do you?"

He nodded excitedly.

"Oh, good," I said.

"You're shy, aren't you?"

I gritted my teeth. "That's not it."

Burt lifted the camera, blinded me again, and he moved over to the fountain outside the children's playroom.

"Oh, you wrote about this!" he exclaimed. "It's beautiful. Just like you described it."

"Burt, I must stop you," I said, faltering.

"Am I too early?" he asked. "I am, I know I'm too early. I can just sit on the couch and wait for the others."

I didn't know quite what to say. But one thing I did know was that Rachana wouldn't take kindly to having guided tours of the house. She had been supportive of my book, but secretly resented the way I had thrown a window open into our private lives. I cornered Burt at the fountain and urged him to put the camera down. Rachana was coming out of the kitchen, and was about to find us.

"You have to listen to me! We don't do guided tours. We aren't a theme park. This is our home!"

The Californian pushed past me. He seemed shaken. "But your book," he said.

"What about it?"

"Well, I loved it. I bought copies for all my friends."

I thanked him once, and then a second time.

"You don't get me," he said.

"I do, and I'm grateful. I really am."

"No, you don't understand me."

"What don't I understand?"

Burt held out his arms, as if he was about to give me a bear hug. "That I'm your number one fan!" he said.

———

EACH MORNING A chicken would flap over the wall and lay an egg in the wide hedge near the swimming pool. It was lured by the promise of safety, and the idea that one day its chicks would run free with grass beneath their feet. The garden was a paradise compared to the mud in which the shantytown's chickens lived on the other side of the wall. While strolling over the lawn, I caught the guardians red-handed. They had caught the chicken and were about to break her neck and stew her into lunch. They strained hard to look submissive. I asked what was going on.

"It's good for eating," said the Bear. "Look at the legs."

"Whose chicken is it?"

"It comes from over there," said Marwan, pointing to the other side of the wall. "That means we can eat it." He held up a sprig of parsley.

"It's been coming in here and eating the worms, so it belongs to the house," said the Bear.

"We want to eat it," said Osman.

It was then that I heard the sound of chicks, chirping.

The chicken pecked herself free from Osman's clutches and ran to her offspring.

"It's a mother," I said. "You can't slaughter an innocent mother with chicks!"

The guardians lined up, saluted, and agreed that it would be cruel to end the life of any mother.

"What shall we do with her?" asked Marwan.

"Keep them safe, and show them a little hospitality," I said.

THE NEXT NIGHT I dreamt of the magic carpet again. It had been weeks since I was last lifted on its silk threads. I lay back, spreading my weight over the geometric patterns, and we soared over the ocean, toward the distant kingdom. But this time we did not fly over the city, or pass the tower, the princess, or the gallows. Instead, we flew west until we came to a vast desert. It was still night, and the sky was empty, not a star, not a sliver of light. I was freezing.

Sensing my chill, the carpet reared up and wrapped me in its edge.

We flew on and on, over a thousand miles of sand. Below there was nothing but dunes, and the occasional silhouette of a Bedouin encampment. Above, the black was touched with gold, as the first rays of dawn pierced the horizon. The sun broke over the sand, and I glimpsed the outline of a city, far more fabulous than the last—an endless panorama of domes, towering minarets, pools of glistening water, and a palace encircled by an iron wall.

The carpet banked to the left, swooped down over the palace defenses, and came to rest on a patch of grass near the royal stables. I could smell the horses, and hear the grooms saddling up the king's prized mount for his morning ride. Because I was in a dream, I somehow knew about things that more normally I might not have known. I knew, for example, that the palace belonged to the great warrior-king Hassan bin Iqbal, who had recently conquered a land far to the east, and had taken its own royal family prisoner. I knew, too, that the king had seven sons, and that each one was the guardian of a piece of knowledge that, when united, would lead to a breakthrough in science that would change the world. But when separated the information had no value at all. The king had reached a higher plane of learning. He had spent years trying to get his sons to pool their resources, but the boys despised each other. Each one was plotting secretly to kill the others, and to become the crown prince. The eldest, who was the crown prince, was about to poison his father.

The carpet flicked up its corner, directing me to the last stable on the main block. I went over, found the door open. Inside, a groom was busy saddling a white mare. Holding the rein in his left hand, he turned to face the light. He froze. As soon as I saw his face, I did the same. He approached, almost in shock.

I was looking at myself.

EACH DAY, ANOTHER egg was laid by the chicken and, each day, another chick hatched. They followed their mother about the garden chirping, avoiding the pack of ferocious cats that vaulted the wall and bred in the long grass on the tennis court.

The guardians gazed lovingly at the hen, tasting the tender meat hanging off her thighs. Then, one afternoon, there was a loud knock at the garden door. A bristly, big-boned woman with a floral head-scarf barged in. She growled something in Arabic, and was taken to the bottom of the garden by the Bear. He pointed at the hedge, where the mother hen and her progeny were scratching for grubs. The woman pulled out a sizeable box that she had somehow been con-cealing under her jelaba, scooped up the chicken, her offspring, and a pair of unhatched eggs, and marched back to the garden door. Before she stepped out, back to her life in the bidonville, she glared at the guardians and me, for laying claim to her birds.

LATE THE SAME afternoon, I drove up to Hay Hassani and parked outside the mattress shop. There were cries across the street. I looked over, and saw a woman shouting. She was waving an empty purse, as if she had been robbed. Suddenly, she caught sight of the thief and ran into the road. But she didn't look. A van swerved to miss her and collided with a cart piled up with eggs. It tipped over, smashing most of the stock. A taxi swerved to miss the cart, and hit an old man pass-ing on his bicycle. He lay in the road, dazed. But no one took any notice of him. Instead, all the participants, including the taxi's pas-senger who had hurt her leg, formed a scrum, blaming each other for the accident.

Sukayna ushered me inside, pulled the curtain down. I told her that I had seen myself living an entirely other life, and that I needed to know more about the holy man who had taken refuge at the house.

The astrologer lit a candle stub and mumbled a prayer under her breath.

"We share the world with Jinns," she said.

"I know... they live in animate objects, created from smokeless fire."

Sukayna pointed out to the street. "Did you see that accident?" she said.

"Yes. People are so careless," I said. "The woman didn't look when she stepped into the road."

Sukayna clicked her tongue. "That wasn't the fault of people."

"What do you mean?"

"It was a Jinn."

"What?"

She repeated herself.

"I saw that all happen," I said. "I can explain it to you."

Sukayna shook her head and folded her arms. "I saw it, too," she declared. "And I know it was the work of a mischievous spirit. He's always there in that same spot, causing trouble."

I pulled the curtain back and glanced out through the mattress shop. The crowd had grown in size. The old man was being carried off to a battered-looking orange ambulance. A policeman was being petitioned by the mob.

"Where you come from," said the astrologer, "you have Jinns as well, but you don't know about them. When misfortune touches your life, you imagine it's random. But it's not."

"Will you tell me about the holy man?" I said.

Sukayna peered at the flame, closed her eyes for a second. "There's another difference between Morocco and Europe," she said.

I looked up, waited for the answer.

"It's that here in Morocco, we work things out. We listen, we watch. But in your countries you do the opposite. You expect everything to be worked out for you, handed to you. You expect other people to use their brains so you don't have to use your own. In your society people are lazy. They want everything now, everything for free."

"But what about my dream? And what about this holy man you mentioned?"

Sukayna washed her hands over her face.

"The answers are in front of you," she said. "Open your eyes and you will see them."

chapter fourteen

"Tell me, Baba," said Joha's son to his father,
"Why do you speak so little and listen so much?"
"Because I have two ears and only one mouth."

Marwan could see I was still having a problem understanding Morocco. He may have been a modest carpenter by trade, but he had the wisdom of a man many times his age. When I told him about the astrologer's caution, that I should use my own brain, he broke a twig from the hibiscus hedge, and scratched a circle in the dirt.

"This is Morocco," he said. "Every point is connected to every other point. It's a whole, balanced and more complete than you might first think."

He drew another circle, but just fell short of joining the two ends. "And this is the West," he said. "It looks very similar, but it's not quite whole. One day the ends may touch but, until that happens, your world will be incomplete."

"What difference does that make?"

The carpenter threw the twig back into the hedge. "In Morocco we have a saying," he said. "We say that a fool thinks he's wise, and that a wise man knows he is a fool."

BURT HAD LEFT Dar Khalifa and gone to Marrakech to buy souvenirs for all his friends. As he walked slowly out through the shantytown, I watched him, knowing instinctively that he would be back. It was just a matter of time.

A day or two passed. Then another. It was a cold afternoon, sheets of rain lashing at the windows. Ariane and Timur were riding their bicycles around the sitting room, gathering speed. Rachana was cooking in the kitchen, and I was drifting off to sleep in one of the low club chairs we had shipped from India.

The doorbell rang. A long, hard buzz followed by a series of shorter bursts. I opened an eye, jolted upright. The next thing I knew, the Bear was leading a gold raincoat into the salon. The figure inside it was drenched from head to toe.

"Hello," said a calm voice, "have I missed you guys."

Burt unbuttoned the coat, and let it flop onto the floor. He was shivering. I fetched a towel and some dry clothes.

"How was Marrakech?"

The Californian unlaced his shoes, pulled off his socks, and splayed his bare white feet out in front of the fire. "It was like stepping into an episode of *Twilight Zone*," he said.

"Did you enjoy it?"

Burt stared into the flames. He didn't look happy. "In California our lives are so comfortable," he said. "The drinking water's clean, the supermarkets are massive, and gasoline is cheap. It's all easy and in a way it's perfect. So much so that we get trapped, and we forget."

"What do you forget?"

"That there's a world out there, out here."

"That happens everywhere—"

Burt broke in: "No, you don't get me," he said. "We were living in a bubble, a bubble of security. It seems real, but it never is. And now terrorists are beating down our door, we're all surprised."

"The world's changing," I said.

"I wish every American could spend five minutes in Marrakech," said Burt. "I wish they could stand in that great square and see, smell, and hear what I did."

"How did it make you feel?"

"Alive," he said. "It made me feel alive. What I saw there was real, *totally* real. There wasn't the bullshit, the sterile wrapping that we use to cover everything. We're so good at wrapping that we take our eye off the ball. We forget what we're actually wrapping up."

Burt moved over to the window and watched the rain. I told him about Ariane's box, the one which holds the "Tale of Melon City"— the container and the content. He asked me to stand up. Then he gave me another bear hug.

"Your head's screwed on right," he said. "You understand the East and the West. You're at home in both. You know both. You know what you are?"

"What am I?"

"You're the bridge."

THE MORE I asked Dr. Mehdi when I ought to leave for the desert, the more he pressed me to stay.

"The time will come," he said dreamily.

"But I'm ready to go now."

"This isn't the right time," the doctor replied.

"Why not?"

"Because certain things are not ready yet."

"What sort of things?"

"The conditions."

AT DAR KHALIFA, Ariane was going up to bed. I tucked her in and kissed her good night. Just as I was about to turn off the light, she said there was something she wanted to ask.

"Can't it wait till tomorrow?"

She shook her head. "No, Baba, unless I know the answer, I won't sleep."

"Tell me then, what do you want to know?"

Ariane nestled her head into the pillow. "I want to know about honor," she said.

"What about it?"

"Can you tell me what it is, Baba?"

I had once asked my father the same question, while lying back on his turquoise couch. I told Ariane.

"And what did he say?"

"He told me this story.

"Once upon a time there was a wandering dervish, a holy man. He was crossing the vast deserts of Arabia when he was taken prisoner by a clan of nomads. They said: 'You are a spy and we are going to chop off your head.'"

"What did the dervish say?" asked Ariane.

"He said: 'I am not a spy. Before you kill me I want to ask a favor. Give me a sword so that I can kill one of your men. Then, when you kill me, you would have done so out of revenge, and your honor would have been saved. Because, as things stand now, your honor is in danger of being tarnished by killing an innocent man.'"

THE CALIPH'S HOUSE may be surrounded on all sides by a sprawling shantytown, but it's located at the edge of Casablanca's exclusive suburb called Anfa. Land in the area is so valuable that every developer in the city has their eye on the shacks. Ripping them down would be a license to print money. The government have regarded the bidonvilles in Casablanca and elsewhere as breeding grounds for fanaticism. The thinking goes that if people live in deprived circumstances, they have less to lose, and are more likely to listen to radical talk.

Whenever I asked them about the future, the guardians looked at me with faraway eyes. They had always been bonded by a communal fear, a fear that one day the shantytown would be torn down, and they would be homeless. Over the time we had lived at Dar Khalifa, there had been moves to sweep away the bidonville. They had failed, perhaps because there had been no plan to settle the inhabitants elsewhere. But things had changed. The guardians and all the others who lived around us had been seduced with new promises.

"They will build a great tower," said Marwan, his eyes wide with wonder. "It will soar up toward heaven, all dazzling and white."

"Who will live in it?"

"*We* will," he said. "We all will."

"Where will it be built?"

"In Hay Hassani, near the mattress shop," he said. "There will be

running water and electricity as well, and television, toilets, and huge windows through which we will look down on the city."

Marwan wiped his nose.

"It will be Paradise," he said.

ONE FEBRUARY AFTERNOON, I was walking through the old Art Deco quarter of Casablanca, when I spotted a young man standing on the corner outside the Central Market. He was a little taller than average and very thin, the buckle of his belt pulled up to the last hole. A tray was suspended round his neck by a frayed length of cord. Laid out on the tray were some homemade cards. They all looked the same—green with red polka dots. I wasn't sure if he was selling the cards or offering a service. So I watched.

A client would approach, hand over a coin, and choose a card. The skinny man with the tray would read the card. More often than not, the client would burst out laughing and would wander away into the throng. My curiosity was piqued. I went over, gave the man the required amount, and chose a card. He turned it over, and translated a short text:

"Every night Joha would bolt his shutters and hang out bunches of garlic. His neighbor asked why he did it. 'To keep the tigers away,' he said. 'But, Joha, there are no tigers here,' said the neighbor. 'Then it works, doesn't it!' said Joha."

I thanked the man, and gave him a tip.

"What is this for?" he said, pocketing the money.

"It's for making me very happy," I said.

JOHA IS A medieval folk hero, a wise fool, whose humor is known in Morocco, in China, and in all the lands in between. In Turkey they call him Hodja, across North Africa Joha, and in Afghanistan they know him as Mulla Nasrudin. He's known in Greece, too, and in

Russia, in Sicily, Albania, and even in Uzbekistan. Tales of his own special brand of warped genius fill the teahouses and caravanserais of Fès, Cairo, Kabul, and Samarkand.

Everyone knows a few Joha jokes, and they tell them to pass the time, to deliver a nugget of wisdom to illustrate a point, or to bring a smile to a glum face. For the Sufis, Joha is a tool, a kind of Trojan horse. The humor deviates the mind, the concentration, and allows something more serious to slip inside the subconscious.

My father brought us up with Joha's exploits. He was obsessed by the character, and published four collections of his tales. He used to say that a short story with a beginning, middle, and an end was like a magic wand: that it could effect a change that would be impossible to emulate by any other method. Why? Because of the way the human mind is wired. Throughout history, every community has told stories, he would say. People told stories long before they understood mathematics or psychology, before they could read or write, even before they had built the first mud hut. These stories kept the human brain in check, balanced it, and maintained a kind of cerebral status quo.

From an early age we were encouraged to choose a Joha tale and to turn it around our minds. "Take it into yourself," my father would say, "and it will become yours."

When I was very young, I asked him if I could go and meet Joha. My father waved a finger.

"You have to think in a different way," he said softly. "With Joha, the message he gives is more important than the man who gives it, or the way in which it is given. Do you understand, Tahir Jan?"

I didn't quite understand, but I said that I did. My father touched a hand to my cheek.

"It's like the box," he said, "the contents are a key, but the box itself is nothing more than something that protects something else. Learn to find the key, and to use it, and you will have received something very important."

Years passed and, very gradually, I learned that Joha jokes were about decipherment just as much as they were about humor. And I learned that the study of seven Joha tales at a time was regarded as a special preparation in itself. The stories usually involved known variables, each one with a second higher meaning. Understand these meanings and, like a cryptologist, you have a chance at deciphering the riddle, a chance of reaching another layer. For Sufis, this ultimate layer—or layers—are the ideal, a kind of jackpot. But at the same time the student of the story can be content with base level, the joke itself.

One rainy afternoon my father had demonstrated how to unpick a Joha tale. If I concentrate hard, I can hear the even tone of his voice:

"Salt had become so expensive that Joha went into the salt business," he said. "He loaded his old donkey with panniers of salt and was heading to market to make a fortune. On the way there, the pair were forced to wade through a river. As they crossed, the salt all dissolved. On the other bank, the donkey rolled on its back, delighted at the loss of its burden.

"The next week, Joha filled the panniers with wool. This time when they waded across the river, the wool became soaked, and the donkey almost drowned. Joha was delighted. 'That will teach you,' he yelled, 'for thinking that every time we cross, you will come out better.'

"I will explain it to you, Tahir Jan. But you must pay attention well. For Sufis, the salt—called *milh* in Arabic—is a homonym for another word that means 'being good.' The donkey symbolizes Man, or the pupil. The river is the process and Joha is the teacher. By discarding one's goodness, a person feels much better. But the drawback is that he loses his chance at prosperity, or attaining enlightenment. The wool signifies the Sufi. When they cross the river the second time, Joha is again the teacher, the one leading the pupil. This time the load is heavier, more spiritually valuable, its weight, gravity, only increased by its passage through the river."

———

UNTIL THAT DAY downtown in Casablanca, I had never heard a Joha tale told in Morocco. I supposed that the character's popularity had died out, killed off by Egyptian soap operas.

When I got back to Dar Khalifa, I asked Marwan if he knew of the folk hero. He burst out laughing.

"Oh, yes, yes, Monsieur Tahir," he said. "Just thinking of Joha makes me laugh."

"Do you know any of the jokes?"

Marwan had already begun. "Joha was a known smuggler, and would cross the frontier every day," he said. "The patrol guards would search his donkey each time, but could find nothing in their loads of hay. Sometimes they would confiscate the hay and set fire to it. Despite having no income, each week Joha became more and more wealthy. One day he became so rich that he retired across the frontier. Years passed and one day the police chief bumped into him. He said to Joha, 'We spent years trying to catch you, but we could not. Tell me, brother, what were you smuggling?' Joha smiled and said: 'Donkeys, I was smuggling donkeys.' "

THE NEXT WEEK, I arrived at Café Mabrook to find Abdul-Latif standing guard. He was holding a kind of homemade club in his fist. I asked what was happening.

"My regular clients are like my family," he said, scowling. "They are like my children. I love each one of them."

"And we come here because we value you so highly," I said. "But please explain what is bothering you."

"A woman came here and looked at me in a certain way!" he replied.

"Was she a beggar?"

Abdul-Latif swished his club. "No, she wasn't begging. She was a *sehura*, a sorceress."

"But what business did she have here?"

The waiter stared out at the street. "She wants to give me the evil eye," he said.

"Whatever for?"

"She's working for the café over there," he said, pointing out the door. "And they want to put us out of business."

Inside, Dr. Mehdi was talking to Hafad, the clock enthusiast. They were discussing a new kind of watch, powered by the heat of the wrist.

"It will never catch on," Hafad said sternly.

"Why not?"

"Well, imagine," he said. "Imagine if you die."

"Yes..."

"Well, it would stop."

I sat down and asked them if they had ever heard of Joha. The surgeon clapped his hands.

"Hah! Here's your Joha," he said, patting Hafad on the back.

"So you know him, Joha?"

"Of course we do," said Hafad.

"Everyone knows Joha," declared Dr. Mehdi.

"He's from Mèknes," said Hafad.

"But Turks say he's Turkish, the Russians claim he's Russian, and the Afghans will tell you he's from Afghanistan," I said.

Dr. Mehdi stood up and slapped his hands together so loudly that everyone else in the café, including Zohra's husband, looked round. I was surprised he had lost his characteristic veneer of cool.

"Well, all the others are lying!" he snapped.

I ordered more café noir and changed the subject. "When shall I leave for the Sahara?"

The surgeon regained his composure. "On Thursday afternoon," he said.

EACH DAY MORE and more e-mail messages arrived from people who had read *The Caliph's House*. My ego was inflated beyond all reason by the attention and the praise. Whereas our lives had been invisible up till then, the location of our home was suddenly published in glossy color magazines in a dozen countries. A few diehard adventurers like Burt managed to find us through the maze of the bidonville. There were others who sought me out not because of the books I had written on Casablanca, but because of my father.

In his effort to popularize teaching stories and the Sufi tradition, my father's work has attracted a wide range of readers across the world. They come from all types of social strata, backgrounds, and professions. Since my earliest childhood, I have met thousands of them, because they have beat a path to our front door.

Most of them are pretty conventional. A few are questionable. And a handful are downright odd.

When my father died from a heart attack a decade ago, his mail—sent to his publishers—was forwarded to me. Over the years, I wrote to hundreds of his readers, explaining that my father, Idries Shah, was no longer alive. The majority took the news with sadness, but were satisfied to have an answer nonetheless.

There was, however, one reader from Andalucia in Spain, who refused to believe that my father was no longer alive. Every month he wrote an airmail letter addressed to Idries Shah, sometimes begging and at other times ordering him to make his whereabouts known. At first I wrote back, assuming the gentleman had not heard the news. But the years passed, and the letters continued with increased regularity.

My father used to say that the answer to a fool is silence.

And so, I refrained from correspondence. Then, on the Monday morning before I set out for the desert, Osman came to tell me there was a visitor at the door. I asked who it was. The guardian motioned the confused outline of a man.

"He's both tall and short," he said.

"You'd better bring him in."

A minute passed. I had turned the dining room into a makeshift office, and was working in there. Osman trudged through the house, and stood to the side to allow the visitor to enter. I finished what I was doing on my computer. When I looked up a tall man with a hunched back was standing over my desk. He had a fatigued face, gray-blue eyes, and a froth of salt-and-pepper hair. I hadn't been prepared and so did not make the connection. I introduced myself. The visitor extended his hand. It was rough and clammy.

"Jose Gonzales," he said.

I narrowed my eyes, then opened them wide in an involuntary action. "As in . . . *the* Jose Gonzales?"

The gentleman seemed content to have elicited a response.

I stayed quite still. Perhaps he half-expected me to show him out.

"My father is dead," I said. "He's been dead quite a while now."

Gonzales didn't flinch. "I have heard this before," he said, in a heavy accent.

"I wrote to tell you."

"Yes."

"And you have not believed me."

The visitor seemed to stoop a little lower. "I am searching for Truth," he said.

"Are you sure that you are not really searching for Idries Shah?"

Gonzales looked at me coldly. He didn't reply.

A year before my father died, he sat me down in a quiet corner of his garden. We shared a pot of Darjeeling tea and listened to the sound of a pair of wood pigeons in a nearby tree. I poured a second cup of tea. As I was putting the strainer back on its holder, my father said: "Some time soon I will not be here anymore. My illness has reached another phase. I can feel it."

I sat there, touched with sadness. I didn't say anything because I could not think of anything appropriate to say.

"When I am not here," my father continued, "some people we have always trusted will betray us. Beware of this. Others will stand forward as true friends, people who were in the shadows before. Many more will ask who I left as my successor. They will hound you, asking for a name. It is important that you tell them that my successor is my printed work. My books form a complete course, a Path, and they succeed when I cannot be there."

He stopped talking, raised the porcelain cup to his lips, and took a sip. I finished my tea, and we walked back to the house. I was going to leave, when he told me to wait.

"One day," he said, "you may meet someone who is misguided. It might not make sense now, but at the time when it happens, you will know. If this happens, take this piece of paper and give it to him."

He held up the sheet, folded it in half once, and then again, and gave it to me. The following November he died. I grieved, but I was consoled by the thought that he was inside me, alive in the stories he had told. Our lives rattled forward. Ariane and Timur were born, and we moved into the Caliph's House. Nine years eventually passed. The paper was kept safe in a box file, along with my own papers.

And so came the morning on which I found Jose Gonzales standing over me. I took a deep breath, and he repeated himself: "I am searching for Truth."

I asked him to wait for me, and I went into my storage room and rooted about until I found the file and the paper. It was still folded as it had been when my father handed it to me. Before I stepped back into the dining room, I opened the sheet and read what was written on it.

It was this story:

There were once three men, all of whom wanted fruit, though none of them had ever seen any, since it was very rare in their country.

It so happened that they all traveled in search of this almost unknown thing called fruit. And it also happened that, at about the same time, each one found his way to a fruit tree.

The first man was heedless. He got to a fruit tree, but had spent so much time thinking about the directions that he failed to recognize the fruit.

His journey was wasted.

The second man was a fool, who took things very literally. When he saw that all the fruit on the tree was past its best, he said: "Well, I've seen fruit, and I don't like rotten things, so that is the end of fruit as far as I am concerned."

He went on his way, and his journey was wasted.

The third man was wise. He picked up some of the fruit and examined it. After some thought, and racking his brains to remember all the possibilities about this uneatable delicacy, he found that inside each fruit there was a stone.

Once he knew that this stone was a seed, all he had to do was to plant, and tend the growth, and wait for—fruit.

chapter fifteen

*More harm is done by fools through foolishness
than is done by evildoers through wickedness.*

The Prophet Mohammed

An hour before I set off on the long journey to the Sahara, Ariane tied a pink ribbon around my wrist. She said that each time I touched my hand to the ribbon, or looked at it, it would mean she was thinking of me.

In a small bag I had packed a few essentials and a letter of introduction from Dr. Mehdi. I pulled the door of the house closed. The guardians were standing to attention in a kind of shambled royal guard. They saluted, and Rachana drove us out through the shantytown, up the hill, to the railway station at Oasis.

We crossed the tracks and I waited for the train to Marrakech. Rachana was standing against the light, Timur on her hip, Ariane between us. There was a blast of a horn in the distance, and the train rolled in, steel wheels grinding against the tracks. I kissed Rachana and the children.

"I won't be long," I said. "I'll be back as soon as the favor is done."

"This isn't about a favor," said Rachana, leaning forward to hug me.

I climbed up, turned back to wave, and the train jolted away out of Casablanca toward the south.

THERE IS NOTHING like a train journey for reflection, and the passage from Casablanca to Marrakech is one of the most inspiring I know. Movement has a magical effect on the mind. It stimulates the eyes, distracts them, allowing real thought to take hold. I stared out the window at a landscape changing by slow degree from urban to farmland, and then again, to a desert panorama—baked terracotta red.

My mind jerked from one memory to another, scraps of people, places, smells, and sounds. A single minute of recollection can be a roller coaster. I thought of the scent of summer flowers, drowsy with bees, at my childhood home. Soaring above the Amazon in a two-seater Cessna. Toes in the sand on a Brazilian beach. Lying on the cement floor of a Pakistani torture prison.

For more than a decade I have traveled with two books. They are always with me, a part of my hand luggage. The first is my father's *Caravan of Dreams*. The other is Bruce Chatwin's *The Songlines*. They are my traveling companions, a source of stimulation on a dark night, or on a train journey south. I value *The Songlines* for the notes in the middle. Each one is a polished jewel, a splinter of wisdom, a piece of something much larger, but complete in itself. I dug out the book, opened it at random as I always do, and read a line that said a Sufi dervish wanders the earth because the action of walking dissolves the attachments of the world, and that his aim is to become a "dead man walking," a man whose feet are rooted on the ground but whose spirit is already in Heaven. I have read *The Songlines* so many times. My eyes have scanned that passage again and again but, until then, I had not really pulled it through the machinery of my mind.

As the train grumbled south over the first miles of brick-red desert, I absorbed it for the first time. It made absolute sense. I slipped the book back in my bag, and gazed out at a herd of scrawny camels standing at the bottom of a low hill. My eyes took a mental photograph of them.

But my mind was far away.

THAT EVENING I retraced my steps through Marrakech's medina, in search of Murad. I wanted to rebuke him for running off with Osman's wife. I have no sense of direction, and it took me three hours to find the corridor at the end of which he lived.

Once there, I stood at the bottom of the ladder and called out the storyteller's name. There was no answer. I called again, and a third time. Then a muffled sound came from the chamber above. I crept up. Murad was lying on the heap of rags. I thought he was drunk at first, because he was lying back, in a kind of stupor. I greeted him frostily, and asked about Osman's wife.

"She was unhappy," he said, "so very unhappy that I agreed to help her escape."

"Where is she now?"

The storyteller shrugged. "As soon as we reached Marrakech, she left," he said. "She was going to her relatives near Ouarzazate."

"But why did you do this? If Osman wasn't so depressed, he might have come to kill you."

Murad coughed hard. "A woman is a flower," he said. "And the saddest thing of all is for a beautiful flower to go unadmired."

That evening, I paid a visit to the Maison de Mèknes, to have a chat with its owner, Omar bin Mohammed. I turned up quite late, but expected to find him reading by the lamp near the door, or chatting to friends out in the street. To my surprise, though, the shutters were drawn. I banged on them. No reply. I assumed he must have gone home for the night. Then the owner of the next shop along rode up on a moped and held up a hand.

"He's shut down, closed, gone away," he said over the sound of the engine.

"Why, where, how?"

The shopkeeper shut off the fuel and his vehicle conked out.

"In Marrakech there is a merchant tradition," he said. "We are proud of it, proud to be shopkeepers. Our Prophet—peace be upon Him—was a trader himself. But every moment you are in business, there is a clock ticking."

"So what happened to Omar and the Maison de Mèknes?"

The shopkeeper unlocked his front door. "His time ran out," he said.

THE NEXT DAY I was up at dawn. I wandered down to Jemaa al Fna, the great square. It was empty. No one. Not a bird, not a beggar, not even a storyteller. I stood there, right in the middle, and I thought of the history and the power of that place—the executions, the stories, the performances. Even when it was empty you could feel the energy. It almost knocked you down. I closed my eyes, shut my nostrils, and put my fingers in my ears. Instead of feeling alone, I felt connected to every person who had ever traipsed across it. When I finally moved on, it seemed as if I was leaving with something new inside me, as though the soul of Jemaa al Fna had slipped in through my skin.

I went to the bus terminal and bought a ticket for the first bus south to Ouarzazate. There was a sense of great expectation. Families hustling aboard with bundles of cloth and bags of dried fruit, packets of dates, blankets in plastic bags, and buckets tied up on strings. The driver tore the corner of my ticket, and wished me peace. I took a seat at the back, behind a large wicker crate filled with chickens. They were alive but very silent, as if they hoped their owner might forget about them. Across from me sat a man with a striped kitten on his lap. The animal had smelled the birds, and was clawing to get nearer to the crate.

We left Marrakech and thundered out into the open country, on what is one of the most scenic roads in the kingdom. The man with the cat said he was a schoolteacher, and that he didn't trust his wife.

"She hates animals," he said. "If she had her way, she would have them all poisoned—everything from the birds in the sky to the foxes in the forest."

He had a don't-mess-with-me kind of face, angry eyes, and a wild, frantic mouth packed with jumbled teeth. I glanced down at the kitten. The hand smoothing back its fur was gentle beyond description. It was hard to believe such a tender hand could be attached to the same body as the face.

"She must have had a bad experience with an animal," I said.

The passenger clicked his mouth. "She doesn't see their beauty," he said. He stared down at the kitten, his angry eyes melting. "But I hope she will change now."

The bus hit a pothole, rocked to the side, and the chickens lost their cool.

"Tomorrow's her birthday," said the man. "I've brought her this kitten from Marrakech. It's from an expensive pet shop. I spent a fortune on it."

"Do you really think your wife will change, after a lifetime of animal-hatred?"

The man held the kitten's head up to my ear. "Can you hear that?"

I listened. "The purr?"

"It is the sound of an angel," said the man. "When my wife hears it, purring in her own ear, how can she resist?"

Dr. Mehdi had told me to head south from Marrakech, to Ouarzazate, and then on past Zagora, until the small town of

M'hamid, the end of the road. Once I got there, he said I was to make contact with his nephew Ibrahim, who would take me to the source of the salt. He gave exact instructions on how much salt to bring back, and how to pack it up.

At Ouarzazate, I found a small hotel where the rooms were little bigger than the beds, and where the owner spent his life in the kitchen, beside a huge cast-iron pot filled with lamb stew. He was called Mustapha. He had scars on his hands from decades of stirring the pot, and a way of talking that was very pleasing to the ear. His sentences flowed like syrup, one pouring into the next.

The walls of the hotel were adorned in paintings of scenes from the High Atlas. I recognized one as the Berber bridal festival of Imilchil. There were no other customers, except for a pair of nervous Swiss tourists, who were traveling with their dog. I went into the dining room, where there was a single table. The Swiss were sitting there, tensely. When they saw me, they got up, apologized politely, and left.

Mustapha stepped out of the kitchen and said the stew was fresh. I ordered a bowl. He brought it to my table and blew the steam off the top.

"It's very hot tonight," he said.

I tasted it. "Delicious."

"I call it Morocco stew."

"But stew is not typically Moroccan."

Mustapha licked a fresh scar on his hand. "There are a mixture of fine ingredients," he said, "prepared with care, over just the right heat. The flavor is subtle, a little delicate, but a delight to the senses."

Mustapha licked his hand again. "Just like Morocco," he said.

I pointed to the painting of a Berber girl in the traditional black and white striped robe of the Atlas.

"I come from Imilchil," he said, "we are a famous Berber family."

When I had finished the stew, I ordered a second bowl.

He refused to charge me. "Your mouth's appreciation is payment enough," he said.

As I ate the stew, I told him about the favor I had been asked to do. I said that I was searching for the story in my heart.

"We are all searching for that," he said.

"How can I find it?"

Mustapha pressed his palms together and touched them to his nose. "I cannot tell you," he said. "But I can offer you something."

"What?"

"A story that was given to me by my grandfather at Imilchil."

He pulled up a chair, took off his apron, and said: "There was once an island kingdom far away from here, where all the camels were tall and proud, and the men were skilled in making pottery, from the soft clay near the shore. The king was fair to his people, and a state of harmony prevailed. No one went without delicious fruit, or fine cloth for their clothes.

"Although the kingdom was prosperous, it was cut off from the world beyond, in the middle of the sea. Whenever anyone needed something not found on the island, a boat would be sent to the mainland to bring it back. But the waters all around were so perilous that these boats often sank, drowning all on board.

"Now, there lived in this kingdom a man called Jumar Khan. He was young and he was handsome, and he had a boat that he used to ferry goods from the next kingdom, far away. He would brave the high waves, and travel there often. And on one such journey he spotted a stallion for sale. It was the color of newly fallen snow, with a jet-black mane, and eyes that shone like coals.

"Jumar Khan had no wife or children to support and he had a bag of gold, the profit from many dangerous crossings. He asked the owner the price of the horse. He had just enough money, but the animal's owner said to him: 'I will sell it to you on the condition that you promise never to sell it to anyone else.'

"Jumar agreed and paid the money. The animal was loaded up onto the boat and, in rolling seas, carried back to the kingdom.

"A few years passed, and everyone praised the stallion. Jumar Khan himself loved it a little more each day. Then, one winter dawn, he set sail as normal, but a giant wave struck and smashed his boat onto rocks. Jumar and the passengers were saved by the beneficence of God. But with no boat, Jumar lost his livelihood and was ruined.

"He might have sold his horse, but he had made a promise never to do so. In any case, he loved it with all his heart, and could not bear to be parted from it.

"One day an important merchant visited the kingdom. He was known by reputation throughout the East, and his name was Sher Ali. While staying on the island, he heard of Jumar Khan, and the misfortunate circumstances in which he found himself. And he heard of the fabulous stallion, and the promise he had made not to sell it. But in the merchant's experience, every object had a value.

"He sent word to Jumar's home that he would like to view the animal, as it was said to be very beautiful. The next evening Sher Ali arrived.

"With no money to afford staff, Jumar received his guest himself and prepared a fabulous meal of succulent meat garnished with vegetables which he grew himself. Sher Ali ate until he could eat no more and, after a glass of tea, he asked about the horse.

"Jumar Khan shifted in his seat. 'Oh, respected guest,' he said, 'as you know it is our tradition to provide a feast for a visitor. And the more esteemed the visitor, the finer the meal is required to be. In my state of poverty, I was unable to provide a meal fitting for a distinguished guest such as yourself,' said Jumar Khan, placing his hand on his heart. 'The only way I could keep my honor was to serve you my beloved horse.'"

THE ROAD WENDED southeast down the Draa Valley. An ocean of palms rippled out on either side, emerald green in a landscape so dry

it seemed miraculous life existed there at all. The local bus ran the route, transporting merchants and their fruit up to Ouarzazate, and ferrying their purchases back down to Zagora.

On our childhood journeys to Morocco, we visited Ouarzazate time and again. It was little more than a hamlet then. But Providence had delivered fortune in an unlikely way. Hollywood had discovered the stark beauty of the region, and used the mud fortresses and adobe villages as backdrops in a thousand movies, from *Lawrence of Arabia* to *Gladiator*.

Film money had delivered to the local people the kind of wealth that fuels the most fantastic dreams. Once he had dished up a third helping of his stew and finished his tale, Mustapha gave me a single piece of advice.

"I cannot tell you what story is in your heart," he said. "But I can tell you that money earned with ease is the devil's currency. Everything it touches is cursed. If you want prosperity, work hard for it, and don't take charity unless you are a day away from being drowned."

"Drowned by water?"

"Drowned by life."

As the bus grunted and wheezed between the potholes, my mind flitted back to the days when our Ford Cortina made the same journey south. My mother spent her time sorting through brocades and kaftans she had snapped up at the previous souq, and my father would be in the front with our gardener at the wheel. He never stopped talking for a moment. Conversation was a kind of lifeblood to him, a way to process his thoughts before he committed them to paper.

My school friends went on family holidays. We never did. We went on expeditions, journeys with a purpose. My father would use them to draw our attention to aspects of life we might otherwise have missed. He used to say that anything the senses showed you could be regarded in a different way.

On a journey down the Draa Valley a generation before, he had asked the gardener to pull over.

"I have to get something," he said, opening the door. He crossed a patch of scrubland and made his way down through a grove of date palms, to the stream. We asked our mother what he was doing.

"Wait and see," she said.

Ten minutes later he was back. There was something in his fist. When we were all looking, he opened his hand and showed us. It was a smooth black pebble, with two veins of white running down one side.

"What is this?" he asked.

"It's a pebble," I said.

"What else is it?"

We shook our heads.

"That's all. It's a pebble and that's that."

My father put the pebble in my hand and told me to look at it carefully. "Do you see anything else?"

"No."

"Really look," he said, "change the way you are looking at it."

"Baba, I'm looking. Really I am."

A few minutes passed. The gardener stepped out to stretch his legs. When he came back, we were still looking at the pebble.

My father weighed it in his hand. "What you see here and you call a pebble is all sorts of things," he said. "It's a fragment of something else, but is complete as it is. It's been rounded smooth by the river, molded by time. If it stays in the river for a few million years longer, it will become sand. To an ant, it is a mountain, and to an elephant, it's almost too small to be seen. And to us it's an object of beauty, something that feels very nice to touch, but it's useful, too."

"Baba, it's a pebble," I said, "and it's not useful at all."

"Tahir Jan, that's where you are wrong," he said. "You see, this little pebble has a thousand uses. You could put it in a pan of milk, and the milk wouldn't boil over. Or you could throw it at a wild dog that's attacking you, or scrape it on the ground to draw a map, or use it as a paperweight. Or," he said quietly, "you could just keep it on a shelf and look at it from time to time, as a reminder of our journey, and of this very beautiful place."

THAT EVENING, THE bus reached Zagora after three punctures and a quick stop to barter chickens at the side of the road. In the countryside of Morocco, there are tokens of modernity—transistor radios, color televisions, and plenty of mobile phones. But the essence of life has not changed in centuries. The man sitting beside me on the bus had five chickens, all trussed up by the feet. Oblivious to their show of discomfort, he pulled them down from the luggage rack and took them onto the road. He bartered them directly for other goods at a line of makeshift stalls.

One was swapped for a jar of honey, another for a bag of clementines, a third was traded for some pomegranates, a fourth for a bottle of olive oil, and a fifth for a rough wicker basket in which to carry his goods.

When I stepped down from the bus at Zagora, I was immediately attended to by a boy of about ten years. He was holding a fishing rod in one hand, and a jar of worms in the other, and he swaggered when he walked.

"I will help you," he said.

"How do you know I want your help?"

He shook the jar of worms, and peered in to see if they were moving. "I know because you are a tourist," he said, "and tourists have money but no wisdom." He tapped his temple. "Nothing in their heads."

"Who told you that?"

"My father did."

"What does he do?"

"He sells carpets over there."

"What's his name?"

"Ashraf."

"And what's yours?"

The boy shook the worms again. "I'm Sami," he said.

A few minutes later, I was sitting in a cramped carpet emporium, across from Sami's father. The shop was a concrete box, airless and so dusty that everyone inside coughed almost all the time. Ashraf's face was hidden by a mask of scruffy beard and dominated by a long, hooked nose.

He poured me a glass of mint tea. "They call me the Eagle," he said.

"Are you cruel and eagle-like with your clients?"

"No, it's because of my nose," he said.

I told him it had been fortunate that I had met Sami at the bus stop.

Ashraf flared his nostrils. "He was fishing," he said.

"For river fish?"

The carpet-seller coughed hard, and gulped down a lump of phlegm. "For tourists."

"Oh, yes, he told me that tourists have nothing between their ears. Empty heads."

Ashraf grinned. "You are different. You are a man of intelligence," he said. He poured me more tea.

"Well, I am also fishing," I told him.

"For what?"

"For a story."

"Then you are in the right place," Ashraf replied. "You see, each of my carpets is a story, a window which looks into another world."

Sami started coughing so violently he had to go outside for air.

When he was gone, his father stood up and pulled down a fine tribal rug, alternating red and white lines, ivory tassels at the ends.

"Look at this one," he said, kneeling again. "It's a story of the desert. The sheep which grew the wool were nourished by the plants that were themselves nourished in the soil, on the banks of the Draa River. The dyes came from berries in the trees, and the knowledge to create this masterpiece came from an ancient wisdom, trapped in the memory of the tribe."

Ashraf coughed again. "There are stories in all my stock," he said.

"But I'm looking for another kind of story ... something with a beginning, middle, and an end."

The carpet-dealer lit a cigarette and filled the cubicle with smoke. "They do have a beginning, a middle, and an end," he said.

"Not in the same way, though."

Ashraf exhaled, and coughed some more. "Two things can look very different," he said. "They can be different shapes, different colors, made out of quite different things. But to the heart they are exactly the same."

chapter sixteen

When a man's sleep is better than his waking,
It is better that he should die.

Saadi of Shiraz

Real travel is not about the highlights with which you dazzle your friends once you're home. It's about the loneliness, the solitude, the evenings spent by yourself, pining to be somewhere else. Those are the moments of true value. You feel half proud of them and half ashamed, and you hold them to your heart. The road south from Zagora was like that. I half-wished I was somewhere else, or that I had a companion to bore with conversation.

A farmer with a pickup full of sheep gave me a lift to his village. The community faced the road, a jumble of square Berber homes, built with the same giant blocks of mud that I have so often seen used in Afghanistan. The farmer pointed to a single lamppost and told me to stand under it.

"A white taxi will come," he said.

"When?"

The moment I asked it, I heard how stupid it sounded. Punctuality and timetables were concepts that hadn't reached the Draa Valley.

"It will come today or tomorrow," said the farmer after some time. "If God wills it."

I thanked him and waited obediently under the lamppost. The February sun was hot on my neck, and the scent of bread baking in a nearby mud-brick oven was almost too much to bear. I had not found any breakfast in Zagora, and so I followed the smell of baking bread. I came to a low adobe building, with a chicken coop and a crazed dog on the roof. A boy ran out, shouted, laughed, burst into tears, and fetched his father.

The man was unusually lean, muscular, and alert, like a greyhound in the starting trap. I wished him peace, and he echoed my words, shook my hand firmly, and looked at the dust.

"Taxi," I said, pointing at the lamppost.

The man repeated the word twice: first as a question, and then as a statement. He shook my hand again, praised God.

In a single movement, he bent round to his house, poked his head inside, barked at his wife, turned round again, and invited me in. I entered the cool, dim room in time to see the hem of a woman's kaftan rushing out the back. It would, of course, have been unseemly for a male guest to have set eyes on, let alone to have met, the women of the house. There was a single room, furnished with a low table and cushions on the floor. In one corner was a nest of embroidery and, in another, a Qur'an wrapped in a scrap of green silk.

An ancient figure was asleep on the cushions. I didn't see him at first, not until my eyes had adjusted to the lack of light. The lean man prodded him awake and whispered. The ancient roused from his sleep, fumbled for a pair of wire-rimmed glasses, and struggled to fit them over his eyes. He looked at the lean man, then at me, jerked upright, and greeted me in French.

"I am waiting for the taxi," I said.

The old man seemed confused. "Where are you going?"

"To M'hamid, the end of the road."

"That's far," he replied, nodding.

We sat in silence. In Morocco, a family's life is put on hold for a guest, even one who has invited himself. I found myself thinking about our world. If we found a stranger, a foreigner, on our doorstep we might be more likely to point him elsewhere rather than invite him in.

The arrival of a guest into a home is quite different in Oriental society. Nowhere is it more pronounced than in Morocco. Hospitality is a ritual built on honor, something of such importance that no family would ever stint in their duty. The ceremony developed through centuries of nomadic movement and intertribal conflict, and is part of the soul of all Arab people.

In the sixth century, before the foundation of Islam, the tribes of Arabia passed their lives fighting one another. These interminable battles might have ended in their mutual extermination had they not developed a code of honor governing their wars. According to the rules which they developed, the object of war was not to win battles or destroy the enemy, but to provide a field for the performance of heroic deeds, which were subsequently immortalized in poetry.

For the early Arabs to fight honorably was more important than to win.

TEA WAS SERVED, boiling hot and thick with sugar. After it came bread and olive oil, followed by a platter of fresh dates. The lean man piled all the food in front of me and urged me to eat. He picked through the dates, chose the best ones, and gave them to me a few at a time. I praised their sweet taste. The older man shooed a hand toward the door.

"We grow them out there," he said.

"I've seen the palms in abundance."

The ancient pushed his glasses up his nose. "This is the desert but God gave us the palms for every need," he said. "We eat the dates, and make baskets from the leaves, and use the trunks as beams in our houses, or we hollow out the wood and make buckets. What more could we ever need?"

At that moment a teenage boy sloped in, greeted us all, and pulled out a new radio. The old man strained to focus on the object, which began crackling music.

"It's music from Casablanca," said the youth.

His grandfather took off his glasses and wiped his old eyes. "The world is not what it used to be," he said dismally.

"All the way from Casa," the boy repeated.

"It's nonsense," said the old man. "This boy here has no interest in what is important. His head is filled with things he hears on that radio thing."

"What is important?" I asked.

The grandfather thought for a long time. He smoothed an arthritic hand over his hair. "Palms," he said. "Date palms."

Another round of tea was poured, and I stood up for Casablanca. The old man scowled.

"It's a place of loud music and loose women," he said.

"Some of the music is not too bad, and not all the women are loose."

He looked up from his lap. "How do you know this?"

"Because I live there."

The young man dropped his radio and ducked his head in respect. "You live in Casa?"

"Yes."

"How is it?"

"It's fantastic," I said.

The boy wriggled. "I want to go there. I want to see the ocean."

His grandfather lay back on the cushions and closed his eyes. I described the ocean.

"It's the most magical thing in the world," I said. "Each time you look at it, it's different. Sometimes the waves are furious, like a wild monster, and at other times it's so calm and blue that it looks like a sheet of glass. And over the ocean lies another world."

"America," said the boy dreamily.

"That's right."

"One day I will cross the ocean to America," he said.

IN THE AFTERNOON, a white communal taxi screeched to a halt at the lamppost and I was pulled inside. Before the door was even closed, the vehicle sped away, and disgorged me at the small town of Tamegroute a few miles on. I got down, dusted my shoulders, and found myself touching the pink ribbon on my wrist. Ariane was thinking of me. I vowed then I would never leave the children at home again if I could avoid it. I had brought them to the kingdom for the purpose of experiencing real Morocco, and not staying in an oasis in its greatest metropolis. From then on we would travel as I had done in my own youth, on our own journeys with a purpose.

In the late afternoon, I found myself at a *zaouia,* the study center beside the tomb of a saint. Tamegroute may not be famous outside Morocco, but it holds a special place in the cultural core of the kingdom. A thousand years ago, the town was already famous, celebrated for its scholarship, and as a rest point en route to Timbuktu. It houses one of the most important libraries of Islamic texts in the Arab world, and dispenses charity to the elderly and the mentally infirm.

A cluster of wrinkled men were sitting on the steps. When they saw me, they moved into action like automata. One of them put out a hand, another staggered to his feet, a third began to sing. I was going to ask them directions to the library. But before I could say a word, a fourth man, much younger than the others, led me aside. He was dressed in a black wool jelaba, the hood up over his head like a monk. His hands were hidden, pushed up opposite sleeves, his face concealed by shadow.

"I need directions to the library."

"I will tell you," he said.

He took me out into the bright sunlight away from the others and seemed to have authority. He handed me a sheet of crumpled paper.

"I work with the patients," he said.

"What is wrong with them?"

"They are fragile, fragile in their heads."

He led me to a patch of shade, pulled off his hood, and I saw his face. It was energetic, unshaven, and a little pallid, the kind of face that keeps your attention because of the eyes. They were green and glittery, like wood opals.

"I am Ilias," he said.

"You look after the patients?"

"Yes."

"Do you heal them?"

"We try to."

"With medicines?"

"No, there is no money for medicines." He kicked a stone from his sandal. "So we talk to them," he said.

ILIAS TOOK ME on a tour of the library, as the sunlight faded into dusk. The building housed an extraordinary collection of manuscripts, most of them Qur'anic commentaries, works of mathematics and astronomy, law books, and historical texts. Many of the books were crafted from gazelle-skin vellum, all written by hand, and some were more than seven hundred years old. In the West there would have been security systems, glass cases, and lists of rules pinned up on the walls. Part of the charm was the library's simplicity, its sense of peace.

Ilias invited me to take tea in a café not far from the *zaouia*. I was impressed by his natural ease. Everyone who saw him appeared to be energized by his greeting.

"You know everyone," I said.

"The town is very small. Even an ant couldn't get lost in Tamegroute."

I laughed, and then asked about the treatment.

"We believe that by talking, we can change the patient's state," he said.

"You ask them about their problems?"

"Certainly we do, and they tell us what they are thinking, how they feel. But we believe in reaching something deeper. We try to wake the sleeping mind."

"How do you do that?"

"We use humor," he said.

Ilias told me that the most successful way of treating the maladies he encountered was to engage the mind with something stimulating, something that could penetrate deep but not be filtered out.

"Humor cuts through the layers," he said. "It has a magical effect. When we have a patient who is fierce, we can change his mood instantly."

Ilias peered at me, his opal eyes catching the last trace of twilight.

I asked if he had heard of Joha.

"Of course!" he cried. "We tell Joha tales every day."

"Do you have a favorite?"

Ilias paused to greet a friend, sipped his tea, and said:

"It was the middle of winter and Joha had no money at all. He couldn't afford firewood, and so he wrapped himself up in his old blanket and sat on his bed. He was very hungry, but didn't even have enough money to make his usual pot of soup. 'At least,' he thought to himself, 'the wind is so strong that my greedy neighbors won't come bothering me for food like they usually do.' He spent a long time thinking of the delicious soup he could not afford to prepare, tasting the flavors in his imagination. Just then, there was a knock at the door. It was the neighbor's youngest son. He had been sent to ask

Joha for some of his soup. 'Damn it,' shouted Joha, 'have my neighbors become so low that they now smell what I'm thinking?'"

As it is customary to tell seven Joha tales in succession, I told the next one.

"Joha was feeling generous. He went to the teahouse and invited everyone inside to come back to his home for a magnificent feast. As the throng of guests neared his house, he realized that his wife would beat him if he didn't warn her of the open invitation. He ran ahead to tell her. When she heard that fifty people were about to descend, she beat Joha's head. 'There's no food in the house!' she shouted. 'How dare you invite people without telling me first!' Gripped with embarrassment, Joha ran upstairs and hid himself. A few minutes later, the guests arrived and knocked at the door. His wife opened it. 'Joha invited us,' the guests said. 'Well, he's not at home,' said Joha's wife. 'But we saw him come in the front door,' said the guests. Joha, who was watching from an upstairs window, shouted down: 'You fools, I could have gone out the back door, couldn't I?'"

A SERIES OF vehicles took me closer and closer to the end of the road at M'hamid. There was another white communal taxi, a truck laden with canned fish, a petrol tanker, and, after that, a horse-drawn cart, on the back of which were squashed a dozen children on their way home from school. The palm groves of the Draa Valley must be seen to be believed. They extend mile after mile, tens of thousands of them, in an oasis of cypress green that runs the length of the river. But then, suddenly, at M'hamid they stop.

It is there that the desert begins.

As soon as the cart pulled into the town, I felt the change. The road I had followed in fits and starts from Casablanca came to an abrupt end. Beyond it was sand, a stark Wild West–Tuareg town, where all the men wore blue robes and the women never stepped out. We had ventured here as children, drawn by my mother's romantic love of *Beau Geste,* and my father's dream to see where the road was swallowed up by dunes. I can remember the "Blue Men" vividly, their indigo robes so drenched with sweat that their skin was dyed blue. We drew pictures of them, and my mother bought up half the robes in the bazaar to take home and turn into quilts.

My father had chosen the desert to recount a story of a Jinn married to a mortal. I have forgotten the twists and turns, but I recall what he said when the tale was at an end: "These stories are technical documents. They are like maps, or a kind of blueprints. What I do is to show people how to use the maps, because they have forgotten. You may think it's a strange way to teach—with stories—but long ago this was the way people passed on wisdom. Everyone knew how to take the wisdom from the story. They could see through the layers, in the same way you see a fish frozen in a block of ice. But the world where we are living has lost this skill, a skill people certainly once had. They hear the stories and they like them, because the stories amuse them, make them feel warm. But they can't see past the first layer, into the ice."

My father would sometimes pause a block of information halfway, as if to let us ruminate, to take in what he had said. He would pretend there was a reason to halt, but the reason was to give us time.

"The stories are like a lovely chessboard," he said. "We all know how to play chess, and we can be drawn into a game so complicated that our faculties are drained. But imagine if the game was lost from a society for centuries. Then the fine chessboard and its pieces were found. Everyone would cluster round to see them, and praise them. They might never imagine that such fine objects ever had a purpose other than to entertain the eyes.

"The stories' inner value has been lost in the same way," he said. "At one time everyone knew how to play with them, how to decipher them. But now the rules have been forgotten. Tahir Jan," he stressed, "it is for us to show people again how the game is played."

DR. MEHDI HAD instructed me to take the letter to Hotel Safari, and to ask for his nephew Ibrahim. A sandstorm had just blustered through, and the people of M'hamid were furled up expertly in their robes, as if the searing wind was an adversary they knew well. There were a few gaudy signs for second-rate tourist lodges, a row of knick-knack shops touting Tuareg junk, and the forlorn-looking Hotel Safari.

I had heard of the place before. For it was there in the main salon that the French Foreign Legion used to come to repose, to mingle with the locals, and to get blind drunk. Their bar stools were still in position, almost as though they had stepped out for a pee. At the end of the bar was standing a young Tuareg with a bandana and the prerequisite robes.

"I'm looking for Ibrahim."

"Hey, brother, you wanna see the desert?"

"You speak very good English."

"I've been around."

"Around the world?"

"Around Marrakech."

"Oh. Seen Ibrahim?"

"You're lookin' at him."

After such a long journey it felt like a grave moment, a messenger at last dispensing with his duty. I fished out the letter and presented it to Ibrahim. He lit a cigarette, held it in his teeth, and opened the envelope.

"Dr. Mehdi sent me," I said. "Got to bring some salt back to Casablanca to purify a wedding garden."

Ibrahim scanned the lines of Arabic, wincing as the smoke swirled into his eyes. "Got a car?" he said.

"No."

"Then how you gonna get to the salt?"

"I will walk."

Dr. Mehdi's nephew threw his cigarette out the window. "The salt lake's fifty miles away."

"Can I borrow a car?"

Ibrahim lit another cigarette. "Fouad could help you," he said.

WHEN I WAS a university student in Kenya, one of my best friends was a shepherd from the northern Turkana Province. He was tall, wiry, and was called Nathaniel. His front teeth had been pulled out in childhood so that he could be force-fed if he ever got lockjaw. I was in my late teens. Nathaniel was about fifty-five.

One day I asked him why he had waited so long to get higher education.

"*Bwana*," he said smiling, "in my village we are shepherds. So we never paid much attention to getting educated."

"So why bother now?"

"Because of the future," he said. "We had a meeting of the village elders and decided that one of us must get educated as a way of protecting us all. So everyone gave a little money and they chose me."

For twenty years I have carried Nathaniel's example in my mind. Long after we graduated, I happened to be in Kenya and had a few days to spare. So I crossed the equator and traveled to the blistering desert of Turkana, where Nathaniel lived. He was on a hillside with his sheep. It was so dry that the animals were forced to eat roots. Nathaniel hugged me. He was pleased to see me, and I him, although he didn't seem at all fazed that I had turned up. We stood on that hillside looking into each other's eyes, the scorching wind on our faces.

Real friends can sometimes dispense with talking. They can take comfort in the awkwardness of silence. Nathaniel said very little to me that day. He took me to his hut, served me some homemade millet beer, and he asked me to pray with him.

We prayed that the future would be as quiet as the past.

I HAD NEVER thought I would ever meet another Nathaniel. But I did at the end of the road, at M'hamid. Ibrahim's half brother Fouad was a subdued Tuareg with oversized hands and a lazy eye. He spoke in short bursts, like machine-gun fire, and had learned his English in far-off Casablanca thirty years before. Back then M'hamid was a one-horse town. As in Nathaniel's village, the entire community had pooled resources to educate a single man.

"There weren't any tourists until recently," he said.

"So why are they here now?"

"German television showed the sand dunes."

"Camel treks?"

"No, no one wants to trek with camels now."

"So what do they want?"

"Sand boarding," he said. Fouad waved an arm at a string of scruffy tourist shops lined along the last few feet of road. "Adventure tours."

"I can't stand tourism," I said.

"Neither can I," replied Fouad. "But it's like a drug. The more cash people make, the more they want."

I asked where I might find a car to cross the dunes.

"You can borrow mine," said Fouad.

I TOOK A room at Hotel Safari, but it was too hot to go inside. So I dragged the mattress up onto the roof and found a burly American already there. He had soaked a pair of trousers in cool water and wrapped them round his head. His arms were bare and tattooed with vivid scenes of a martial artist in training. Across the back of one hand was written "LOVE" and across the other "FATE."

I flung the mattress down and lay on my back. The stars were like a million grains of salt cast on a black canvas, the moon a sliver of lemon rind.

The American said his name was Fox. "I'm from Iowa."

"Hello," I said.

"Ever been there?"

"Where?"

"Iowa."

"No, I haven't."

"Know anything 'bout it?"

I thought for a long time. "Des Moines," I said.

"That all?"

"Yup."

Fox pulled a Moleskine notebook from his breast pocket. He twanged back the band, scribbled something in pencil.

"What are you writing?"

"A note to myself." He paused, then read: "*Des Moines sucks.*"

"I'm sure it's not that bad."

"Oh, but it is," said Fox.

"What are you doing here, at the end of the road?"

"I'm a surfer."

"You're a long way from the waves."

"Sand. I surf sand."

`

"Wow," I said.

"That's the Sahara desert," said Fox, "the greatest sandbox on earth."

He asked if I surfed sand.

"No, I'm here doing a favor," I said.

"Like what?"

"I've come to get some salt for a friend."

"Salt?"

"Salt."

"Can't you get it where you come from?"

"Yes, you can. But this salt is different."

"How?"

"Er, it's special?"

"Why?"

"Because it's going to be used to chase away the Jinns."

The American put away his notebook. "So you believe in the Jinns?"

"Not really. Not properly."

"So you're telling me you've come all the way to the Sahara to get something you could have gotten at home for someone else's superstition?"

"Er, um."

"Well?" said Fox.

"Yes, I guess that's about it."

chapter seventeen

Joha's watchman found his master breaking into his own bedroom in the middle of the night.
"Master, what are you doing?"
"Hush," said Joha, "my wife says I walk in the night. I'm trying to see if it's true."

Ariane and Timur have a shelf full of books in their bedroom. Before they sleep, one of them goes over, pulls down a favorite, and begs me to read it. Timur likes *Where the Wild Things Are*. He stomps around gnashing his teeth, pretending he's a Wild Thing. Ariane likes the book, too, but she won't admit it. She once whispered to me that she thought the Wild Things were sweet but a little bit naughty, and not very pretty at all. She prefers her *Barbie Princess Book*. Whichever book they choose, they ask me to read it again and again and again. They can never tire of the words, and really only delight in a book when they know it by heart.

When I was a little older than Ariane, my father said that the more you read a story—the same story—the more it works on your mind. Like a beautiful flower bud, he said, the story only opens up, and flowers, with time. Seeing my children enjoy the same tales over and over helped me to see that this repetition is a kind of natural setting inside us all. But as adults in our world, and with the strain of reading rather than oral repetition, we choose a new text over a known one.

Our competence in reading is something of which we are especially proud. We publish hundreds of miles of books each year, and fill cavernous libraries with them. Mass education has, of course, led to the upsurge in writing. The more written texts we have in a single room, the more valuable we regard it, and the more knowledgeable we think we are because so much writing is available to us. We cling to the belief that the more we read, the wiser we become.

My father would say that the Western world spends far too much time reading, and far too little time understanding. It would infuriate him if someone asked when his next book was due out. He would say: "I will write another book when you have understood the last thirty books I have published." On this subject he observed a key difference between Oriental and Occidental minds: Eastern society values that which is tried and tested. Stories that have been in circulation for millennia are regarded as having real value, as being containers of inner wisdom—whereas Western society constantly demands new material. Much of the time it's the same old stuff packaged in a fresh way. The result is wordage for the sake of wordage. For my father it was almost too much to take.

"This world we are living in, Tahir Jan," he used to say in bewilderment, "it's upside down."

FOUAD SAID TOURISM was destroying the desert, but it was bringing in so much money that no one dared speak up. The sand boarding, the rally drivers, and the litter left by campers were having a grim effect. The next morning we left Hotel Safari and walked through the empty streets to where the car was parked. I was laden down with blankets and supplies. Once, long ago when I broke down in the Namib desert, I learned the value of preparation.

All the tourist shops were shut up tight. The air was still cool, sounds muffled by a sprinkling of the ubiquitous sand.

As we strolled through the heart of M'hamid, Fouad talked in short staccato bursts.

"There is no respect," he said.

"From whom?"

"From the Tuareg and from the tourists."

"Why?"

He tilted his head in thought. "If aliens came from outer space," he said, "and gave money to the Tuareg, they would be happy, but they would not respect them."

"Who?"

"The aliens."

"Ah."

"And the aliens would probably have no respect for us," he said.

"Do you blame the tourists, though?"

Again, Fouad tilted his head in contemplation. "No, Monsieur," he replied. "I don't blame them."

"Then who do you blame?"

Fouad smiled. "I blame the aliens," he said.

THE CAR WAS buried in a sand drift. It looked as if it had been in there for weeks.

"When did you last use it?"

"Two days ago."

"So much sand in two days?"

"It's the wind," said Fouad.

He opened the back, grabbed a shovel, and worked on the drift.

"I will tell you something," he said after five minutes of shoveling.

"What?"

"Just because two people speak the same language, it doesn't mean they understand each other."

"The tourists and the Tuareg?"

He nodded. "If I learned the language of cat, I would not think like a cat."

It was still rather early for philosophy.

Fouad let out a kind of grunting sound. "A hundred years ago our worlds were separated," he said.

"By distance?"

"Yes. By distance. Now they are closer."

"Much closer—a short flight."

Fouad touched my arm, his lazy eye leering toward me. "But they are still very far apart," he said. "In their minds."

FOUAD'S CAR WAS one of the reasons I moved to Morocco.

In Europe or the United States, it would have been condemned a generation before. There would be a hundred laws against it. Merely looking at it would get you arrested. But for the proud people of M'hamid, it was in fine roadworthy condition. Just about everything that could be torn out or smashed by human strength had been ravaged.

There were no wing mirrors or windows, dials or carpeting, and the only seat was the one the driver used. Fouad told me he had bought the vehicle cheap on account of the noise. He asked if I knew the way to the salt lake. I shook my head.

"I will drive you," he said.

We set off.

I huddled in the cavity where the passenger seat had once been. Fouad, cloaked in his long blue robes, sat beside me, the wheel gripped tight in his hands. The engine noise was jarring beyond words, matched only by the smog we left in our trail.

There was something a little disconcerting about heading off into an ocean of sand, especially into the Sahara—the widest desert on earth, which stretches from the Nile Valley all the way to the Atlantic. Most of us are road people. We don't realize it, but we are wedded to the notion of having tarmac beneath the wheels. Driving on sand is rather like driving over snow. You aim the vehicle in the vague direction you want to go, and hope that you don't get stuck.

Fouad pointed out the tracks left by a thousand sand surfers. "They go to the high dunes," he said angrily. "These tracks will be here forever."

I asked him about camels. I had seen very few.

"The Tuareg aren't interested in them now," he said.

"Why?"

"Because they don't have a clutch pedal."

An hour after leaving M'hamid, we were adrift, sand all around. I quickly understood why the Bedouin call the desert *sahel,* "ocean." To my eyes, each track was the same. But Fouad knew better. He said he could smell the dry salt lake.

"But it's miles away."

"It rained a week ago."

"So?"

"So I can smell the salt."

"What does it smell like?"

"Like the ocean."

Another hour and we came to a kind of encampment. A low stockade had been crafted expertly from thorns, and was guarded by a thirsty-looking dog. It went wild at the noise of the car, came running out, its legs a blur of movement. Its master called it to heel.

We got down.

Fouad said the place was a sacred spring. "Drink the water and you will remember."

"Remember what?"

"Anything that ever happened to you."

"How much does it cost?"

Fouad shot a line of words at the dog's owner. A mouth filled with big white teeth said a number.

"Thirty dirhams."

"Give me a cup."

A homemade bucket was lowered down into the well. It was a long time before we caught the sound of wood touching water.

"It's deep," I said.

"But the water is low. I have not seen it this low."

"Have you drunk it?"

Fouad said he had.

"Did you remember everything?"

"Yes. Every detail."

The bucket was swung up and passed to me. Its water smelled of sewage. "How much do I have to drink?"

"As much as you want."

I took a gulp, swilled it around my mouth. It tasted of sewage, too. I would have spat it out, but the Tuareg seemed proud of their sacred spring, and I didn't want to upset them.

Fouad leaned toward me. "What can you remember?"

I thought back. I was sitting cross-legged on the floor playing with a little garage and a toy car, making the sound of the engine with my lips. How old was I...three, four? Then I was running through the woods, my hands filled with chestnuts, pricked by their shells. After that I was in a rose garden, riding my red bicycle between the flower beds.

"I remember my childhood," I said.

"Drink some more of the water," said Fouad.

It tasted foul, but I forced down another gulp, closed my eyes, and thought back. I was in Morocco, in the Sahara. My mother was knitting, and my sisters were nearby playing leapfrog in the sand. I looked around. My father was sitting by himself. He seemed sad. I went over. He picked up a fist of sand, let it drain through his fingers.

"We are basket weavers," he said. "That's what we do, we weave baskets. My father weaved baskets before me, and his father before him. Tahir Jan, take pride in the baskets you weave."

Fouad claimed the water had helped my memory.

"I don't think it was the water," I said.

"It always works."

"No, these memories were already inside me."

We left the encampment, the sacred spring, and the ferocious dog, and drove on across the flat surface of sand. The recent rain had brought shoots and the odd patch of green. The only flourishing plants had succulent round green pods, the size of oranges. I asked Fouad if they were good to eat.

"Touch them and you will go blind," he said.

Two more hours and we came to a vast salt pan. A white crust stretched as far as the eye could see. There was no water, although in the middle the salt was darker, no doubt moistened by the rain.

"This is the lake," said Fouad.

"The salt! It's the salt I have to get!"

I was overcome with a frail rally of emotion. I got down, fell to my knees, and scooped up a handful of the salt crystals. There was a plastic bag in my pocket. I took it out and filled it half full.

"Shall we go?" said Fouad.

We looked at each other, and then I scanned the desert. I could see from one horizon to the next. There wasn't another human in sight. I felt foolish. The journey from Casablanca had taken me to a distant destination, only to spend a moment there. I was as bad as the tourists I so disdain, who travel to India's Taj Mahal, to the Eiffel Tower, or to Big Ben, snap a photo, and leap back onto the tour bus.

"You have the salt," said Fouad. "You can go back to Casablanca."

"I would rather spend a night in the desert," I said.

WE DROVE A little farther to a crested sand dune, with a clutch of thorn trees on its leeward side. It was early afternoon. The sun was extremely bright. I couldn't understand how the Tuareg went without sunglasses.

Fouad laughed at the thought. "You people need much more than us," he said.

"But sunglasses just make life more comfortable."

"Comfort...comfort is from your world," said Fouad.

He gathered some sticks, tossed them in a heap, ready for dusk. Then he joined me in the shade. I asked him how the Tuareg spent their time doing nothing. He didn't reply for a long time.

"We listen to the sounds," he said at length.

"To the silence?"

"There is never silence."

"But how can you stand having no books, no television, or Internet?"

Fouad grinned. "When life is too quiet, we talk."

"Do you tell stories?"

"Sometimes."

"Can you tell me one?"

"You like stories?"

"I'm sort of collecting them," I said.

Fouad leaned back, and the shadow of a gnarled branch fell over his face. "I can tell you the 'Tale of Hatim Tai,'" he said.

I closed my eyes, and the stage of my imagination was set.

"Long ago in Arabia," said Fouad, "there lived a wise and powerful king. His name was Hatim Tai, and he was loved by every man, woman, and child in the land. In his stables were the finest stallions, and in his tents the very softest carpets were laid. Hatim Tai's name was called from the rooftops, and tales of his generosity filled the teahouses. Everyone in the kingdom was content, well fed, and proud.

"Whenever they saw the king's cortege riding through the

streets, the people bowed down. And if anyone needed to ask a favor they could do so, and their great monarch always granted whatever they asked.

"News of Hatim Tai's generosity spread far and wide and reached the ears of a neighboring king. He was called Jaleel. One day, unable to take the stories any longer, he sent a messenger all dressed in black to the court of Hatim Tai. The messenger handed over a proclamation. It read: 'O King Hatim Tai, I am master of a far greater land than yours, with a stronger army and far richer treasure store. I will descend upon your kingdom and kill every man, woman, and child, unless you surrender immediately.'

"Hatim Tai's advisers all clustered around. 'We will go to war with the evil Jaleel,' said the grand vizier, 'for every fighting man would gladly lay down their life for you.' King Hatim Tai heard his vizier's words. Then he raised a hand. 'Listen, my courtiers,' he said. 'It is me that Jaleel has demanded. I cannot allow my people to face such terror. So I shall allow him to take my kingdom.'

"Packing a few dates and nuts in a cloth, Hatim Tai set off to seek shelter in the mountains as a dervish. The very next day, the conquering warriors swept in, with Jaleel at their head.

"The new king installed himself in the palace and offered a ransom for anyone who would bring him Hatim Tai dead or alive. 'How could you trust a king who would run away like this,' he shouted from the palace walls, 'rather than stand and fight like a man?'

"Hatim Tai wore the dress of a peasant, and lived a simple existence in the mountains, surviving on berries and wild honey. There was no one who would have ever turned him in to Jaleel's secret guard, for they loved him so.

"Months passed and still there was no sign of Hatim Tai. Then one day, Jaleel decided to hold a feast. At the festivities he doubled the ransom. He stood up and scorned the memory of Hatim Tai, declaring again that the generous king had run off rather than face battle. No sooner had he finished than a child stood up and shouted:

'Evil King Jaleel, our good King Hatim Tai disappeared to the mountains rather than spilling a drop of our blood.' Jaleel fell into his chair. Even now he was a hermit, Hatim Tai was showing compassion.

"Jaleel again doubled the ransom for the wise king, declaring that anyone who could capture him would be buried in gold. At the same time, he raised taxes and forced all the young men into his army, and many of the young women into his harem.

"Hatim Tai was gathering berries in the mountains near the cave which he had made his home, when he saw an old man and his wife, gathering sticks. The old man said to his wife: 'I wish Hatim Tai was still our king, because life under Jaleel is too hard. The tax, the price of goods in the market. It is all too much to bear.' 'If only we could find Hatim Tai,' said his wife, 'then we could end our days in luxury.'

"At that moment, Hatim Tai jumped out before them and pulled off his disguise. 'I am your king,' he said. 'Take me to Jaleel and you will be rewarded with the ransom.' The old couple fell to their knees. 'Forgive my wife, great king,' said the old man. 'She never meant to say such a terrible thing.'

"Just then, the royal guards came upon the group and arrested them all. They found themselves in front of Jaleel in chains. 'Who are these peasants?' he cried. 'Your Highness,' said the old man. 'Allow me to speak. I am a woodcutter and I was in the mountain forest with my wife. Seeing our poverty, King Hatim Tai revealed himself to us and ordered us to turn him in, in exchange for the ransom.'

"King Hatim Tai stood as tall as his chains would allow. 'It is right,' he said. 'This old couple discovered me. Please reward them with the ransom as you promised you would.'

"King Jaleel could not believe the depth of Hatim Tai's generosity. He ordered for the king to be unchained. Kneeling down before him, he gave back his throne and swore to protect him until the end of his days."

———

WHEN FOUAD HAD finished the story, he hunched his shoulders and stared at the fire's flames. It was almost dusk. The first star showed itself, glinted like an all-seeing eye above. On earth there was the call of a wild dog far away. Lying there on a blanket, cloaked in darkness, I understood how the *Arabian Nights* had come about. Campfire flames fueled my imagination, as they had done throughout history for the desert tribes.

Fouad pressed his right hand to his heart.

"I love the story of Hatim Tai very much," he said. "On some nights that I am here alone, with a small fire to keep me warm, I tell myself that story. Each time I hear it, I feel a little more at peace."

He took a pinch of the salt I had collected and sprinkled it on the ground, to keep the Jinns at bay.

"When I have heard it," he said, "I sit here and think what a good man King Hatim Tai must have been."

"Do you think the story's true?"

"Yes."

"Why?"

"Because it *is* Truth."

FOUR DAYS AFTER leaving the salt lake, I arrived back in the chaos of Casablanca.

A dense winter fog tinged with pollution had engulfed the city. The result was gridlock traffic and a great deal of bad feeling. At every crossing there was broken glass with at least one pair of enraged motorists shaking their fists. As my taxi slalomed between accidents, I felt a sense of pride. Casablanca had not changed in the few days I had been away, but *I* had. I had seen oceans of date palms, oases, and dusty Berber villages, and had slept under the Saharan stars.

At Dar Khalifa, the children huddled around and asked what I'd brought them. I fished a hand into my pocket and pulled out a thread of yellow fiber. I gave it to Ariane. She asked if it was a strand of a princess's hair.

"Of course it is," I said. "And it is also an ant's rope, and a piece of fiber from a cactus growing in the greatest desert on earth."

Timur pushed forward. "For me?" he said.

I rooted around in my pocket a second time and pulled out something smooth black with a streak of gray running down the side.

It was a pebble. "I've brought you this," I said, kissing his cheek.

"What is it, Baba?"

"It's so many things."

THAT EVENING I telephoned Dr. Mehdi. It was Saturday and I couldn't wait until the following Friday afternoon for our usual rendezvous. The doctor gave me the address of his house.

"Have you got the salt?"

"Yes!"

"Please come at once," he said.

The doctor lived in a square prewar villa on a quiet street overlooking a row of derelict factories. He led me into the salon and apologized for the clutter. The place was like a museum, filled with orderly piles of books and French magazines, with wooden boxes, papers, maps rolled up, knickknacks, mementoes, and lamps. Every inch of wall space was hung with paintings. Some were large, broad strokes of bright abstract color, others somber and small.

"You have so much art," I said.

"Where?"

"On the walls."

Dr. Mehdi pointed to a chair. "I don't see it," he said.

"How can you *not* see it?"

"Because it is a part of me."

He apologized for the mess a second time, picked up a newspaper, and let it drop on top of a dirty plate.

"My wife has gone to Fès to see her sister," he said. "And the maid has run away."

"I've brought the salt."

"Wait a moment," said Dr. Mehdi. "First tell me about your journey."

"It was wonderful. I went right down into the Sahara. I slept in the desert. It's another world."

"Who did you meet?"

"All sorts of people."

"Who?"

"There was a carpet-seller and his son in Zagora, a man called Mustapha who made good lamb stew in Ouarzazate, a healer in Tamegroute, a man and his father in a village who gave me some bread, an American called Fox from Iowa, and a Tuareg called Fouad."

Dr. Mehdi washed his hands together. "Excellent," he said.

"Look, look, I've got the salt."

"Wait a moment . . . tell me, what did you learn?"

"Um, er . . . all kinds of things."

"Such as . . . ?"

"I learned about a man called Jumar Khan and his magnificent horse, and about the generosity of Hatim Tai, and I learned about dates in the Draa Valley, and about the desert, and . . ."

"And . . . ?"

"And I learned about solitude," I said.

The doctor seemed pleased. "In a week you have seen so many things, met so many people," he said. "In the same time you may have stayed here in Casablanca and seen nothing new at all."

Dr. Mehdi stood up and walked over to a bold modernist painting of a man with three hands and a single eye offset on his forehead.

"I don't see this anymore," he said, "or any of the others, because they are always here. My mind filters them out. The only way I would see them would be if they were gone."

He led me out into the garden. It was laid with rubbery African grass, and had miniature lights hidden in the path.

"Show me the salt," he said.

I opened my satchel and brought out the plastic bag. Dr. Mehdi untied the knot and dug his fingers into the gray powder. He held it to his nose, felt the consistency, nodded.

"The salt lake," he said. "I used to camp there as a child."

"Is there enough salt for the wedding?"

The surgeon took a deep breath. "There is no wedding," he said.

"What?"

"The favor I asked you was less of a favor to me, and more of a favor to yourself."

"I don't understand."

"Think of the things you have seen, the people you have met, and the stories you have heard," he said, emptying the bag of salt onto the path. "You are a different man than you were seven days ago."

chapter eighteen

Your medicine is in you, and you do not observe it.
Your ailment is from yourself, and you do not register it.

Hazrat Ali

The door-to-door dentist arrived in the bidonville and set up a
stall in the sun. He was fine-boned and fragile and looked like
the kind of man who, in childhood, pulled the legs off spiders for
amusement. His face was blotchy red, his neck slim, and his teeth very
rotten indeed. He laid out a moss-green cloth and placed upon it an
assortment of instruments and prosthetic devices. His tools ranged
in size and shape, and were covered in varying degrees by rust.

There were giant pairs of pliers, calipers and steel-tipped picks,
lengths of bright orange rubber hose, spittoons, tourniquets, and
clamps. Beside the impressive array was a miniature mountain of
secondhand human teeth.

I found Zohra hovering about at the stall. One of her molars had
recently fallen out, the consequence of taking six sugar lumps in her
tea. A tooth was selected from a mountain and placed on her palm.

The dentist spat out a price.

"*B'saf!* Too much!" snapped Zohra.

Another figure was given.

The maid weighed the tooth in her hand. The dentist passed her a mirror and she held it in place. She blushed.

"*Safi, yalla,* all right then, let's go."

"Where's he going to fit it?"

"In my house."

I WALKED DOWN to the beach across dunes thick with marram grass and watched the waves. We live close by the ocean, but I don't go there very often, except to fly my kite. It seems too easy, as if I haven't earned such a tremendous sight. That afternoon, when I crossed the sand and strolled down to the water, I didn't do it for myself. I did it for the young man I had met, who dreamed of crossing the ocean, of going to America.

I ambled down the line where light sand met dark, and I thought about what Dr. Mehdi had said, about the power of seeing with fresh eyes. At first I had resented him for discarding the salt, something I had traveled so far to fetch. But, his wisdom had gnawed away at me.

He was quite right.

The best medicine is sometimes not medicine at all.

FOR ONCE, THERE had been tranquillity in my absence. Rachana said the guardians had been preoccupied with watching a stork which had begun to build a nest on top of the roof. They spent all their time straining against the bright winter light, to get a glimpse of the great white bird.

As soon as I went into the garden, they dragged me over to their viewpoint.

"*Allahu Akbar!* God is great!" Marwan shouted. "This is a blessing on the house, and a great thing for us all."

"A bird's nest?"

"This is no ordinary bird," Osman chipped in.

"It's a stork!" shouted the Bear.

"Can you believe it, a stork, here!" said Marwan.

"What's so good about a stork?" I asked. "There are egret nests by the dozen, and you don't ever talk about those."

The guardians gathered round and shook their heads.

"You do not know, Monsieur Tahir."

"Don't know what?"

"Our tradition."

THREE DAYS AFTER getting back from the desert, I got the feeling someone was following me. I was certain of it. The first was when I was buying a sack of oranges in Hay Hassani. I had paid the money and was taking the fruit to the car, when I saw a red baseball cap duck behind a pickup truck. I didn't think much of it at the time. But later that day I spotted the cap again, in Maarif. I was going to Café Lugano to meet Abdelmalik. This time I had turned sharply and saw it darting round a corner.

A couple of days passed. I almost forgot about the red cap. Then I went to see Sukayna at the mattress shop in Hay Hassani. She had given me some powder to sprinkle in the corners of the sitting room. She said it would help the house to heal itself. When I asked her what it was, she hadn't wanted to tell me. I pressed her.

"It's very special salt," she said.

"From the ocean?"

"No, from the Sahara."

As I was leaving the mattress shop, I saw the cap ducking out of sight again. I didn't get a look at the face, but ran after it. After a minute or two the man lost me in the backstreets of Hay Hassani's forest of white apartment blocks. I returned to Dar Khalifa with the salt, concerned that someone would want to spy on me.

Zohra was holding court in the kitchen, and was smiling broadly

again. The tooth was fitted, and looked quite good. I asked if the surgery had been painful. She winced.

"Worse than childbirth," she said.

Osman came to the kitchen to inspect Zohra's dentistry. His mouth was a dentist's casebook. He asked the maid about the pain.

"You could never stand pain like that," she said.

Osman straightened his back.

"Of course I could."

"Impossible," she replied. "You are just a man."

The guardian asked me if he could have an advance on his wages. He took the money and stormed off to find the dentist. When he was out of earshot, Zohra said, "Moroccan men are like cooking pumpkins."

"How is that?"

"Quite hard on the exterior, but all pulp on the inside."

THE GUARDIANS CLEARED all the dead twigs from the hibiscus hedge and laid them out on the roof for the stork. Then they filled a washing tub with water and hauled it up there, too. I quizzed them on what they were doing.

"Storks are very lazy," said the Bear. "They don't like building nests because it takes so much work."

"But I'm sure he can handle the task."

"It's not a he," cracked Marwan. "It's a female and she has come to lay an egg."

"How do you know?"

Marwan rubbed his eyes. "I just know these things," he said.

I asked why storks were such an omen of good fortune.

The Bear explained:

"There was once a judge who killed his wife by strangling her. He buried her body and married a young woman. As a punishment, God turned the judge into a stork."

"Where did you hear that?"

"Everyone knows it," said Marwan.

Confused, I went to the kitchen where Zohra was cuddling Timur in her arms. I asked her what she knew about storks. She had never heard the story of the judge who murdered his wife.

"Those men spend too much time talking rubbish and not enough time working," she said.

An hour later, I went back into the garden and glanced up at the roof. I did a double take. The stork had disappeared. Marwan and the Bear were weaving something with the twigs. I called up to them. They didn't answer. I called again, louder.

"We are helping the stork!" shouted Marwan.

"Why?"

"We told you, storks are very lazy!"

OSMAN DIDN'T SHOW up for two days. On the way to the market, I stopped at his home and tapped on the door. There was no reply. I banged again, heard groaning inside.

"It's me," I said. "It's Tahir."

The door was pulled back by a feeble hand. Osman peered out, squinting into the light. His face was hung, his eyes ringed with gray circles, his lips tightly shut.

"You look terrible," I said.

Osman put a hand over his mouth. "The dentist," he mumbled.

"He came?"

"Mmmm."

"Was it painful?"

A look of unimaginable fear swept over the guardian's face. His entire body seemed to quiver. He struggled to stand up straight.

"It was nothing to a man like me," he said.

AT THE MARKET I spotted the figure in the red cap again. This time he wasn't moving, but standing across from me at a butcher's stall. He had turned his back and was chatting to the butcher, who passed him a cow's hoof. I stepped up and tapped his shoulder. He turned. I froze.

It was Kamal.

I have never met someone so adept at hiding his emotions.

"Hello," he said.

I was almost too shocked to speak.

"Are you . . . are you following me?" I said after a long delay.

Kamal passed the hoof back to the butcher, and shook my hand. "Good to see you," he said.

I breathed in deep. "And you."

A few minutes later we were installed inside the window of a smoky café opposite the Central Market. Kamal tugged off the cap. His head was shaven clean bald. He could have passed for fifty. He wasn't a day over twenty-eight.

"What have you been doing with yourself?"

He unwound the cellophane from a packet of Marlboros.

"Waiting," he said.

"Waiting for what?"

"The right opportunity."

"I knew our paths would cross again," I said.

"Casablanca's very big but very small."

"Did you get a job?"

Kamal flicked his ash on the floor.

"A whole life change," he said.

"Really?"

"Sure."

"What?"

"I'm leaving Morocco."

"Oh?"

"Yup."

"Where are you going?"

"Down south."

"To the Sahara?"

"To Australia."

"What are you gonna do there?"

Kamal flicked his ash again, bit his lower lip. "Start a family," he said.

A month after our last breakfast at Café Napoleon, Kamal had met an Australian backpacker at a hostel near the port. He didn't say it, but he had been fishing for a foreigner, a passport to a new life. She was a medical student, the daughter of a property tycoon, and had been touring around the country alone.

"She loves me," he said.

"And do you love her?"

Kamal didn't answer right away. He paused as if to add a touch of doubt. "Sure I do," he said.

I pressed a couple of coins onto the table, and we shook hands. As we shook, we looked at each other's eyes. I don't know about him, but I was remembering the madcap adventures we had shared. We left the café. Kamal put on his red baseball cap, straightened it, and stared at his watch. He crossed the street.

I have not seen him since.

OSMAN RETURNED TO work and showed off his new smile. The other two guardians were envious, but too busy fretting about the stork to make a point of it. The bird had flown away toward the ocean and disappeared, despite the fact a ready-made nest was awaiting it on our roof. Marwan said he and the others knew a great deal about storks merely by being Moroccan, that the birds were a national obsession.

Somewhere in my library I knew I had a book about African birds. I went in search of it. When finally I found it, I flicked to the page on Moroccan storks and read a passage to the guardians. They weren't impressed.

"That's how you are," said Osman scathingly.

"What do you mean?"

"In the West it's always like that."

"Like what?"

"You read something in a book, some writing, and you think you are an expert."

"I'm not an expert," I said.

"Osman's right," said the Bear. "Our knowledge isn't the kind of thing you can find in a book. It's given to us through generations of . . ."

"Of conversation," said Marwan.

I went inside and slipped the book back in its place. The guardians hardly knew it, but they had touched upon one of the greatest differences between East and West. In the Occident learning tends to be done through reading. In the Orient, the chain of transmission is made through generations of accumulated conversation.

THAT NIGHT I took Ariane and Timur up for their bath. As they splashed about, I told them to never take water for granted. I described the desert, what it was like to sleep under the stars, and how it felt to have the first rays of morning sunlight on your face.

"Baba, why do we live in Morocco?" Ariane suddenly asked.

"To be a part of something very real and very ancient," I said.

After their bath, I dried them and got them ready for bed.

Ariane put her hand on mine. "I know you are worried," she said.

"About what?"

"About finding your story."

I kissed her head.

She pulled on my shirt until my face was level with hers.

"I already know what story is in my heart," she said. "The one about the lion and the water."

Before turning out the light, I read them the story of "The Lion Who Saw Himself in the Water," a teaching tale that my father had told me, and fathers have been telling children at bedtime for a thousand years or more:

"Once upon a time long ago there was a lion called Sher. He lived deep in the jungle and was the proudest lion who had ever lived. He had a great mane of hair, long, long teeth, and claws that were as sharp as razors. All day he would prowl up and down scaring the other animals, until they told him that he was the bravest creature in the kingdom.

"One day it was very hot and all the animals went down to the water hole to drink. They drank and they drank, and they drank and they drank, until they could drink no more. Sher the lion had been preening himself, but at last felt that his tongue was very dry. He strode down to the edge of the water hole and opened his mouth to drink. But just before his tongue touched the water, he saw a terrifying male lion looking back at him, its mouth open wide in a growl. Sher the lion jumped back in fear and ran into the jungle to hide. The other animals wondered what was the matter.

"One day passed, and then another, and the summer heat grew worse. Sher the lion became thirstier and thirstier, until he could stand it no more. He walked down to the water hole once again, and opened his mouth wide to drink. The lion was there as before, glaring at him angrily, roaring. But this time he was too thirsty to care. He drank and he drank and he drank until he could drink no more."

The moral of the story of course is not to be afraid of what you cannot understand. By the time I had finished reading, Ariane and Timur were sound asleep.

They always fell asleep before the end.

———————

AT DAWN THE next day, the stork returned. The guardians regarded it as a miracle, and forced me out of bed to come and see. The bird was sitting awkwardly on the nest, rearranging itself, trying to get comfortable.

"She's happy," said Osman under his breath. "She'll stay here now."

"I wonder why she's chosen our roof," I said.

Marwan cleared his throat. "Dar Khalifa has *baraka*," he said.

Explaining the idea of *baraka* is not easy. It's a notion found in Islam, but must surely be pre-Islamic: the idea that a person, creature, or thing is blessed. The blessing runs so deeply that it touches every cell, every atom, so that any association with that thing extends the blessing on to you.

When we bought the Caliph's House, the guardians believed it was inhabited by Jinns. Their fear had been so great that they almost never entered the actual house. The idea of living there before the spirits had been expelled was almost too much for them to bear. Not so much because of what the Jinns would have done to us, but what revenge they might have exacted upon them.

But now that Dar Khalifa had been exorcised, the guardians—and the people living in the shantytown—regarded it as a place with *baraka*. The Bear hinted that the house may have always been blessed, a possible explanation why the Jinns had chosen it in the first place. When the renovations were over, I would take pride if a visitor praised the work we had done. Renovations were like frosting on a cake, fodder for the eyes. *Baraka* was something far deeper, something connected to the soul.

ALL THE TALK of the stork and *baraka* got me thinking about Sukayna. There had been no chalk graffiti in a while, but I wanted to use the lull to investigate the matter of the holy man she had mentioned. I sent a message to the astrologer and the next day there was a ring on the bell.

When I went to the front door, I found a line of people already there. It consisted of the three guardians, the two maids, the gardener, and a blacksmith who was making some furniture for us at the end of the garden. They had formed a reception committee. Sukayna shook the men's hands and kissed the women's cheeks. Amid much whispering, she stepped inside.

First, I showed her the so-called heart of the house, the courtyard where the exorcists had sacrificed the goat. Sukayna lit a candle, placed it on the floor. She moved very slowly, touching her fingers over the plaster, absorbing the energy. I led her through into the main courtyard, with a large room at either end. It was the original section of the Caliph's House, that would once have stood alone, far from the city of Casablanca.

Sukayna removed her slippers and walked barefoot. In her clinic at the back of the mattress shop, she had struck me as a calm person. But she seemed all the calmer the moment she entered the courtyard garden. We had installed an elaborate mosaic fountain on the far wall, which backed onto the shantytown. The sight of the fountain with its dazzling colors, the sound of water flowing into the pool, and the coolness of the liquid touching the skin stirred the senses.

The astrologer stepped over, dipped her hand in the water, closed her eyes, and said, "I am overwhelmed."

"What do you feel?"

"The energy, the *baraka*."

"How did the energy get here?"

"The saint," she said. "I can feel him."

"Where?"

"In this garden, in the walls."

We ambled down the narrow path to the far end, to the room where the Jinn was believed to have resided. As she entered the room, which is now used for guests, Sukayna's eyes widened. She touched the walls, opened her mouth a crack, swallowed.

"What do you feel in here?"

"Good and evil met in this room," she said.

"The exorcists battled the Jinns in here for hours. They spilled blood, and they sucked the Jinns from the walls."

"I know," said Sukayna. "I can feel it."

"Have the Jinns gone?"

She nodded. "There are no bad spirits now."

I pointed out where the stairs went down, the great mystery of the house. They ended nowhere, at a blank wall.

"Why are there stairs?"

Sukayna stepped down, running her hand along the wall. She was concentrating very hard, her back muscles tight with anticipation. On the last stair she lit another candle, held her palms upward in prayer, and, after several minutes, she touched the three walls with both hands.

"Where do the steps lead?"

"I will tell you," Sukayna replied.

She climbed the stairs, and we sat in the garden courtyard, the sound of water flowing behind. Sukayna wiped her eyes, smiled.

"There was a holy man," she said. "He was traveling along the coast, to a shrine in the north. As he neared Casablanca, a winter storm hit. Waves as high as mountains, rain so heavy that it could knock you down. The sage was drenched, freezing cold. He was by himself with a donkey."

"What did he do?"

"He looked for shelter. There were no houses, just the bare shore, sand, and waves. He staggered inland a little way and, through the pouring rain he saw a house, this house. He called out, and the owner, the Caliph, welcomed him, gave him dry clothes, food, warmth. He stayed here for several weeks."

"When did this happen?"

"A long time ago, a hundred years or more. Before he left, he touched the house with his hand. It wasn't the same as you or I touching something. It was far more powerful. His touch transferred energy, baraka. You can feel it, it's still here."

"What about the stairs, though? Where do they lead?"

Sukayna stood up, and led me back to the room. "Do you see how high the ceiling is here?"

"Yes, it must be twenty feet."

"Is there such a high ceiling anywhere else in the house?"

"No."

"These steps do not go down to anywhere," said Sukayna.

"Then why are they there?"

"They are a symbol," she said.

"Of what?"

"Of our condition."

"What?"

"Down there is what is below and, up there, is what is above."

"But the ceiling is much farther than the bottom of the stairs."

"Heaven is much further than the fire of Hell," said Sukayna.

"What about here in the middle, where we're standing?"

"This is the realm of men."

THE NEXT EVENING, I went out to the front of the house because I heard someone ringing the bell. I saw a boy running away fast down the lane. Marwan was there yelling for the prankster to leave us alone. I wished him a good evening. Just as I was turning to go back into the house, he lowered his head.

"Monsieur Tahir, do you have a moment?"

"Yes, of course."

"I want to show you something."

"Yes, Marwan, what?"

The old carpenter stuck a hand in his pocket and rummaged around. He pulled out a long nail with a kink in the middle.

"A nail?"

"Yes, a simple nail."

"It looks a bit bent," I said.

"It is."

"Ah…"

The carpenter passed me the nail.

"When I was a young carpenter, this nail was new and shiny," he said. "I took it from a bag of nails at my master's workshop, and I hammered it into a big piece of wood. I was inexperienced and foolish. The nail bent over as I struck it with the hammer. I pulled it out of the wood with pliers. As I did so, my master, a great carpenter named Moualem Abdul Majid, came over. I tried to hide the nail, but he saw me. He picked it up.

"'This nail is you, Marwan,' he said. 'It's shiny and good-looking, but it's got a fault running down the middle. We could straighten it out and give it another chance, put it to some good. Over time it would prove its worth, but there would always be the twist in the middle, a reminder of a time when action came before thought.'

"The great master struck the back of my head with his hand. 'Put that nail in your pocket,' he said, 'and carry it with you always, as a way of remembering this lesson. Whenever you find yourself too full of pride, put your hand in your pocket and have a good feel at the bend in the middle of the nail.'"

"Marwan, how long have you carried the nail around with you?"

The old carpenter blinked. "Since 1966," he said.

FATIMA NEVER SPOKE about her life. I took it as a form of modesty, blended with a cultural reticence of voicing personal matters to a man from outside the family. One morning a girl of about ten arrived at the door. She asked for her sister. "Who is your sister?" "Her name is Fatima."

The young maid ran out of the kitchen and a conversation in whispers followed. The sisters hugged, then wept, and slipped into Fatima's room. The little sister remained in there for a week. We tried to coax her to come out and enjoy the space, but she refused, as if the outside world drowned her in fear.

At last, after seven days and nights in Fatima's room, the girl emerged. It was the first time I got a good look at her. She had small wood-green eyes, jet-black hair running down her back, and a long, slender neck leading to a delicate frame. On her left cheek there was a gash about three inches in length, and on her arm a terrible bruise. We asked what had happened. Fatima didn't want to say. I sensed that talking would be betraying family honor. But that night, after her little sister had gone home, Fatima told her story to Rachana.

One night about five years before, her father came home and announced that he was taking a second wife. He had chosen his bride, a girl of about eighteen, and set the wedding for the following month. Once the festivities had taken place, the younger bride moved into the minuscule family apartment. It was then that the fragile status quo began to be rocked. The new bride lavished the little they had in terms of communal funds on beauty parlors for herself. Rather than reining her in, the father brokered a marriage for Fatima to a business contact. The wedding took place, two days after Fatima had met her groom for the first time. She settled down for married life. But then, three weeks after the wedding, her father fell out with her husband, and ordered her to come home. Fatima was still legally married, but was forbidden to ever contact her husband.

"Surely you could contact him?" Rachana had asked.

"My father will beat me, just as he beat my little sister," she replied.

"Then you should go to the police."

Fatima's eyes widened at the thought. "In Morocco, a family is closed. An outsider can never see in," she said. "It is like a house without doors or windows."

EARLY THE FOLLOWING week, I received a telephone call out of the blue. An Italian voice was on the other end. It was Señor Benito from Tangier, the man who had sold me his edition of Burton's *Arabian Nights*.

"I am journeying to Casablanca," he said.

"Please stay with us."

"You are very kind."

"Are you coming for work?"

"No, no, just to visit an old friend."

The next day, a pair of well-loved Louis Vuitton cases were lugged into the house by Marwan. Señor Benito followed them, coutured as before in an immaculate off-white linen suit, a silk handkerchief flowing from his top pocket. Over the suit he wore on his shoulders a navy cashmere coat. He held my fingertips, thanked us in advance for our hospitality, and sat on the corner of the sofa.

Zohra brought in a tea tray, stepped forward, and shook Señor Benito's hand firmly. He raised an eyebrow.

When she had gone, he produced a box of chocolates from his bag. "For your children," he said.

Ariane and Timur, who had been watching from the security of their playroom, were lured forward by the confectionery. Ariane had a statue made from Lego in her hands. It was odd-shaped and multicolored. Señor Benito presented the chocolates and asked Ariane what she had made.

"It's a dinosaur," she said, "and it's a princess as well."

"If only adults had the imagination of children," said Benito. "Our world would be very different. We would be capable of much, much more."

Ariane dropped her dinosaur and the Lego smashed into many pieces.

"What is it now?" asked Señor Benito.

"It's the sky filled with stars," she said.

The Italian blew his nose on his fuchsia handkerchief. "In Europe we are a little embarrassed by a child's imagination," he said. "We see it as something at fault, something to be corrected, like eyes which need reading glasses to see. And we forget that it's inside us for a reason."

"But we've built our world to suit adulthood," I said.

"Well, if we could go back," said Benito.

"Back where?"

"To the time before, when we thought like children..." He glanced down at Timur, who was making a pattern out of chocolates on the floor. "Imagine what possibilities there would be."

I poured more tea.

"The imagination of children," he said. "It's a kind of programming, an original setting for humanity. It's inside us all, asleep."

chapter nineteen

If a gem falls into the mud it is still valuable.
If dust ascends to heaven, it remains valueless.

Saadi of Shiraz

The first night that Señor Benito stayed, the sound of dogs fighting in the bidonville kept us from sleep. Their frenzied chorus only set off the donkeys, who feared an invisible terror in the dark. The din was so tremendous that I got out of bed and went down into the garden. I found Osman there on a ladder, propped up on the wall. He was shouting ferociously into the blackness.

"Osman! What's the matter?"

"The noise!" he hissed. "It's not good."

"I know, it's keeping us awake," I said.

"No matter of you, Monsieur Tahir, but the stork...we fear for the stork."

The following morning, Zohra said dogs barking in the night meant they had seen death, and donkeys braying was a sign that the devil was there.

"Tsk! Tsk! Tsk! Tell me you did not hear dogs," she said.

"But I told you, I did, and I'm sure you did, too."

"What I hear with my ears is different," she said.

"Why?"

"Because I can pretend it was a dream."

Down at the stables, the guardians were calm. The stork had been insufficiently frightened, or insufficiently motivated, to fly away in the night.

"*Alhamdullillah*," said the Bear. "Thanks be to God."

"The stork is already giving us good fortune," said Marwan, who was not normally as superstitious as the others.

"What proof is there?"

Osman held up a seed tray peppered in young green shoots.

"Because our seeds are flourishing," he said.

"They've come up because of the rain," I replied.

"No, no, Monsieur Tahir, that is not right," said the Bear.

"Of course it is."

The guardians fell into line and shook their heads.

"One day you will learn to see as we do," said Osman.

SEÑOR BENITO CAME down from his room just before eleven. He said he hadn't heard any sounds in the night.

"I sleep with a metronome beside the bed," he said distantly.

"Whatever for?"

"It drowns out all noise," he said.

"Doesn't it keep you awake?"

"On the contrary," he replied. "I have done it since childhood, and I would be unable to sleep without it."

He asked if I would care to join him in the town.

"Where are you going?"

"To see my old friend."

"Where does he live?"

"It's not a person, but a place," he said.

We drove down the Corniche, past the palace of the Saudi royal family, past the lighthouse and the Catholic cemetery, the great mosque and the port, and turned right into the shadow world of real

Casablanca. The buildings may be dilapidated beyond belief, but they have a somber sophistication that's impossible to match.

Benito suggested I park on Boulevard Mohammed V, the main drag, built almost a century ago by the French. Back then it was a showcase of Franco-colonial might, and is still lined with some of the very finest Art Deco buildings ever constructed. We strolled past the Central Market, down walkways once fitted out with the most opulent imports from Paris, and arrived at a small restaurant. It was tatty on the outside, not the kind of place one would ever look at twice. A sign on the outside advertised its name.

Benito straightened his already straight back. "Let me introduce my old and very dear friend, Le Petit Poucet," he said.

We stepped inside. The ceiling was low, paneled with painted glass, the windows hung with lace curtains, a time warp of 1970s decor, when the place must last have been refurbished. The chairs and tables were solid and plentiful, the clientele nonexistent. A manager was combing a single strand of hair across a curved expanse of baldness at the back of the salon. As soon as he saw us, he stowed the comb in his top pocket and made a beeline for the door. He kissed Benito on the cheeks, shook my hand, and gestured to the dining room.

"Your usual table, Monsieur?" he said grandly.

We were led past a low trolley on which an assortment of tired salad leaves had been artistically arranged, and found ourselves at a corner table, over which was hung a pen and ink sketch. The manager pressed fingertips to the ends of his mustache and cooed like a turtledove.

"To see your face again gives me such joy," he said, "like the taste of water on a parched man's lips."

The Italian thanked him, ran a thumbnail down the list of white wine, and whispered: "The Muscadet, please, Saad."

"An excellent choice, Monsieur Benito."

An instant later, the bottle was in a cooler on a stand. The cork was removed and the tasting glass poured with much ceremony. Benito swilled the wine around the glass, then around his mouth. He nodded. The manager filled the glasses. They clouded with condensation. Benito lifted the stem in the thumb and forefinger of his right hand, his malachite eyes staring into mine.

"A toast," he said. "To the little pleasures in life."

We clinked glasses.

"I thought this place shut down decades ago," I said.

"You know it?"

"Only by reputation. A grocer once described a very fine meal he had taken here. It's strange, because he suggested it was closed."

Benito ran the tip of his finger through the condensation on the side of his glass. "Perhaps the man had the power to see into the future," he said. "I think I am the only customer now, and I only drop in once or twice a year."

"How long have you been coming here?"

Señor Benito stared into his Muscadet. "Since the glory days of Casablanca," he said. "The days when that street out there was brilliant white and was the center of the French empire." He took a swig of his wine, washed it around his mouth. "Back then this room was packed with the European elite."

"I heard Edith Piaf lived in Casa at one time," I said. "Do you think she ever came here?"

"Edith, of course, she used to come in with her boyfriend, the boxer Marcel Cerdan. She liked that table over there." He pointed to the back of the restaurant. "She was one of many. Albert Camus was a regular, too, and Saint-Exupery."

"The one who wrote *The Little Prince*?"

"Yes, *Le Petit Prince*." He motioned to the wall behind my head. "That's a page from his notebook," he said. "It's just a photocopy now, of course. The management sold the original to pay for a hole in the roof."

"It's all changed now," I said.

"Oh, how sad!" exclaimed Benito. "It makes me weep."

"When did the glory days end?"

"With the episode of the penis."

"Penis?"

"In the fifties there was a great deal of unrest, not only here in Casa, but across Morocco. The French knew their time was running out, and they didn't like the thought of waving good-bye to all this."

"What was the episode...?"

"Which?"

"With the penis?"

"Oh, yes, that," said Benito. "It was terrible." He covered his eyes with a hand and sniggered. "There were riots, and the bodies were stacking up. We were all shocked because the glory days were under threat. Then one night some students were eating down here somewhere at a cheap restaurant, a hole in the wall. They ordered the goulash, I think it was. It was cheap and cheerful and rather ghoulish! They'd all chewed their way through the meal. As he was finishing, one of the boys realized that the meat on his spoon was actually a human penis."

"Oh my God."

"I know, it was grotesque. The police raided the kitchens."

"What did they find?"

"Pots full of human flesh."

SEÑOR BENITO TOOK the afternoon train back up to Tangier, and I went downtown to buy a bottle of Indian ink. I had found an old-fashioned stationer's across from the cobbler's shop that stocked the brand I have used for twenty years. Fortunately, the rather strict pied-noir who ran the stationer's appreciated the importance of fine writing ink. He said that filling a fountain pen with low-grade ink was like cheap wine—an abomination that ought to be punishable by death.

As I came out with my bottle of ink, I saw Noureddine standing outside his shop, the navy blue hat pulled down to his eyebrows. My eyes moved from his face, up to the tree, and into its naked branches. The small brown bird was gone. I crossed, engaged in lengthy greetings, and asked about the bird.

The cobbler looked to the sky. "It flew away," he said sorrowfully.

"When?"

"A week ago."

I expressed condolence.

"Who am I to say why good and evil happens?" he said.

I told him about the stork. His eyes lit up, he tugged off his hat.

"You are a blessed man, Monsieur Tahir!"

Just then I remembered his promise, to tell me his favorite tale from the *Arabian Nights*. I reminded him.

"*Alf Layla wa Layla*," he said, the façade of melancholy fading a little.

"Do you have a moment to tell me the story?"

Noureddine pushed open the shop door and steered me inside.

"My friend in the tree has flown away," he said, "but your visit is like a hundred little birds singing to me!"

He went into the room behind, ferreted out a grubby old chair, patched with scraps of rubber soles, and invited me to sit.

"'Maruf the Cobbler,'" he said. "To hear it will wash away your troubles, and ease your mind. You will leave my shop calm like a summer day. And to tell it, ten times the joy will be showered on me."

The ancient cobbler asked me if I was comfortable. I said that I was. He crawled under the counter and locked the door twice. I closed my eyes and the story began:

"Once upon a time there lived in Cairo a cobbler called Maruf. He was a good man, God-fearing and honest, and he was married to a crone, a woman named Fatima. She treated him very badly, and offered him no respect. From morning until night she complained, scolding him for being a lowly repairer of shoes.

"Unable to take any more of her unpleasant behavior, he fled from his home one morning and ran into the hills. Once there, he fell into a fit of sadness, begging the higher forces to save him from the horrifying woman who was his wife. After ranting for some time, he fell down on the ground overcome with fatigue.

"Suddenly, he found that a great creature was bearing over him. It was what we call a Changed One."

"A Jinn?"

"Yes, a Jinn," said the cobbler. "Seeing Maruf weeping, he cried out: 'I am the guardian of this place, and my name is Abdul Makan. I am ready to fulfill your command.' Hearing the creature's homage, Maruf stood to his feet. He explained his situation, and described his unhinged wife. The apparition ordered him to climb upon his back. He did so, and they flew up into the sky.

"After many hours of flight, they descended at a magnificent city. Maruf had no idea of where they had put down. He had not been away from Cairo before. As soon as their feet touched the ground, the Jinn vanished. Maruf realized that he was very far from home, as all the people there looked Chinese.

"The cobbler's appearance was very different from the inhabitants of the town. Soon, a crowd gathered. They threw stones at Maruf and jeered. He lay on the ground, weeping. But just then a wealthy-looking man approached. He scolded the crowd for not treating a stranger with respect, introduced himself as Ali the son of Ali, and said he would do all he could to help the impoverished Maruf.

" 'This town is called Ikhtiyar,' he said. 'If you are rich here, people treat you with respect, and if you are poor, everyone will shun you. To go from poverty to wealth is almost impossible, although I myself arrived here a pauper and I have managed to turn rags to riches. I borrowed a little money from the merchants in the bazaar, invested it, and paid it back as soon as I could. And I can help you to do the same as I have done,' he said.

"Maruf thanked God for sending Ali his way. Before he knew it, his new friend had dressed him in the finery of a prince. So well attired it was easy for him to borrow money from the merchants in the bazaar. When they asked why he was so well dressed but so short of funds, he simply replied that his caravan laden with riches was delayed en route to Ikhtiyar.

"The difference between Ali and the cobbler was that Maruf had no understanding of trade. Worse still, the newcomer had an insatiable streak of generosity. As soon as he had money in his pocket, he handed it out to all the beggars who approached him. As the months passed, he borrowed more and more money. And the more he borrowed, the more he distributed to the poor and the needy. The moneylenders were calmed by the prospect of the treasure caravan, and were impressed by the stranger's charity. As they saw it, a man who could squander a sack of gold on beggars must be worth many thousand times more.

"As time slipped by, the merchants in the bazaar began to wonder if they had been tricked by Maruf. A group of them went to the king and explained the situation. Greedy at the thought of gaining the treasure caravan for himself, the king summoned Maruf to his court. The monarch's vizier designed a test. The stranger would be presented with a large emerald, unequaled in size and quality. If he realized its true value, he would be rewarded. If not, he would be beheaded.

"Maruf arrived at the palace, where he was received by the king, and offered the enormous gem. But instead of accepting the stone, he waved it aside. 'Keep it for yourself,' he said, 'for I have far larger jewels in my caravan.' 'Dear stranger, where exactly is your caravan laden with riches?' asked the king. Maruf the cobbler touched a hand to his great silk turban and said: 'It will be here any day now, Your Majesty.'

"Unable to contain his greed, the king of Ikhtiyar decided to marry his loveliest daughter, Princess Dounia, to the fabulously rich stranger, despite the grand vizier's disapproval. But when Maruf received the invitation to marry the royal princess, he said: 'How could I sustain such a treasure as your daughter until my own treasure caravan arrives?' The king, who was now beside himself with avarice, opened the royal treasury and demanded that Maruf take what he needed for the wedding.

"Celebrations on a scale never seen continued for forty days and forty nights. The poor were rewarded with charity beyond their wildest dreams, and the rich were buried in gold, all at Maruf's insistence. Watching the royal treasure vaults being emptied, the grand vizier pleaded with the king to test Maruf one last time.

"A plan was devised, involving Princess Dounia, the cobbler's new wife. As they lay together in their palace suite, she asked Maruf about his caravan. Not wanting to lie to his beautiful new bride, he told her the truth. 'There is no caravan of treasure,' he said. The princess, who had fallen in love with Maruf's generous spirit, said: 'Dear husband, take this sack of gold and flee. Send word to me of your whereabouts and I shall come to be with you as soon as I can.'

"Dressed as a simple cobbler again, Maruf crept out of the city at dawn. A little later, the king sent for his son-in-law. Princess Dounia went into the throne room. 'Father,' she said, 'Maruf received a group of royal outriders in the night. They were dressed in the finest livery.' 'What did they want, my dear?' 'They came to tell my husband that his caravan had been attacked. Fifty of his soldiers had been killed and two hundred camel-loads had been stolen.' 'What a tragedy,' said the king. 'On the contrary,' replied Princess Dounia. 'Maruf hardly seemed to care. As he left to escort the rest of the caravan into the kingdom, he declared that two hundred camels was but a small fraction of the whole.'

"Maruf himself rode day and night away from Ikhtiyar. He eventually came to a farmstead, where a peasant was tilling the land. Seeing the stranger, the peasant greeted Maruf and asked him to wait while he fetched refreshments. As a gesture of thanks, the cobbler took the tiller and continued with the plowing until the farmer returned.

"He went up and down with the oxen. Then, suddenly, the plow hit a stone. Fearing its blade had been broken, Maruf looked down and saw a slab of stone with an iron ring in the center. He pulled the ring and the stone came away, leading to stairs. He crept down cautiously and found a huge chamber filled from the floor to the ceiling with treasure."

At that moment, a fist knocked at the door. Noureddine glanced up, cursed, and apologized once and then again.

"It is the landlord of this building," he said gloomily. "I shall have to sit with him a while."

I excused myself and said I would return later in the day. The cobbler unlocked the door. He shook my hand and looked me in the eye.

"Do you promise?" he said.

"Promise?"

"Promise that you will come back."

SOMETIMES WE ONLY understand a thing when it is no longer there. Through my childhood and until his death, a week into my thirties, I heard my father speaking thousands of times. On some occasions he was addressing a crowd, on others a small group, or just me. He wasn't the kind of person who took part in idle chatter. His conversations usually had a point, a central idea, which he revealed as he went along. When he spoke, I felt it wise to listen well, although much of the time I couldn't grasp the full depth of his address.

In the years since his death, I have found snippets of the conversations bubbling up in my mind. I can hear him, stressing certain words or phrases, giving caution for a time that he envisaged would one day arrive. My great fear then was that I didn't remember conversations as they came and went. But now I understand that the snippets which stuck form a structure of their own. Just as with the teaching stories he passed on, the shreds of advice and the observations have a framework and a cause.

Of all the fragments of conversation, the ones most vivid are those that offered guidance. My father was a believer that every person had an in-built ability to achieve in the most astonishing way, but that most people never realized their ambition because certain circumstances held them back. He considered it an imperative to get the correct set of circumstances in a life if one was ever going to realize one's full potential. Teaching stories were for him a way of preparing the individual for the process of learning, the path to achievement.

"People think I am a writer," he would say, "and when they think that they are missing the point. I write things down but the writing is just a tool. It's nothing more than ink arranged over a surface of wood pulp. If they had real insight, they would see that I am really a basket weaver. I have always told you that, Tahir Jan. I take reeds from the river that have been nurtured by fresh water and grown in good soil, and I turn them into baskets, a product that has so many uses. I know how to make baskets from something so simple because my father taught me, and his father taught him.

"Make baskets of your own," he would say, "make them all kinds of shapes and colors. But never forget that your baskets are made of something that is there for anyone to cut and use. And never imagine that you created the reeds yourself. You are only the person who shapes them into something that can be of use to others."

At six in the afternoon, I returned to the cobbler's shop.

The old man was stitching a workman's boot, gritting his teeth as he forced the needle through the layers of Taiwanese rubber. As soon as he saw me come in, he tossed the boot aside, slapped his hands together, and bolted the door.

"Praise be to God for your virtuous return!" he cried.

The chair was dished out from the back room once again and, a moment later, the cobbler had conjured us back into the tale.

"As I have told you," he said, "Maruf found himself in a dark and wonderful cavern, abundant with precious gems and gold. He could not believe his eyes, so great was the wealth. He ran his fingers through rubies and sapphires overflowing from iron coffers, and became almost hypnotized by the sheer amount of gold. But there was one item that caught his attention by its dazzling brilliance: a rock crystal box, no bigger than this." Noureddine motioned something round with his hands, the size of a pencil box.

"Maruf picked it up, unfastened the golden catch, and found inside a gold ring. He slipped it onto his finger and was knocked backward by a tremendous noise, and blinded by a flash of lightning.

"Before him towered a colossal dark-faced Jinn, with a golden earring in his ear, and a scimitar in his fist. 'I am your servant, O Master!' roared the creature.

"Craning his neck back, Maruf shielded his face with his hand. The Jinn explained that the treasure which lay beneath the furrowed field had once belonged to a king called Shaddad. He had served him until his kingdom had fallen.

"Maruf ordered the spirit to transport the treasure up to the surface. It was done in the blink of an eye. The Jinn then materialized a multitude of camels and fine stallions from a legion of spirits. A moment later the treasure was loaded onto the caravan.

"The peasant arrived back at the field in time to be showered in jewels. He assumed that the visitor was a prosperous merchant who had until then been in disguise. Maruf commanded the Jinn to transport the treasure caravan to Ikhtiyar. It took an entire day and a night for the train to enter the royal city, such was its enormous length.

"As soon as the king spied the caravan from his royal balcony, snaking its way forward, he danced with jubilation. His daughter, the

Princess Dounia, although confused, assumed that her husband had lied in order to test her loyalty.

"Once the caravan had arrived, Maruf himself appeared. He repaid the merchants in the bazaar with precious gems, and distributed sacks of gold to the beggars who lined the streets. But the grand vizier, who had secretly wanted to marry his own son to Princess Dounia, tricked the cobbler into admitting the truth. As soon as the king's adviser understood the power of the ring on Maruf's finger, he stole it and summoned the Jinn himself. The creature appeared in a flash of light, and was ordered to transport Maruf to the farthest corner of the world.

"But Providence shined upon the cobbler," said Noureddine, gazing out at the street. "For realizing what had taken place, Princess Dounia stole the ring from the vizier and summoned the Jinn again. She commanded the spirit to return her husband, and to bind the grand vizier in chains.

"In less time than it takes to tell, Maruf was transported back across the world and into his apartment in the palace. With time, Princess Dounia bore a son. And, with her father's death, Maruf succeeded him as king."

The ancient cobbler tugged off his dark blue hat and scratched his nails across his head. I thanked him for the tale. He held an index finger in the air.

"But the story has not ended," he said.

"There's more?"

"Of course," said Noureddine. "It's an epic from *Alf Layla wa Layla.*"

"But I have to go and pick up the children from their friend's house," I said, shifting in my seat.

"Rushing a good tale is a terrible crime," replied Noureddine gravely.

"Then I shall return tomorrow," I said.

We shook hands, and the door was ceremoniously unlocked.

"There is one crime worse than rushing a story," the cobbler said as I was leaving.

"What?"

"Not finishing a story once it's begun."

chapter twenty

Do not look at my outward shape,
But take what is in my hand.

Jalaluddin Rumi

The next morning, I was standing outside the cobbler's shop by eight o'clock. The traffic was like a seething juggernaut, choking anyone stupid enough to be standing on the road. I waited for twenty minutes but the cobbler didn't show. I was about to turn round and go home, when his apprentice appeared.

"Where's the cobbler?"

"He was taken ill in the night," he said.

"Is he at home?"

"No, Monsieur, he's been rushed to the hospital."

The boy wrote the name of a public hospital on the back of a shoe receipt, handed it to me. An hour later, I was going up and down the hospital corridors, the smell of bleach heavy in the air. There were so many patients that they had spilled out into the corridors, many lying on makeshift beds. I wasn't sure why I was there. The story could have waited. But something inside prompted me to go.

At the end of the last corridor on the right, I came to a ward edged on both sides by beds. I don't know how, but somehow I knew Noureddine was in there. I could feel him, pulling me in. His bed was near the window. He was asleep, the blue woollen hat on the nightstand beside a jug of water and a strip of pills. I crept closer, until I was standing over him. His face was calm, the deep furrows on his brow smoothed a little by sleep. He must have heard me approaching. His eyes flicked open. He strained to focus, paused, smiled.

"My dear friend," he said.

I held his hand, and whispered a greeting. He looked very tired, as if he might not live.

"Sit down," he said.

"Where?"

"Here, on the edge of the bed. I must hurry," he said faintly.

"With what?"

"With the story. Quickly, moisten my lips."

I poured a glass of water and held it to his mouth.

The old cobbler pushed himself up higher on the bed. "*Bismillah rahman ar rahim,*" he said softly. "In the name of God, the Compassionate, the Merciful...

"Are you ready?"

"Yes, yes."

Noureddine wove his fingers together on his chest, and began. "Where was I?"

"Maruf had become king."

Noureddine peered into the middle of the room.

"Ah, yes, I see it," he said. "Maruf and Dounia were happier than they could have imagined. They had luxury, a fine healthy son, and a people who loved them very much. But good fortune can be turned upside down in the blink of an eye. And it was. Queen Dounia became gravely ill. She knew she would not survive. On the last day of her life, she whispered to her husband, who nursed her day and night, 'Dear Maruf, when I am gone, look after our son with great care, and make certain you guard this well.' So saying, she passed him the magic ring, and took her last breath.

"After the funeral, which the entire kingdom attended, a long period of mourning began. Maruf felt very alone, although he had the little boy to keep him company. He called for the peasant on whose land he had found the treasure cave, and appointed him grand vizier.

"Days turned into months. Maruf did his best to raise the child and rule over the kingdom, but the loss of Dounia had struck a heavy blow. One night, he retired to his chamber and fell into a deep sleep on his bed. But he woke up with a start, as a strange smell wafted into his dreams. A woman was lying beside him. 'Dear Maruf,' she said, 'do you not remember me, your wife from Cairo? It is I, Fatima.'

"Almost dumb at seeing the hag, Maruf leapt out of bed. 'How did you get here?' he cried. The crone explained how she had resorted to begging when Maruf had deserted her. She had existed on charity and, the more she did so, the more she realized how good life had been when she was married. Years had passed. Then, the night before, she had repented, shouting out loud how foolish she had been to constantly nag her beloved husband. Suddenly, a gigantic creature, a Jinn, had appeared from nowhere. Taking pity, the spirit had transported her to the kingdom of Ikhtiyar, where she found herself lying in the king's bed.

"Maruf then explained how he had been transported to the very same kingdom, how he had been married to the royal princess, been forced to flee for his life, found the treasure and the magic ring, been sent to the wilderness at the edge of the world, been made king, and how his wife had borne him a beloved son before taking her last breath.

" 'I shall return you to our own land,' Maruf said to his wife, 'and shall ask my Jinn to construct a magnificent palace for you and adorn it in precious silks.' 'Oh, husband,' said the crone, 'my dream is to stay with you, here at your side.' Feeling pity for the woman,

Maruf agreed to allow her to stay. He had the Jinn build her a separate palace not far from his, where she lived in opulence beyond her wildest dreams. And, while her husband attended to matters of state, she grew a little uglier and a little more gluttonous each day.

"As for Maruf's son, who had by this time reached seven years of age, the wretched Fatima despised him. One night, hearing that her husband was entertaining officials from another kingdom, Fatima crept into his palace and gained entry into his bedchamber. There, on a plump silk cushion, she discovered the magic ring with the power of summoning the great Jinn.

"But, unhappily for her, the sound of her large clumsy feet woke the little prince, who was sleeping next door in his own chamber. Spying his hideous stepmother and understanding instantly what was about to occur, he fetched his small sword and lunged at her. The sword may have been short, but was sharp as a razor and was quite capable of slicing an old woman's throat. It did so, and the little prince saved the ring, which the vile Fatima was about to use to take the kingdom for herself.

"And with that," said Noureddine, taking a sip of water, "Maruf lived out his days until he was at last called to Paradise."

THE NEXT WEEK I met a woman from Chicago called Kate. She had come to Morocco to meet her sister, who was in the Peace Corps down in the Sahara, and she was lost. The heat, the dust, and the smoky cafés filled with dejected husbands had been too much for her. She had sat down in the middle of the street near the port and begun to weep. That was where Hamza's brother-in-law, Hakim, found her. He was a parking attendant, and the woman was making his job very difficult. The cars wanting to park could not get into their places, and parked cars couldn't leave because the woman was blocking the way. Not knowing quite how to handle a distressed

American lady, but stirred nonetheless by a sense of civic responsibility, Hakim bundled her into a taxi and brought her to our home. He told me later that he didn't know how to explain his intentions, as he spoke no English. The only word he could remember, he said, was "help." So he shouted it at her as loudly as he could.

By the time the little red taxi trundled down our lane, Kate was much calmer. Hakim reported the details and I thanked him for assisting a foreign lady in distress. Then I took our visitor into the salon for a cup of mint tea. She was in her forties, a little taller than average with a mane of copper-red hair and a pair of small, delicate hands, the nails polished red. She apologized for causing a scene, but said it had all been too overwhelming for her.

"Was it the heat?"

"No, it wasn't that," she replied. "It was my ignorance, a sense of my own tremendous ignorance."

I asked what she meant.

"In the United States we know the system," she said. "But down there at the port I felt like a dancer about to go onstage to perform a dance for which I knew none of the moves."

"How did it make you feel?"

"It crushed me, and I always thought I was so in control," she said.

It was then that Kate said something that interested me very greatly, something I have thought about every day since.

"When I was a child my father couldn't afford a good education," she said. "We went to average schools. I remember on my first day of grade school he sat me down on my bed and said he would teach me a way to understand the world, and to be wiser than almost anyone in it. He knew the secret, he said."

I sat forward, put my glass on the table, and listened. "What was it . . . the secret?"

Kate smiled. "He told me to read a lot of fiction," she said.

"Whatever problems whack you in life, he said the answer was fiction."

"Stories?"

"Well, yes, stories, and all sorts of stuff."

"Why fiction?"

"He said it was psychotherapy. As a child I didn't know what that meant. But I read books all the same, and I found that they worked in a silent way, balancing my mind."

Kate told me she had never written fiction, but had become a film director and was making movies.

"I'm a believer in the idea that Hollywood's a mass psychotherapist," she said. "The stories go into the subconscious and work away. People don't realize it, but when they go to the movies on a Friday night they're really paying a visit to their shrink."

We went out into the garden and watched a pair of collared doves working on their nest. Kate told me about a movie she had been making in Kansas.

"You know what's so strange to me?" she asked.

"What?"

"That as a film-maker you know the story you've created is total fiction, with actors and props, but even so you're drawn in. You find yourself suspending disbelief, slipping into the story." Kate looked at me and frowned, as if to show she was making a very serious point. "That's the power of fiction," she said, "it keeps us on track and sings to the primal creature in us all."

ONE MORNING WHEN I was a child, my father came out to the lawn where I was playing with my box of wooden bricks. He picked up one of the smaller bricks, a yellow one, and said: "This brick is the house in which we live." He picked up another, a larger, red one. "And this brick is the village out there." Then he took the actual box in which the bricks had come and placed it on the grass, a long way from the others. "This box is Afghanistan," he said. "Do you understand?"

"Yes, Baba."

"Are you quite sure that you understand?"

I nodded.

"Tahir Jan," he said, "I am showing you this because it's an important thing. I will explain it to you. If I go into the kitchen and take a dry sponge and put it in a bowl of water, it will suck up a lot of water, won't it?"

"Yes, Baba."

"But if I take the same sponge and put it in a bowl of ice, it won't suck up anything at all. That's because the sponge isn't designed to suck up ice. Its structure—lots of little holes—can't take in ice, only water."

He sat down beside me, motioning with his hands.

"Ice is water, but just in a different form," he said. "To make it into water—so we can suck it up easily—we need to change its form. The water is knowledge, Tahir Jan, and the sponge is your mind. When we hear information, a lot of it," he said, "sometimes it's too hard for us to suck up. It's like ice. We hear it in the same way that the sponge touches the bowl of ice, but it doesn't get inside. But as soon as you melt the ice, the water penetrates deep into the middle of the sponge. And that's what stories do."

My father always spoke very carefully to children so that they understood. He would pause and study the feedback, making sure what he said was getting through. I wasn't quite sure what he was aiming at, and was rather keen to get on playing with my bricks.

"Stories are a way of melting the ice," he said gently, "turning it into water. They are like repackaging something—changing its form—so that the design of the sponge can accept it."

He pointed to the bricks. "When I told you that brick was our house, that other one was the village, and that box way over there was Afghanistan, you knew what I meant, didn't you?"

"Yes, I did, Baba."

"And you knew that they weren't really the house, the village, and Afghanistan . . . but they were two bricks and a box?"

"Yes."

"Well, that's how stories are. They are symbols. The different people and the things in stories represent other things, bigger things. In the same way that we can talk about a sponge and ice, which means something else, we can use the bricks and the box to explain in an easy way an idea that's very complicated to understand.

"Try and remember, Tahir Jan, that there are symbols all around us. Look out for them, examine them, and work out what they mean. They're a kind of code. Some people will try and tell you the symbols don't exist, or they'll say that something they do not understand is nothing more than what it first appears to be. But don't believe them."

When Sukayna visited us and told me that the stairs and the high ceiling were symbols, I understood exactly what she meant, because I remembered sitting on the lawn with my box of bricks. The astrologer's idea, the symbols of Heaven and Hell, sounded preposterous.

But the more I turned it in my mind, the more sense it made.

In Morocco, and in the Arab world, symbols are all around, just as they are everywhere else. But the difference is that the Oriental mind can make sense of them, decipher them. People are trained to recognize symbols, to understand through a chain of transmission that stretches back centuries. The Occidental world once had the same chain but somewhere along the line, one of the links was broken and the chain collapsed. The result is that the symbols which ornament Western society—and are quite plain to Orientals—can't be decoded any longer by the Western mind. They are regarded as nothing more than pretty decoration or, in the case of stories, as simple entertainment.

A FEW DAYS AFTER Noureddine went into the hospital, I heard from Osman that a date had been given for the demolition of the bidonville. It was to take place the next month, a week after the move to a newly built tower block up the hill in Hay Hassani. The guardians and Zohra, who all lived in the shantytown, were unable to contain their excitement.

"We are going to have hot water in the bathroom," said Osman, "and special windows that do not let in the cold."

"And there will be an elevator that zooms up to the top," said the Bear.

"And from there, we shall have a view of the whole of Morocco," Zohra added.

"What will happen to the land on which the bidonville is built?" I asked.

Marwan swept his hand out sideways. "Flattened," he said. "Then there will be buildings, lots of them."

"What kind of buildings?"

"Villas for the rich," said Osman.

"People with a lot of money."

"Casa Trash," I said.

The fact that the Caliph's House is located where it is—slap bang in the middle of the city's prime shantytown—gives us a window into a world where people are less financially fortunate. As time has passed, we have developed an abiding respect for everyone who lives in the bidonville. The people who live there may not have pockets lined with money, but their heads are screwed on right. Their values are rock solid.

If the shantytown is at one end of the equation, then Casa Trash can be found far at the other extreme. Their lives are created from an alphabet of name brands, cosmetic surgery, and sprawling black SUVs. Female Casa Trash is dressed in the latest Gucci or Chanel, is heeled in Prada, and is so thin that you wonder how her organs function at all. Her vision is obscured by oversized sun goggles, and her mouth is masked in lipstick of such thickness and viscosity that it hinders her speech.

She can be found in a handful of chichi haunts, such as Chez Paul, picking at platters of imported salad leaves, smoking designer cigarettes, and rearranging her curls. She never looks at the friend she has come to lunch with because she is on her phone and too preoccupied scanning the other tables, making sure she's been seen.

The male variety of Casa Trash carries at least two portable phones, and has a diamond-encrusted Rolex on his wrist. He drives a black German 4x4 with frosted windows and aromatic rawhide seats. He wears a black leather jacket, tight Levi 501s, and so much aftershave that your eyes water as he passes. To show just how important he is, he speaks in little more than a whisper. His hair, weighed down with handfuls of gel, shines like a bowling ball, and his teeth have been chemically whitened to create a Hollywood smile.

Casa Trash almost never come to the Caliph's House, partly because they are not normally invited, but also because for them the idea of fording a full-on shantytown is tantamount to committing bourgeois suicide. When they do come, we find them at the door, the women shaking in their high heels, the men inspecting the chassis of their car for damage.

On one occasion in the first week of March, a Casa Trash couple did penetrate our defenses. They had seen an article about me in *Time,* and had known a previous owner of Dar Khalifa. They drove at high speed through the bidonville, schoolchildren scattering in the nick of time before the black Porsche Cayenne crushed them into dust. The husband whispered he was an industrialist. He lit a cigar as thick as his wrist and asked me if the area was safe. Just before I answered, he pulled out a pair of mobile phones, and whispered into them both at once.

His trophy wife seemed to have spent much of her adult years on a surgeon's table. The skin on her face was so tight and so loaded with Botox, I feared it might split right then. Her lips had been cosmetically edged with a dark pink line, her teeth capped, and it looked as if a pair of tennis balls had been pushed down her blouse.

The guardians were whitewashing the front of the house when the Casa Trash couple arrived. On the way into the house, the husband slipped his car key to Marwan, and barked an order fast in Arabic to wash the vehicle down. I led the couple into the house for a show of forced hospitality. As we moved through the hallway, the Casa Trash wife waved a hand back toward the shantytown.

"Those poor little people," she said, "living in those squalid little shacks. It's a shame on our society."

"But the homes in the bidonville are spotlessly clean inside," I replied defensively. "Everyone who lives there is well dressed and clean as well. Despite the lack of running water."

The wife twisted a solitaire diamond on her finger. "You must remember that they're not true Moroccans," she said.

"I don't understand you," I said, my hackles rising.

"They're thieves," whispered the Casa Trash husband between phone calls. "Nothing but thieves."

Thankfully the couple left almost as soon as they had arrived. When they were gone, I went outside. The guardians were gloomy because the stork had disappeared again. As I was standing there outside the house, a little girl approached down the lane from the bidonville. She couldn't have been more than about seven. Her cheeks were rosy, her hair tied back in a ponytail. In her hand was a posy. They were not the kind of flowers you find in the fancy French florists in Maarif, but were in a way all the more beautiful. The little girl approached me, half nervous and half proud. When she was about two feet away, she motioned for me to bend down. I did so. She kissed my cheek, placed the posy in my hand, and said, "*Shukran.*"

I didn't understand why she had thanked me. I asked Marwan, who was standing there.

"She was thanking you, Monsieur Tahir," he said.

"But for what?"

"For not looking upon us with shame."

THE NEXT AFTERNOON, I dropped in on the hospital where the cobbler was convalescing. I made my way through the dim corridors echoing with the sound of bedpans and patients moaning, and traced the route back to his ward. He was lying asleep in a bed beside the door, his face gray rather than its characteristic dark brown. He was struggling to fill his lungs. An oxygen mask had been fitted to aid his strained breathing, and a drip was feeding his arm.

I stood there for quite a while just looking at him.

The man in the next bed had his legs strapped, and his head was bandaged tight. He seemed delirious, but his eyes managed to follow me as I crossed the room to take a chair over to the cobbler's bed. I leaned forward and held the old man's hand. It was cold, the fingers were almost purple. As I sat there, clearing my mind of the insignificant debris that tends to fill it, I remembered visiting one of Rachana's relatives in an Indian hospital some years before. The lady was in intensive care. We were permitted to go in a few minutes at a time. At the far end of the sterile room were a series of three small incubation units. Inside them were triplets, a day old—two girls and a boy. The father was there, his face ashen, dejected. The nurse said the little girls were expected to live. But the boy was so frail his chances were slim.

I visited two or three days in a row to see Rachana's relative.

Every time I dropped by, I heard the babies' father talking to the boy in a whisper. He paid hardly any attention to the girls, just spoke to his son. By the end of the week the little girls were both dead. Their brother, although feeble, was expected to survive. All the while, his father continued talking to the boy. He didn't stop for a moment.

I asked one of the nurses what he was saying. She said, "He's telling him the epic tale of the *Mahabarata*."

"But the child isn't awake."

"It doesn't matter," she replied. "The words slip into the subconscious."

Sitting at Noureddine's bedside, and remembering the experience in India, I pushed a little closer to the bed. Holding his hand, I recounted a tale my father had told me as a child, when I was lying sick in my bed—the story of "The Man Who Turned into a Mule."

THE NIGHT AFTER visiting the cobbler, I dreamed of the magic carpet again. Weeks had passed since I had last been wafted up into the night sky, carried away to its distant kingdom. As soon as I saw the carpet lying there, laid out on the lawn, I ran to it, stepped aboard, and sensed its fibers bristle with eagerness to get away. With the breeze rustling through the eucalyptus trees, we left the Caliph's House far behind, and traveled out over the Atlantic, what the Arabs call *Bahr Adulumat*, the Sea of Darkness.

The carpet flew faster than before, pushing up higher and higher to where the air was thin. The stars above were bright like lanterns and, as we flew at great speed, I glimpsed the curve of the earth's atmosphere. Suddenly, we plunged. Spiraling down, my cheeks pinned back, like a skydiver in freefall. At first I screamed, but there was no one to hear me. No one except for the carpet. I clung onto its edge, spread-eagled, but I became too hoarse to shout. Then, gradually, our rate of descent reduced, and we were flying horizontal once again.

The carpet skimmed over a thousand domed roofs, over streets and across grassland. I sat up, and then a very strange thing happened. I found I could understand what the carpet was saying.

"Everything I show you has a meaning," it said. "Sometimes we know at once what something represents. But at other times, we have to turn the signs around in our heads and decipher them. Do you understand me?"

"Is that you, the carpet, talking to me?"

"You know it's me," said the carpet, bristling, "and you heard what I asked."

"I understand," I said. "But I don't really know what's going on."

The carpet banked right, and soared down a black street lined with windows, each one shrouded in gauze. In every window was a candle. It made for a chilling sight.

"What is this place?" I asked.

"You know it," said the carpet.

"No, I don't."

"Yes... remember my words, that what I show you has a meaning."

"Well, what could this mean?"

"Think! Think!"

"I don't know!"

"Yes, you do, but you must let your imagination tell you."

I closed my eyes as we flew, faster and faster down the pitch-black street, each house a facsimile of the last—six windows with a solemn candle in each, the flames flickering as we passed.

"The street is Death," I said, "and the windows are Hope."

"And the candles that burn in them?"

"They are..."

"Yes?" the carpet yelled. "What are they?"

"They are Innocence."

The next morning, I sat up in bed, my eyes circled with fear. All I could think of was the princess at the gallows. What did *she* represent? I thought hard, imagined all kinds of lunacy. Then it hit me. It was obvious, right in my face.

The girl standing at the gallows was my own ambition.

chapter twenty-one

"The king spoke to me this morning!"
exclaimed Joha at the teahouse.
"What did he say?"
"Get out of my way, you idiot!"

I returned to the hospital a day later to find the cobbler's bed stripped of its sheets and the nightstand cleared. My stomach felt sick with bile. The man at the next bed was still there, his legs suspended with wires and weights.

I stopped a nurse and motioned to the empty bed.

"Mr. Noureddine," I said, "has he been moved?"

"He was very old."

"I know. But where is he? In another room?"

She looked at me, her eyes reading my dread. "He is in Paradise," she said.

I WAS TOO sad to stay in Casablanca a moment longer. I told Rachana to pack some clothes, and Ariane and Timur to fetch their favorite toys.

"We are going away," I said.

"Where?"

"I'm not sure."

"How long are we going for?"

"A couple of days, a week, a month."

A short time later we were all in the car sitting in the lane. The cases had been piled in the back and the seat belts fastened. The children were already fighting. I had left money with Osman to pay the guardians for four weeks, and had given him a note for Dr. Mehdi, to be taken to Café Mabrook the following Friday afternoon. It said simply: *Gone to search for my story.*

We drove down the lane and through the bidonville. The fish-seller had rolled his cart down the track from the road. It was surrounded by a cacophony of cats. The knife sharpener was there, too, and the man who wrote letters for the illiterate, and two dozen children playing marbles in the mud.

Rachana asked again where we were heading. I didn't answer, but thought back to the security of my childhood. I was squeezed up in our red Ford Cortina, between my twin sister, Safia, and a giant brass candlestick my mother had got cheap in Marrakech. The car was low to the ground, whining, weighed down with mountains of bargains. My father was haranguing the gardener on the taste of Kabuli melons in Afghanistan, and my mother was knitting a fluorescent pink shawl. My older sister, Saira, was on the backseat, her head pushed out the open window, about to be sick. The car was freewheeling downhill across farmland, the soil nut-brown and moist. There was a screen of tall trees, their leaves quivering in the breeze that precedes the rain. After it was a signpost. My Arabic was almost nonexistent, but Slipper Feet had ground its alphabet into my head. I read the sign: "Fès."

The word caught my father's eye, too.

"Fès!" he cried out halfway through a sentence about Afghan pilau. "It's the dark heart of Morocco. It *is* the *Arabian Nights.*"

For a third time Rachana asked the name of our destination. I had a flash of the storytellers crouching outside the great city walls, then another of the tanneries, which look like something out of the Old Testament.

"Baba, where are we going?" asked Ariane.

"We are going to the dark heart of Morocco," I said.

AFTER THREE HOURS on the highway, we descended across the same nut-brown fields I had seen as a child. The sky boiled with anvil clouds, the earth below it lush from months of rain. Ariane spotted a rock in the middle of the highway, then another, and another. They were all the same shape—smooth and oval, about the size of a tortoise... Then I realized. They were tortoises, and were about to be flattened by the giant red truck we had struggled to overtake a mile before.

With Ariane in fits of tears at the thought of the execution of her favorite animals, I did an emergency stop, threw the car into reverse, and leapt out. The truck was close and closing in, freewheeling down onto the nut-brown plain, the driver's crazed face already visible in the cabin. I jumped into the fast lane, scooped up the first tortoise and, in the same movement, another three. The truck was now so close that I could see deep into the driver's bloodshot eyes. They told a tale of a life dependent on *kif.*

My arms juggling tortoises, I spun to the side, and managed to lay the little reptiles in the soft grass at the edge of the highway. Ariane had calmed down on the backseat. She said that a witch had once turned a handsome prince into a tortoise for laughing at her warts.

"Who told you that, Ariane?"

She thought for a moment.

"The Queen of the Fairies did," she said.

THERE CAN BE no place in the Arab world quite so bewitching as Fès.

We reached the ancient city as twilight melded into night. There were no stars, and no more than the thinnest splinter of a moon. A blanket of darkness shrouded the buildings, muffling the last words of the evening call to the faithful. Arriving at Fès by night is almost impossible to accurately describe. There's a sense that you're intruding upon something so secretive and so grave that you will be changed by the experience.

We found a small guesthouse deep in the medina through Bab Er-Rsif, one of the central gates. I hauled the cases there and shepherded Rachana and the children through the labyrinth, to the door. The owner offered two rooms for the price of one. He said it was because we had brought *baraka* into his home—in the shape of children.

"A house without children is like a landscape without trees," he said. "It may be beautiful, but there is emptiness."

He bent down, kissed Ariane and Timur on the head, and then on each cheek. I found myself thinking about it later. If we were in the West and a man you didn't know covered your children in kisses, his motives might be considered questionable. In Morocco, however, a gentle innocence still prevails, as it did in the Western world until a generation ago.

Just before we turned in for bed, the owner rapped at our door. I half-wondered if he wanted to kiss the children good night. But he had come to say that a man was waiting for me downstairs.

"Who is he?"

"A foreigner."

I went down. A single forty-watt bulb struggled to illuminate the hallway, projecting long shadows over the walls. The man was standing near the door, wearing what looked like a Stetson. He was smoking a cheroot.

"It's Robert," he said.

"Robert?"

"Robert Twigger."

I shook his hand. "My God, it's been years. How did you find me?"

"The medina grapevine," he said.

AT DAWN I crawled out of bed, woken by the *muezzin*, and made my way to the vantage point above the old city, at the Merinid Tombs. The first blush of pink light had touched the medina, where the only sign of life was the smoke rising solemnly from the bakeries in the twisting maze below. My father had taken me to the same spot thirty years before. He said that watching Fès was like peering into a world that had disappeared centuries ago.

"This is the city of Sindbad, Aladdin, and Ali Baba," he said, "of Jinns and ghouls and the medieval Arab world."

"But the *Arabian Nights* were set in Baghdad, Baba."

"That's right, but Fès now is how Baghdad was then."

"It's dangerous," I said.

"Tahir Jan, what you think of as danger is the soul. Stretch out to touch it. Embrace it."

We had stood at the Merinid Tombs each morning for a week. On the last day, my father touched my shoulder as we walked back to the red Ford.

"Fès will be important in your life," he said.

"How do you know?"

"Because it's a center of learning, a place where transmission takes place."

"But, Baba, it's just an old city," I said.

My father's face froze. "Never do that," he said coldly.

"Do what?"

"Never call a diamond a piece of glass."

He opened the car door for me, stared into my eyes so forcefully that I found it hard to breathe.

"Fès is where the baton is passed on," he said.

THE FIRST TIME I met Robert Twigger was fifteen years ago when I was homeless in Japan. He was a poet with a fondness for martial arts, the friend of a friend. I had traveled to Tokyo to study the culture and language of the indigenous Ainu people, the original inhabitants of the Japanese islands. Unfortunately I had severely misgauged the cost of living. Tokyo at the time was the most expensive city on earth. A cup of coffee, albeit flaked with gold leaf, could set you back a week's wages.

Ten days after arriving, I had blown my entire savings, most of it on a single elaborate meal of Kobe beef, from a herd so pampered that each cow boasted its own private masseur. When Twigger found me, I was squatting in a disused office block, living on ornamental cabbages I had stolen from Ueno Park, where they grew in the flower beds. I would cook three up at a time, and stir in a couple of heaped spoons of monosodium glutamate. It wasn't what most people regard as luxury. But then real luxury is in the eye of the beholder.

Twigger took me in. While I lived on his floor, brewing up my infamous soup for us both, he would spend all his time preparing for the harshest martial arts course in the world. It was a form of aikido, a course designed to harden the Tokyo Riot Police. During the months I lodged with him, Twigger would spend the evenings talking of a dream that had gripped him since infancy—to find a lost race of cave-dwelling dwarfs thought to reside in Morocco's Atlas Mountains.

For a decade, he subjected himself to routines of wild preparation. He took to sleeping on a bed of nails that he had made himself, learned to shoot a pistol blindfolded, and even canoed across Canada upstream to build the muscles in his arms.

From the beginning, he was certain the dwarfs were part of a pygmy race that had once inhabited all of North Africa. His interest in the subject had arisen as a child. He had read a curious monograph by the nineteenth-century scholar R. G. Haliburton, entitled *The Dwarfs of the Atlas Mountains*. The paper suggested that the dwarf people were afforded an almost sacred status, and that their whereabouts were kept secret from outsiders.

Twigger believed that a local community somewhere in Morocco must have known stories of the small people. After all, he said, the subject had been a sensation when it first reached the West, little over a century ago. Trapped in the communal knowledge of the society he felt sure there was a clue waiting to be unearthed, a clue that could lead him to the lost tribe of Moroccan pygmies.

We met for coffee the next morning, at a café outside Bab Er-Rsif. The place was filled with a dozen unshaven men in tattered jelabas, each one nursing a glass of café noir, with a cigarette stub screwed into the corner of his mouth. Rachana had taken the children to a hammam. She said male cafés were worthy only of men who frequented them.

I couldn't understand what Twigger was doing in Fès.

"You're not going to find your lost pygmy tribe here," I said, once we had both been served coffee.

"I know that."

"So what are you doing in town?"

"Looking for clues," he said.

"In the old city?"

"Kind of . . . in cafés like this one."

I swilled a mouthful of coffee. "I'm not quite sure I see the connection."

"It's in the folklore," he said.

"Meaning?"

"Meaning you've got to tap into the substrata."

I ordered another round of coffee. Twigger lit a cheroot and sucked at the end.

"Anthropologists are a pathetic bunch," he said. "They never find anything because they don't know how to look."

"How do you look?"

"With my eyes closed."

THAT AFTERNOON, I had a chat with the owner of the guesthouse in which we were staying. He said his brother had committed the entire Qur'an and the Hadith to memory by the age of twelve, that his ability to remember was so defined he had created a business from it.

"What kind of business?"

"He remembers things for people."

If you required an important date to be memorized or the text of a legal document, or a poem you especially liked, Waleed would remember it for you. He made a small charge depending on the length and complexity of the thing to be memorized. Like a social hard disk, he performed a function with the ear and the mouth that is more usually done by the eye and the hand.

Late in the afternoon Waleed turned up at the guesthouse to take a nap. He had just memorized a seventeen-page document, and was feeling a little drained from the feat. He was big-boned and calm, with a waxy face that reflected the low-watt lighting. As soon as we had been introduced, he asked for my parents' names and my date of birth.

"Don't worry," I said, "I won't need reminding of that information."

Waleed tapped the front of his head. "It's for the register," he said.

I asked him why people didn't write things down like everywhere else, why they preferred trusting his service to a sheet of paper. Waleed stretched out on the divan that ran along the far end of the entrance hall.

"It's a tradition," he said.

"What is?"

"Using the mind."

"But if something happened to you, all the information would be lost."

Waleed tugged off his yellow slippers. "Just as it would be if there was a fire, a flood, or a thief."

"But paper liberates the mind," I insisted.

"You're wrong," he replied. "The written word is weakening society, turning it to pulp."

"But writing makes books," I said. "And books are the most precious thing we have."

"Books are an insult to the mind," said Waleed.

"They are magical."

"No, they're the reason for society's collapse."

Waleed was part of a tradition almost lost in the West, a tradition that predated writing. Most of us spend our lives rallying against the deadening effects of television and computer games, and we celebrate the written word. Waleed was a link in a far more ancient chain, a chain that existed since the dawn of humanity and is now under threat—that of the spoken word.

For Muslims, the power of memory is important because it enables them to memorize the Qur'an, an achievement regarded as a blessed act in itself. According to Islamic tradition, the Angel Gabriel recited the Holy Book to the Prophet Mohammed over a period of about twenty years. Mohammed, who was illiterate, committed the entire text to memory as he received it, just as his disciples did, and Muslims continue to do today.

But at the battle of Yamahah, little more than a decade after Mohammed's flight from Mecca, so many of his followers were killed that there was a real fear the knowledge of the sacred text would be lost altogether.

It was then that the Qur'an was written out for the first time.

WALEED HAD SAID the only man in Fès with a better memory than he was a storyteller called Abdul Aziz. He was in his eighties but had a mind so crisp that he could supposedly remember every word he had ever heard spoken.

"Where can I find him?"

"I will take you," said Waleed.

Two days later, we packed the children into the car and, with Waleed directing, we drove out of Fès, down a series of bumpier and bumpier tracks into the low hills which encircle the town. There were olive groves on either side, and the odd stone wall speckled with moss.

After forty minutes, we rattled to a stop.

"It's the end of the road," said Waleed. "We walk from here."

The sun was dazzling, the air tinged with the scent of warmer months approaching. We strolled through a meadow of citrus-yellow flowers. Ariane fell to her knees and made a posy. She gave it to Waleed.

At the end of the field there was a ramshackle house, its brick walls pocked with holes, its roof about to cave in. The path leading to the place was littered with tin cans and shards of broken glass. A dog raised the alarm, ran out barking, a smudge of brown.

A moment later, the silhouette of a man was in the door. He was tall, alert, and walked with a cane. The sun was in our eyes, and so I didn't catch his face at first. Waleed stepped forward, kissed the old man's hand, and made the introductions.

"I present to you Abdul Aziz," he said solemnly.

The man shook our hands and welcomed us. His hair had been dyed orange with henna, and his face was dominated by a sore on his right cheek. It was an inch across and glistened in the light.

He rounded us up with his arms.

"It is a blessed day," he said.

Three stone steps led up to the house. The door was badly warped and had a crack down the middle so wide you could see through it into the salon.

We went up the steps.

The inside was cozy and scant, the home of a man with no interest in the material. There was a picture of fantasia, a swirling rush of paint, men charging with their guns; and a dark lacquered cabinet packed with an assortment of plates. At the far end of the room stood a copy of the Qur'an on a carved wooden stand.

Abdul Aziz opened a cupboard and wrestled with a long object, tied at both ends. He slid it out. It was a carpet. The strings were unfastened and the rug laid over the floor. The design was Persian, a central medallion with interlocking arabesques at each corner. It was exquisite, the colors cochineal red, sapphire blue, with a hint of lilac along the edge. Just before ranting praise at seeing such a beautiful thing, I put a hand to my mouth and swallowed my words. In the East, an object admired by a guest is presented to him as a gift.

Abdul Aziz invited us to sit on the carpet, then limped away to prepare the tea. When he came back a few minutes later, he found me stroking a palm over the knots.

"It was given to me a long time ago," he said.

"The work is very fine."

"I keep it in the cupboard," he replied, "and bring it out when guests come to visit."

"It's Persian."

"Yes, from Isfahan."

"Have you been there, to Isfahan?"

"No, no. A man from Iran gave it to me. I helped him through a trouble in his life." Abdul Aziz paused, poured a glass of tea, and tipped it back into the pot. "I told him a story," he said.

He poured the tea again, leaned forward and kissed Timur on the cheek. I said that I heard of his powerful memory. He waved a hand to the window.

"A memory is no more than a tool," he said. "It's worthless in itself. A good memory is not the power to think. What has value is the thing you are holding in your mind."

"How many stories do you know?"

The old storyteller stared at the carpet's interlocking arabesques, the corners of his mouth rising in a smile.

"Many hundreds," he said dimly. "Thousands. I don't know. But a single good tale is as valuable as them all."

I asked about the tradition of storytelling in Fès.

"The stories that touched the ears were as great as the buildings that still entertain the eyes. They were sacred in their own way."

"Are there any storytellers left?"

"One or two, but they can't support themselves. Some have paying jobs. They tell tales in the evenings after their work is over. But they are not celebrated any longer."

"I am searching for the story in my heart," I said.

Abdul Aziz lifted his head until his eyes were in line with my own. "I haven't heard of that in many years," he said.

"Most people don't seem to know about it."

"Of course they do not," said the old man, raising the pot high to pour more tea. "They have lost the tradition. It's like a piece of slate that's been wiped clean."

"Could you tell me my story?" I said.

"How can I do that?" Abdul Aziz replied. "For only you will know it."

"Can't you see it?"

He shook his head. "Of course not."

"But how will I know it?"

The storyteller raised a finger. "Be patient," he said.

The dog ran inside and rolled over. Moroccans usually keep dogs outside. They say that when they enter a home, the angels leave.

But Abdul Aziz was a doting master.

"An audience of dogs would listen far better than a crowd of people," he said. Abdul Aziz ran a hand over his dog's belly. "These days people tell stories haphazardly," he said. "But it was never like that. Before the traditions faded, they used to choose them more carefully, selecting a tale for a particular person, and a particular setting, to have a special effect."

"You mean teaching stories?"

The old man traced one of the carpet's lines with the tip of his finger. "All stories are teaching stories," he said.

Ariane and Timur were growing restless. They wanted to run out to play in the meadow, to hurl each other into the carpet of yellow flowers.

"I will tell them a story," said Abdul Aziz. "I think that they will like it and that it will like them."

He stretched back, stroked a hand down over his throat, and said:

"Once upon a time there was a kitchen in a palace, as grand as any the world has ever seen. There were pots and pans hanging on all the walls, and delicious ingredients piled up, waiting to be prepared. In the middle of the kitchen stood an enormous chimney, and below it was a magnificent iron stove.

"Fifty chefs worked day and night to prepare the food for the table of the king. There were pies filled with peacock meat, roast lambs, skewers of venison, and platter upon platter of meatballs, for everyone knew that the king's favorite dish was meatballs in creamy white sauce.

"Now," said Abdul Aziz, "one of the junior chefs had just finished preparing the last platter of meatballs. He opened the great iron door of the stove and slipped it inside. The dish began to sizzle away as the fat melted and the temperature rose. The heat grew more and more suffocating, and the meatballs began to bake. They cried out to their leader: 'Help, help, do something, please, because we are being cooked alive. We will do anything for you, but first you must save our lives!'

"The meatball leader, who was the largest of them all, raised himself as high as he could and called to his fellow meatballs: 'Have faith, O meatballs, I shall save you. I promise that we shall not be cooked, but salvation will occur in the most extraordinary way!' 'What will our salvation be, O great leader?' 'There will be soothing medicine to cool your burns and a fragrant bed for you to lie down upon and rest.'

"Just then, the door of the oven was swung open and a cool white sauce was spooned over the meatballs. They gasped with joy, and thanked God for saving them from the terrible fire. 'You did not listen to me, my fellow meatballs,' said the meatball leader, 'for I promised you a cooling medicine, and look, it has come.' But then the heat began to rise once again, and some of the meatballs, the ones nearest the edge of the platter, were roasted alive. 'O leader,' cried the others, 'please save our souls. We will follow you to the end of the earth. Just save us from this terrible heat.' 'Be calm, my meat-balls,' said the meatball leader. 'Calm yourselves and the fire will be cooled. I promise you.'

"At that very moment, the door of the oven opened again, and the great platter was carefully removed by the chef. He shook it a lit-tle, to make sure the meatballs were not sticking to the bottom, and tipped it onto a bed of saffron-colored rice. The platter was adorned with fragrant leaves and herbs. The meatballs were carried at shoul-der height from the kitchen through the palace corridors, and into the throne room, where the king himself was dining with his guests.

"The meatballs couldn't believe the change in their fortune. 'I told you all that our bad luck would be reversed,' declared the biggest meatball. 'You just need to believe in me for I am your leader.' The other meatballs squeaked words of praise, as they nestled into the soft cushioning bed of rice. Suddenly the platter was laid down in front of the king himself.

"Some of the meatballs were dazzled by the glint of jewels on the necks of the guests, and others became overcome by the sound of the musicians playing on a dais in the room.

"But then the brotherhood of meatballs were removed a few at a time, spooned off the platter onto individual plates. And, far worse, hungry mouths around the table began gobbling them up. 'O leader, our leader,' cried the remaining meatballs, 'what is happening to us?! Our numbers are being culled and in the most shocking way. We are being exterminated.'

"The king himself dug a fork into the platter and skewered six meatballs in one blow. 'Treachery!' the last few meatballs cried. 'How could this be happening to us?' By this point, the meatball leader was sick of hearing of the problems his meatball followers were facing. He shouted to them: 'You were cooled by the medicinal white sauce, were you not?' 'Yes, yes, we were!' shouted the last remaining meat-balls. 'And you were removed from the terrible fire and placed on a bed of cool, calming rice, were you not?' 'Yes, yes, we were,' said the meatballs. 'Well, when are you going to understand that you are meatballs and that as such you are destined for the stomachs of hungry men?'

"A moment later, the meatball leader was scooped up and swallowed whole by the king. The last meatballs on the platter continued to shout and scream and protest their unwillingness to be eaten. But by then no one was left to listen to their cries."

chapter twenty-two

Tie two birds together.
They will not be able to fly even though
they now have four wings.

Jalaluddin Rumi

There was only one day I can remember on which my father said nothing at all. We had been in Fès for more than a week, staying at the plush Palais Jamai Hotel. My sisters and I spent most of our time playing hide-and-seek in the Andalucian gardens which overlook the medina. My mother sat on the terrace, knitting. My father was nowhere to be seen. Whenever we asked where he was, my mother would rest the knitting needles on her knee and say: "He's out doing his work."

I never thought to ask what his work actually was. I would hear him talking almost all the time, and assumed that people paid him to talk. Sometimes a stranger would turn up at our home in the late morning. They would sit primly on the slippery turquoise couch, and my father would start talking to them. He would continue through lunch and the afternoon, through the evening, and then late into the night.

When he wasn't talking, he was typing on a robust old manual typewriter. The sound of inked keys striking paper at lightning speed haunts me even now.

On the day my father didn't say a single word, he sat on a chair in the gardens of the Palais Jamai, drinking coffee and making notes in blue-black ink. Every so often he would glance up and watch us running through the flower beds. But he didn't really see us.

He was seeing stories instead.

The next day the blue-black notes were in his hand at breakfast. It was clear he was ready to talk about what his mind had processed. We were just about to scamper into the garden, when he said: "Who likes stories?"

We put up our hands as if we were in class.

"We all do," I said.

"All children like stories," said my sister.

"Do you think stories are just for children?" he asked.

"Yes, Baba."

"Well, I'll tell you something. Stories are for everyone, not just for children," he said. "But sometimes people forget that. When grown-ups hear stories, sometimes they don't realize that they are very clever things, things that can help them to learn other things."

"Are stories like going to school, Baba?"

"Well, yes, in a way that's just what they are. But stories have been around long before there were any schools or schoolteachers. They have been around since the beginning of time."

"Baba, shall we go and tell people?" I asked.

"Tell them what, Tahir Jan?"

"Tell them stories are clever and that they are for them."

My father held up the paper he was holding. "That is a very good idea, and just what I was thinking. What I want to do is to get grown-ups telling other grown-ups stories again where we live. Just like people do in Morocco." He paused, touched the paper to his chin.

"I want to start a College of Storytellers," he said.

ROBERT TWIGGER TRACKED me down the next afternoon. He had just finished a marathon session going from café to café in search of clues, and was wide-eyed from all the caffeine. I still didn't see the connection between folklore and pygmies, but Twigger swept my questions away with his hand.

"Folklore is like the thick green soup humanity climbed out of," he said. "It's packed with nourishment, with information, and clues. The thing is that we belittle it. We laugh at the idea of being able to tap into it. But imagine if we could decipher folklore in a place like this."

"In Fès?"

"Yes! Imagine . . . everyone who's ever lived here has rubbed off and left a kind of footprint in the folklore. They've impacted it, touched it. Everything they've ever seen, discovered, known, it's all there, all in the thick green soup."

"But how would you go about deciphering it?"

Twigger took a deep breath. "That's a big question."

"Do you have an answer?"

"Perseverance," he said.

AT THE GUESTHOUSE, the owner's brother, Waleed, was stretched out in the hallway again. I staggered in through the door with a dozen bags filled with bargains from the medina, Rachana and the kids treading in my steps. Waleed sat up, kissed Ariane and Timur, and asked if I was a Christian. It was a strange question to get hit with out of the blue. I told him that my family were Muslim, and that Rachana had been raised Hindu. Waleed seemed pleased by the answer.

"That's good," he said.

"I have a lot of Christian friends, though," I said. "I have friends from all religions."

Waleed groomed a hand over his chin. "Morocco is the place

where all religions live freely," he said. "There were Jews here two thousand years ago, long before the Arabs. Many have gone to Israel now, but in their hearts they are Moroccan."

I put the shopping down.

"I don't notice people's religion," I said. "It's not important to me."

"You are right, Monsieur Tahir. We have Muslim friends, and Hindu friends, and friends who are Christian and Jew."

"Very good."

"But there are new people here in our city."

"Oh?"

"Yes, they are Christian, but they are not like the Christians we have known before."

"What's different about them?"

"They are trying to make us into Christians. We have told them that we are very happy being Muslim, that we don't want to change."

"Are they missionaries?"

"Yes, missionaries," said Waleed. "That's what they are. They sing songs and play guitars and wave their arms in the air."

"Happy Clappies," I said.

"That is their title?"

"Well, some people call them that."

"What can we do, Monsieur Tahir, about these Happy Clappies?"

"Just ignore them," I said.

Waleed scratched his neck.

"If we ignore them, will they listen?"

THE COLLEGE OF Storytellers drew together an assembly of raconteurs, folklorists, and oral historians, both in Europe and in the United States. Over the years it existed, the college promoted the transmission of stories from almost every country in the world. At the same time, it encouraged people to consider how stories worked on the mind, how they helped in problem solving, and how the same tale can be found in completely different regions of the globe.

At one of the meetings held in a community hall in London, I was introduced to a man called Wilson. He was six foot three, as thin as a barge pole, and hollow cheeked, as if a mysterious tropical illness had eaten all the flesh from his face. He had a hard-to-place accent, and was wearing yellow gum boots.

The College of Storytellers' great attraction was the throng it attracted. It ranged from members of the establishment to the eccentric, and beyond, to a realm peopled by the gloriously odd. But the great thing was that everyone who turned up at the meetings was passionate about storytelling.

Wilson slapped me on the back and said he had just got in from South Africa. "Been transcribing some Zulu tales," he said vaguely. "They have their own form of the Ugly Duckling, don't you know?"

"Are you going to tell a story here today?" I asked.

Wilson pulled out a briar pipe and stuck the bit between his teeth. "Got a little tale from the Mekong Delta I thought I'd share," he said. "After all, a good story's like a rat trapped in a larder."

"How's that?"

"It gnaws away until it's set free."

The next week, Wilson telephoned the flat where I was living in north London. He said he had been unable to sleep for two nights, that another tale was gnawing away. I was busy with university exams and hardly had enough time to eat, let alone listen to stories. But I have never found it easy to give an excuse down a telephone line.

"You'd better come over," I said.

Three hours later, Wilson's finger was holding down the doorbell. His gaunt cheeks were redder than before. It may have been because he had walked from the East End, a distance of ten miles. On his feet were the yellow gum boots, and on his head was a lizard-green trilby.

He sat on the sofa in my cramped studio flat. There were papers strewn everywhere and dozens of books, each one open at a particular page.

I excused the mess. "I've got finals," I said weakly.

Wilson took out his pipe, filled it with tobacco from a leather pouch, and set fire to the bowl. The papers and books disappeared in a fog of silver smoke. He related a few stories gathered on his travels, in West Africa, New Zealand, and Nepal. Then, pulling off his gum boots, he said: "I'll tell you something."

"What?"

"We could have learned a lot from the Ainu in Japan," he said. "They didn't have a writing system, but they used stories to remember things. Any important event or bit of knowledge was put into a story, packaged neatly up in a frame, and was told and retold. As time passed people forgot what was true and what was imagined, which stories were based on reality and which were not. But then," said Wilson, refilling his pipe, "it didn't matter to them."

"What didn't matter?"

"Whether something was true or not."

Just before dark, Wilson put on his yellow gum boots, shook my hand, and strode off back to the East End.

"I'll see you at the college's next meeting," I said as he turned to leave.

"I shouldn't think so, old boy."

"Why not?"

"Because I'm heading off to New Guinea at dawn."

Our paths never crossed again. I didn't forget the afternoon Wilson had spent smoking his pipe, telling stories in my flat. I can't remember what tales he told me. But his observation about fact and fiction rubbed off, as did his notes on the Ainu, a subject that preoccupied me later on.

During my own travels I have found fact and fantasy blended together throughout the developing world. Where they converge and coexist there may be poverty, but there tends to be a kind of harmony, too, a balance, as if the culture is held in place by an invisible counter-weight laid into the fabric of the society.

STEP INTO FÈS's medina and it's almost impossible not to be affected by what you find. Certainly, it may appear to be disorderly at first but, as your eyes acclimatize, you begin to understand that there's very little disorder at all. The old city moves to an ancient rhythm, a routine that has become streamlined through time. Like a shard of once-sharp glass smoothed by decades on the seabed, Fès is sensible, rounded, complete within itself. Walk through the streets and you can tell who belongs there and who does not. The locals have a special look in their eye, a confidence, an arrogance.

And they have plenty to be arrogant about.

Before we bought the Caliph's House and moved to Casablanca, I had negotiated for a vast merchant's house in Fès. The building was so large that I toured it without muttering a word, silenced by the enormity and by the grandeur. There were three large courtyards and a harem, each replete with mosaic fountains, painted wooden ceilings, stucco plasterwork, and bougainvillea vines. The house was owned by seven greedy brothers. To buy it, I would have had to coax each one to sell. It was a possibility, but I was still so unripe that I stormed out of the first coaxing session after only an hour and a half. A local would have dug in his heels, swilled down another glass of sweet mint tea and put in days of negotiation.

There is no city on earth that gets me quite as excited as Fès. Medieval Moroccan architecture, serene beyond words, is crafted on a matrix of perfect geometric design. It is an incomparable joy to slip from the tangled streets through a doorway no taller than a barrel, and to find yourself in a shaded palace, utterly cloistered from the outside world.

The appeal of Moroccan houses has not gone unnoticed by the West. Over the last decade thousands have been sold in Marrakech, in particular to Americans, British, and French. There is an abundance of coffee table books of what are usually called riads, although many are not strictly riads at all. "Riad" simply means garden, and is used to describe a house with a central courtyard, typically with four symmetrical flower beds inside. The flower beds signify the world beyond, for Muslims believe that Paradise is a garden. Any visitor to the Arabian desert can imagine how the nomadic Bedouin would have fantasized about such a place, with cool shady trees, birdsong, and fountains issuing an abundance of fresh water.

ONE MORNING, THE owner of the guesthouse lurched up the stairs and asked if I wanted to buy a house.

"My cousin is selling," he said.

"What kind of place is it?"

"A nice one, old, very old."

"How old?"

"Five hundred years."

"What state's it in?"

"Go and see for yourself."

He made a telephone call and as soon as he replaced the handset, his cousin popped up. He was called Badr, and was dressed like a rock star, his hair spiked up with gel, clothed in denim with a lot of gold chains and pungent aftershave. Badr moonwalked through the medina's streets. He said he had watched Michael Jackson videos continuously since he was six, and had perfected his hero's moves. I had to run to keep up, dodging the oncoming traffic: an endless flow of mules laden with crates, old men pushing barrows, and wide Fassi women weighed down with their shopping.

From the guesthouse we walked straight for a while, turned left, then right, then right again, and left, then right, right again, left, another left, and straight, until we came to a small olive-green door.

Badr slapped it with his hand. The door opened.

"Go on in," he said.

I stepped down and found myself in a blacked-out corridor, fumbled my way forward and round a sharp bend, and emerged into a courtyard, blinded by sunlight. On three sides there were towering double doors leading to rooms, and a marble fountain in the middle. Above the courtyard was a second story, with another three rooms and a wrought-iron balcony. The walls had once been adorned with hand-cut mosaic in red, yellow, and black.

Damp laundry crisscrossed the courtyard, hung up on strings. From what was hanging there you could imagine how many people, and who, resided in the building. There must have been at least four women, three men, and six children living there.

"You have a big family," I said.

Badr did a break-dance move fast. "I will show you the tomb," he said.

"*Tomb?*"

"That's right."

He opened a door on the opposite side of the yard, pulled out a box filled with old shoes, and a broken chair.

"In here."

I poked my head inside. It was very dark. Badr fetched a candle, lit it, and pushed past me. There was a small cavity, ten feet by ten, with a stone slab in the middle.

"Who's buried down there?"

"The founder of the house."

"Was he a relative of yours?"

Badr squinted. "Not sure," he said.

The idea of living with a tomb in the house was original but unnerving.

"I don't think my wife would like having a dead person in the house," I said.

"There's another place," Badr said fast, "another cousin. It's bigger."

"Where is it?"

"Not far."

We left the tomb, shuffled back through the blacked-out corridor and into the street. Badr winked at a veiled girl who was peering out from the house opposite. She shouted something loud in Arabic and pointed to the sky.

A few minutes later we were crossing a second threshold. I turned the corner, and found myself in a courtyard filled with orange trees. A pair of shriveled women were sitting outside one of the salons. They stood up, gave greeting, and invited us to look around.

Badr led me up one of the two flights of stairs to the roof. In Fès, houses are built on multiple levels, with a clutch of rooms arranged on each floor. Any recess too small for human habitation tends to be filled with a spider's web of junk. On the way up, we passed a dozen or more bedrooms, each one lined with sofas and beds. There was a color television in each one, blaring soap operas from Egypt.

A small flap opened onto the roof. We struggled to get through it. There were three chicken coops up there, a pair of dogs, and what looked like a tractor engine. I looked out across the medina, each house with a central *halqa,* an opening to the sky, nestled cheek by jowl to the houses around it. Badr pointed to the distance.

"One day I'll live over there in the new town," he said.

"And leave all this history behind?"

"History's for my parents and their friends," he said.

"You've lived here all your life. So you don't see the beauty."

"There is no beauty here, there's just dirt and damp."

"I know people who'd give their front teeth to live here," I said.

"Who?"

"People who appreciate history."

"Tell them to come here then," said Badr. "There are plenty of people who want to sell their family homes."

We traced our way back down through the house, passed the

rooms alive with television. I made a joke, asking if there was a tomb there as well. Badr said there wasn't a tomb.

"But there's a big kitchen. I will show you."

We stepped down into a kind of cellar. It was dim and stank of dead rats and damp. The ceiling was falling in. There was a pool of light at the far end.

"That's the kitchen down there," said Badr.

"And what's this room we're standing in?"

"These are the slave quarters," he said.

chapter twenty-three

I have never seen a man lost on a straight path.

Saadi of Shiraz

Waleed took me aside and told me his sister was dead. We were sitting in a café in the new town, waiting for another of his cousins to turn up.

"Her name was Amina," he said softly. "She was two years older than me, a student with perfect school grades, and very nice teeth."

"I'm very sorry to hear she's passed away. When did it happen?"

Waleed the memory man crossed his arms and stared into his coffee. "It's not an easy question to answer," he said.

I changed the subject, asked him about his children. He broke into a smile.

"There is Ali, who's seven, and Dounia. She's five. They are like sunshine on a cold day," he said.

"Raising kids is a big responsibility."

"Children are like clay, it's for us to mold them." Waleed seemed pleased with his analogy.

"Values are important—a sense of right and wrong," I said.

"They must understand the beauty of honor and the ugliness of shame."

Waleed's cousin swept in, ate three croissants, and left. He didn't say a word.

"He seemed nice," I said when he was gone.

"He was very close to my sister," said Waleed. "They were supposed to get married. Both families were planning the marriage."

"It must have been very hard for him when she died."

Waleed nodded. He put his head in his hands. "It was terrible," he said. "My sister was very lovely deep down. The shame, the shame."

"I don't understand," I said. "What has shame got to do with it?"

Waleed raised his head. His eyes were full of tears. "Amina disgraced us, brought great shame on the family. We are laughed at by everyone," he said.

"How could people laugh when your sister died? That's so callous."

Waleed didn't look at me. He raised his glass, staring at the pattern on the rim, and said: "Amina eloped with a Frenchman. She lives in France."

"You mean she's not dead?"

"In our eyes she is," said Waleed.

WORD SPREAD THROUGH Fès that I was searching for a house to buy. It wasn't strictly true. I dreamed of owning an old courtyard home in the medina, but I knew Rachana wouldn't be gripped by the idea. And, besides, we didn't have any money to spare for frivolities. As far as Rachana was concerned, the Caliph's House was already far too big.

Waleed's cousins saw it as their duty to find me a suitable home. Their enthusiasm to help me realize my dream was fueled by a lust to see their own communal dream come true, the dream of leaving the medina and moving into the new town.

That afternoon, another cousin took me on a tour of houses so deep in the old city that it seemed as if the modern world had never quite penetrated. The tourists who come to Fès tend to do a circuit of the main historical sights. They rarely journey into the inner regions of the labyrinth.

Waleed's cousin Abdur Rahman said that every house was for sale.

"Without the foreign money the city will collapse," he said. "It's already falling down."

He was right. Hundreds of buildings were supported by wooden buttresses and scaffolding. As families have grown, additional floors have been added onto the top of old buildings, applying massive downward pressure which has pushed out the walls. We must have visited twenty houses in the space of a morning. The different buildings all melted together in my head, a tapestry of fountains, mosaics, balconies, carvings and painted wood, orange trees, and marble floors.

I wasn't going to ask about Waleed's sister Amina, but Abdur Rahman mentioned her name.

"She was seventeen," he shouted as we waded through a herd of pack mules heading toward us. "She was the favorite, and was very loved. Waleed's parents had planned to marry her to another of our cousins. They had been engaged as children."

"I met him," I said.

"He doesn't say much," said Abdur Rahman, "and Amina thought he was boring. She ran away to France with a guy she met at McDonald's."

"I can imagine the family being angry."

"No, no," he replied. "You can have no idea how angry they were. They beat their chests, wept, screamed, tore out their hair. Then they did the hardest thing of all."

"What?"

"They buried their dead daughter."

IN THE AFTERNOON, I bumped into Twigger. He was haggling with a shopkeeper for a pair of embroidered mule panniers. I asked him if he had a mule to go with the baskets.

"All in good time," he said. "You have to go slow. I've been bitten by the used-mule business before."

"In Morocco?"

"No, in Outer Mongolia. Got ripped off big time. The second-hand mule business is always run by thieves."

"What's the secret of a good pack mule?"

"You've got to check for sores."

"Where?"

"Everywhere, but epecially on the rump and down the back," he said. "If you see sores, walk away. However sweetly the damn mule looks at you, walk away. When you're buying a used mule you can't get too attached."

Twigger threw down a wad of low-denomination dirham notes and grabbed the leather panniers.

Then he asked if I wanted to buy a palace.

"It's around the corner," he said.

"How much?"

"The price of a broom cupboard in London or New York."

Two minutes later we were inside the great salon of a vast family home. There were three principal courtyards with four cavernous rooms off each, marble fountains long since dry, and the very finest painted cedar ceilings. The walls in each room were paneled with mosaic six feet up from the floor, millions of hand-cut pieces laid in geometric patterns.

The house was empty, except for an old man who used the upper drawing room as a workshop for making sandals. He lived in the same room with a flock of pet doves. The birds nested in a cavity behind the fabulous painted ceiling. Every so often, one of the birds would swoop through the room. The place was splattered with decades of bird excrement.

The shoemaker said he never went outside.

"Don't you go shopping in the medina?" I asked.

"Oh no, no," he said fearfully. "I never, ever go out there."

"How do you get food, though?"

"A neighbor goes for me."

"How long have you lived here?"

"Since I was born . . . sixty years ago."

"Do you realize you live in a palace?"

"This is my home," he said.

"But it's a palace."

"Is it?"

"Where are your family?"

The man threaded a needle with twine. He didn't look up. "Those birds up there are my family," he said.

JUST BEFORE WE left Fès, I was strolling through the medina, taking pictures of the traditional artisans turning sheets of metal into exquisite appliqué lamps, when I spotted a shop front. It was out of place. Fès's medina has a worn-in appearance, a uniformity reached through more than a thousand years of life. The shop front stood out because it was impeccable, and because it gave no hint of the wares on offer. The only clue was a small black and white sign hanging in front of the door. It read "Services."

I couldn't resist going in.

A fresh-faced young man was sitting inside. He was boisterous and big, and it looked as if his shirt was about to split down the back like the Incredible Hulk. His giant hands were holding a miniature Bible, his lips reading the words silently. There was a guitar in the corner with a rainbow-colored strap.

When the door opened, the giant looked up, sat straight with a jerk, greeted me. I inquired what services were on offer. He removed his reading glasses with both hands, placed them on the desk.

"We connect people," he said in a well-mannered Southern voice.

"Are you an agency?"

"Um, yes, sir, you could kinda call us that."

"What's your product?"

"The Truth." The giant placed his hand on the Bible and grinned. "We're in the wisdom business," he said.

At the guesthouse, Waleed insisted the shop was known throughout Fès.

"I told you before," he said. "We Moroccans are quiet people. We love all religions. They are our brothers. It says in the Holy Qur'an that if you cannot find a mosque, you should go and pray in a church. Our Book says that Moses and Jesus are prophets and must be respected," he said. "We live peacefully. You have seen us. But, Monsieur, you must understand we do not have a place for these people."

"Which people?"

"These Happy Clappering people."

WE LEFT FÈS and drove northeast on one of the windiest roads I have ever experienced. Ariane and Timur swayed about in the back. They played "I Spy" for a while, and then both threw up. I pulled over so that we could sponge them down, and take them out for a pee. I took Timur into the undergrowth at the side of the road and pulled down his trousers. All around us was a forest of thick, healthy stems. Most of them were about four feet high. They were marijuana plants.

Morocco's Rif is famous for *kif*, marijuana resin. The crop supplies much of southern Europe since it was discovered in the sixties by a tie-dye generation, traveling in multicolored Volkswagen camper vans. The police are in force these days, arresting tourists foolish enough to smuggle the resin home.

Northern Morocco couldn't make for a sharper contrast from the south. Gone was the desert, replaced by a patchwork of fields, tilled by bent-over women wearing conical hats. There were orange groves and farmsteads, ripe old men astride tired old donkeys, rocky outcrops, clear streams, and oceans of sheep.

In the flaxen light of late afternoon, we approached Chefchaouen, a small town built by Muslims fleeing from Andalucia five centuries ago. It sits cradled between two summits, above the Oued Laou Valley. Entering it was like stepping into a lost fragment from Andalucian Spain. The place was designed as a secure citadel for the Islamic faith, a mainstay from which its forces could regroup and plan their assault on Portugal, the rising Catholic power.

The town's architecture, cuisine, and unlikely Mediterranean feel are results of its curious Latin heritage. Until 1920, when Spanish troops occupied northern Morocco, Chefchaouen was cut off from the Christian world. The invading Spanish found a time capsule of their own culture. They heard spoken a form of tenth-century Catalan—a language brought south by Andalucian Jews—which had died out on the Iberian Peninsula four hundred years before. And they found Granada leatherwork, pottery, and other crafts long extinct from their native Iberia.

The streets were steep and cobbled, shaded by trellises overlaid with clematis, the houses rinsed with indigo, their doors studded, their roofs tiled with terracotta. We strolled up and down the medina's alleys, struck by the tranquillity.

I had visited Chefchaouen the year before, on the trail of an American convert to Islam. He was called Pete, and had traveled to Morocco in search of a young woman he had met in a Texan nightclub. Unlike most of the foreigners who travel to the mountain town, Pete had no interest in *kif*. There was only one thing on his mind—the expansion of a radical Islamic message.

I had tried to explain to him that Islam preaches moderation, that the religion had been hijacked by terrorist forces, as every genuine Muslim knows. But Pete had been sucked into a subworld of hatred, a realm awash with old-fashioned anarchy.

RACHANA, THE CHILDREN, and I sat at a café on Chefchaouen's main square, Uta el-Hammam. We ate Spanish tortilla followed by soupy blue ice cream. I found myself thinking about the Happy Clappers. They may not have found any followers in a staunchly

Muslim country like Morocco, but their message—the Bible—has a remarkable cultural value that is sometimes overlooked. Until World War II, the majority of Christians attended church services on Sundays. They did it without question, and were exposed to a body of work rich in stimulation and in storytelling. The Old Testament in particular was drummed into young minds by preachers and vicars on both sides of the Atlantic, stressing moral values and correct behavior, against a backdrop rich in symbolism.

Churchgoers on a Sunday morning learned how to dissect a story and grasp its inner meaning, just as Arabs still do expertly today. Sitting in their pews, Christians were surrounded by an extraordinary tapestry of symbolic material. There were symbols in the sermon, in the wall hangings and the stained glass, in the carvings on the pulpit, and in the wine and the wafer, the blood and the body of Christ.

These days the young generation are enlightened in so many ways, but symbols are something they hardly know, except for in computing. They have become separated from an ancient kind of thinking, oblivious to symbolism in religion, in stories, and in art. The chain has been broken, so it's no wonder a young man or woman may not understand what a wafer has to do with the body of Christ, or what a sip of watered wine has to do with his blood.

But all is not lost.

I am certain that symbolism can be taught again, that by reintroducing a knowledge of how it works, Western society would learn once more how to tap into layers of accumulated wisdom that form a backdrop to their lives. It would be like teaching a language that has been forgotten so that an ancient literature could be accessed again, or like learning a formula with the intention of breaking a code.

ARIANE FINISHED HER blue ice cream and licked the bowl with her tongue. She said when she was bigger she would live in a house in

Chefchaouen with a pink pet dinosaur called Floss. She reminded me of myself. We had rumbled through the town more than once on our travels as children. If I closed my eyes, I could see us, sitting on the square, wrapped up in tie-dyed sweaters, licking blue ice cream.

On one visit, my father got talking to a hippie who had followed Jimi Hendrix to Morocco back in '69. He had been too stoned ever to find his hero or to get back home. He was working in a café on one of the backstreets, a café which doubled as hash den, and was trying to find a ride back to England. When he saw our red Ford Cortina pull in, he ran out in a stoned stupor and kissed the front license plate.

My father used to say that hashish had rotted generations of great Arab minds and was set to have the same effect in Europe and beyond. He tried to warn the hippies of the scourge they were facing. When he saw the tie-dyed waiter clutching the front of our station wagon, he told him to give up the weed and to think for himself.

"But I don't want to think for myself, man," said the hippie despondently.

"What?"

"I'm searching for a guru, man," he said. "He'll tell me what to do."

"You don't need a guru, you just need to regain control of your own mind."

The hippie stood up. He was swaying. He pulled a frail gray kitten from his jacket pocket, and touched its head to his lips.

"But you don't understand," he said.

"What don't I understand?"

"I have heard of a guy who can help me."

My father rolled his eyes.

"Yeah," said the hippie, swaying. "He's in England."

"Where does he live?"

"Not sure, man."

"What's his name?"

The hippie stuffed the kitten back in his pocket. He thought for a long time and looked as if he was about to pass out.

"He wrote some books. I've got 'em all, man."

"But what's his name?"

"He's called..."

"What?"

"He's called Idries Shah."

BACK AT THE Caliph's House everything was quiet. The guardians had taken to buying sardines from a bicycle that was pushed through the shantytown twice a day. The crate tied to the back was slithering with fish. The sardines were placed carefully on the stork nest, in the hope of enticing the great bird to return.

When he saw my car approaching down the lane, Osman leapt out the garden door and smothered the children in kisses. He seemed very happy. We went into the house. Zohra fussed around us, grabbed Timur and forced a packet of chewing gum down his throat. The Bear stood in the doorway and asked politely if he might tell me something. I feared a resignation, or news of a family crisis, or a wedding, the kind of thing that tended to result in me parting with large amounts of cash.

"Is it that you are all moving to new apartments?"

"No, Monseiur Tahir," said Marwan. "The move has been canceled."

"Then why are you so happy?"

"It's Osman," said the Bear.

"What about him?"

"His wife..."

"What now?"

"She has come back," he said.

"And he accepted her?"

The Bear nodded.

I punched the air and went out to congratulate Osman.

In Moroccan society it is not fitting for a man to be too familiar with another man's domestic arrangement, unless the two men are married into the same family. Osman was washing my car, sloshing water everywhere. I moved in to shake his hand. He offered his wrist because it was dry.

"I am very happy for you," I said.

Osman grinned so broadly that I glimpsed the back of his throat. "God has blessed me," he said.

THE TWO MAIDS began a new war of attrition for Timur's affection. It started with an offensive initiated by Fatima. She presented my little son with a bow and arrow. I didn't want to undermine her kindness, and so I didn't confiscate the toy. Timur took to stalking Zohra around the house, firing sucker darts at her bottom. Anyone else would have scolded him, but Zohra loved the attention. The next day when she turned up for work, she gave Timur a gift—a soldier set: handcuffs, bandoliers, revolvers, and matching grenades. He seemed very pleased, much more so than I, especially when I saw the brand name: "Osama Bin Laden," followed by the familiar phrase, "Made in China."

Timur grabbed the weaponry and hurried upstairs. He said he was a pirate, and that his bedroom was Treasure Island. Then he rounded up the guardians and shut them in the guest bathroom. He said it was his prison, and charged about on his tricycle, firing sucker darts at anyone who got in the way. Ariane wasn't impressed, especially when she was shot on the back of the head by one of the darts. She came down, screaming. I confiscated the weapons. But then, Fatima rushed out and bought Timur a plastic M-16 assault rifle, the cutting edge of the Osama Bin Laden range. Fortunately, I managed to get my hands on the gun before Timur had seen it. I was beginning to worry for his safety.

"Don't you see that these toys are dangerous, Fatima?"

The maid put a hand to her mouth and giggled.

"He likes them," she said.

"Of course he does, because he's a boy, but they're a bad influence. You have to remember that he's not even three yet."

Just then, Zohra stepped into the house. She was dragging a black plastic bag. Something shiny and long was poking out the end. It looked like a length of plastic guttering pipe.

"It's for little Timur," she said lovingly.

"What is it?"

She pulled back the plastic bag, revealing a terrifying weapon. It was a toy bazooka.

TWO WEEKS PASSED. Spring seemed to come and go in a day, ushering us into an early summer. I bought two dozen cans of paint and some brushes, and encouraged the guardians to work. For once, they didn't resent me. The Bear even went as far as thanking me.

"You are a good man, Monsieur Tahir," he said. "God has seen your kindness."

"He will remember it on Judgment Day," said Marwan.

"Do you three want something from me?" I asked accusingly.

"No, no," they replied, three voices as one.

"Then why are you thanking me?"

"Because we love you, Monsieur Tahir."

AS IT WAS Friday, I went to see Dr. Mehdi and the other regulars at Café Mabrook. I walked through the bidonville, greeting the imam and some of the people we know who live there, down to the Corniche, and across to the café. But something was wrong, very wrong. Café Mabrook was missing.

Where it had stood since the beginning of time there was now a crater. Beside it was a sign. It said in French: "The City of Casablanca apologizes for any inconvenience."

I stood there, staring at the hole, and the sign, rocking back and forth on my heels.

"Bastards!" I snarled to myself. "How could this be allowed?"

Hafad sidled up, and then Zohra's husband. A few minutes later Dr. Mehdi appeared.

"When did this happen?" I asked bitterly.

"Last night," said Hafad.

"Where's Abdul-Latif?"

"He's away from Casablanca, visiting his family in the Atlas."

"He doesn't know about this?"

"Not yet," said Hafad.

"We have to do something," I said boldly.

"What?"

"Um, er, we could start an action committee," I said.

Dr. Mehdi put an arm around my shoulder. "I've got another idea," he said.

"What is it?"

"We could forget about Café Mabrook, and go somewhere else instead."

There was a round of applause from the other regulars. They sauntered off down the Corniche in search of a new haunt. I stayed outside Café Mabrook for a few minutes, as if paying my respects in private to a deceased friend.

Then I ran after the others.

chapter twenty-four

When you arrive at the sea, you
Do not talk of the tributary.

Hakim Sanai

From time to time life sends you someone who is so unexpected that you wonder how you ever lived without them.

In May, Rachana and the children went to India to visit my in-laws and I felt free from all responsibility. I decided to travel south on rough local transport and have another go at finding the story in my heart. Until then I had been quite lackadaisical in my search, and felt it was time to strive for real progress.

Over the years I have learned that real adventure can only come about through zigzag travel. One of life's great sensations is walking along a road without any idea where it leads or what will happen next.

So I made my way south of Casablanca, on the road to Marrakech. A truck carrying cement bound from Mèknes picked me up. It was so decrepit that the driver had to stop every half hour to pump air into the tires. He said that once, long before, the truck had been new and he had been young.

"Where did the years go?" he said, as he fed the wheel between his calloused hands. I asked him if he had a story in his heart.

"The only thing I have in my heart is a pain," he said. "It comes every morning and every night. It's due to smoking too much when I was a young man. It serves me right. Young men are fools but it is old men who pay for their mistakes."

The truck driver pulled the key from the ignition and let his tired old vehicle slide to a graceful halt. We both jumped down into the dust and choked until our faces were red.

"I think I'll stay here," I said.

"You are young and foolish," said the driver. "Stay here and you will choke to death on the dust."

"I'll go to that café."

"The coffee will kill you," the driver grunted.

"Well, I may meet someone interesting."

"There's never anyone interesting in places like this, just thieves," he said, forcing his weight down onto an ancient foot-pump.

He paused to press his calloused palm onto mine, and I crossed the road in search of coffee. The café had no name. It was the kind of place frequented by drivers of worn-out cement trucks from Mèknes. The walls were bare, peeling lilac paint, dust, and broken chairs. I sat down. The waiter didn't come over at first, as if he was too busy or didn't want the business. I spent five minutes eagerly trying to catch his eye. It seemed absurd as I was the only customer. Eventually he sauntered to my table with an ashtray and a glass of water.

"The dust is very bad," he said, choking. "It drives a man mad."

I commiserated, asked for coffee, and sat back on the broken chair, waiting for something to happen. In Africa the bleakest outlook can be changed miraculously in a moment. It is a question of maintaining faith, faith in the bizarre.

The coffee arrived, thick and bitter just as I like it. I took a sip, then another, before wiping the dust from my face. Then I looked up. The waiter was looming over me.

"I told you," he said, smirking. "The dust, it will drive you mad."

Just then, as I wondered how I might escape the waiter and his obsession with dust, a well-dressed figure entered. He was six foot two, broad shouldered, and moved with confidence. He looked Moroccan, an aquiline nose and black hair groomed back with a touch of gel.

Outside I heard the rumble of a worn engine sparking fitfully into life. I looked out the window. The cement truck from Mèknes was pulling away from a cloud of diesel fumes. When I turned back, the waiter was leading the suave man to my table.

"You have a connection," he said.

"Do we?"

"Yes."

"What is it?"

"You are both travelers."

"So?"

"So you should sit together."

He pulled out a chair and the man sat down. In an American voice he said, "Only in Morocco would two travelers be expected to share a table in an empty café."

We chatted for almost an hour, and in that time I learned that the man was named Yousef, but preferred to be called Joe. He had lived in northern California since his teens, but had been born in the medina at Marrakech. He returned each year to see his family at their ancestral farm nearby.

He asked why I had paused my journey in such an uncelebrated place. I explained my interest in the folklore of Morocco and the Berber concept of searching for the tale within your heart.

"This is as good a place as any to find it," I said.

There was silence for a while. Then Joe glanced out the window.

"There are streams running under the ground," he said.

I wondered if Joe was a madman, a well-dressed madman. Rachana says that madmen can smell me. They always make a beeline for me, usually pinning me to a wall at a party or into my window seat on a long-haul flight.

"I don't follow you," I said.

"In the south of Morocco people believe that there are streams running under the ground."

"They believe that everywhere, not just in southern Morocco."

"No, no, it's you who don't understand," he said politely. "The streams don't run with water."

He tapped a finger to the glass on the table. "Not this," he said.

"Then what do they run with, if it's not water?"

"With words," he said.

I sensed my back growing warm, the feeling you get when ideas connect, the spark, the moment of breakthrough.

Joe looked at me hard.

"The streams irrigate Morocco," he said, "like water on farmland, they have allowed the civilization to grow, to thrive. Why is Morocco what it is? Why does it mesmerize everyone who comes here, with its colors, with its atmosphere?"

Joe paused for a moment, sipped his coffee. "It's because of the streams," he said.

THE SUFIS SAY that teaching stories belong to human society as a whole, and that if tapped, their power is sufficient to unlock man's entire potential. They say that until their minds are stirred with stories, people are asleep. The stories are a kind of key, a catalyst, a device to help humanity think in a certain way, to help us wake up from the sleep.

The subterranean streams that Joe spoke of reminded me of the Sufi idea, which was no coincidence. For Morocco has been home to Sufis since the advent of Islam thirteen centuries ago. The streams were reminiscent, too, of the Aboriginal "Songlines," invisible pathways linking the land with the history of a people who lived upon it.

The more I thought about them, the more the waterless streams made sense.

I had hoped that Joe would invite me back to his family's farm. He had said it was no more than a stone's throw from the café. But he didn't extend an invitation. Perhaps he thought I was the maniac. After two cups of coffee he stood up, thanked me for the conversation, and excused himself.

Over the following days, I traveled from one small community to the next, struggling to make myself understood, pleading for stories. Much of the time, the people I encountered sent me on a little farther to someone else, like the illiterate fool in the story with a note he couldn't understand, a note that read "Send the fool another mile." Some of them did tell me tales. Others did not. Frequently, I would be taken in, dusted down, and fed with a banquet by people who had almost nothing.

Zigzag travel has tremendous highs, and its lows can be depressingly deep. The lowest point was waiting for a bus that never came near a small town called Guisser, northeast of Marrakech. I had spent almost all my money, and hadn't found a bank as I had hoped. It was getting dark. I didn't know what to do. Then out of the twilight stepped a navy blue uniform with a matching cap. I braced myself for trouble, or at least to give an explanation. I wished the policeman a good evening, told him I was waiting for the night bus to Casablanca.

"There isn't a night bus," he said. "There's no bus from here. What will you do?" asked the officer.

"I suppose I'll sleep here," I said.

He held up a hand.

"You will stay in my house," he said, taking me by the arm and leading me up the main street to a concrete apartment building. We climbed stairs, more and more of them, until we were on the uppermost floor.

Keys jingled and the front door swung open. "I live here alone," he said. "My family are in Marrakech."

The officer cooked up a pot of mint tea, and we sat together in silence.

"Shouldn't you be on duty?" I asked.

"Oh no, the town's safe," he said.

We went through the salvo of questions, familiar to any traveler: Where are you from? Where are you going? Why are you in our town? I knocked back the replies in quick succession and said: "I'm here because I am searching for the story in my heart."

The officer's face lit up. "I have a story," he said. "It has been told and retold in my family for a long time."

"Would you tell it to me?"

"Of course I will!" said the policeman, pouring more tea. "I will tell it to you at once."

I sat back, and the officer cleared his throat.

"In the name of God, the Compassionate, the Merciful," he said. "There was once a young man who was very restless. He traveled from one village to the next hoping to find a teacher who could teach him something of value. People would see him going from one place to another, and they treated him kindly, because he was a good young man, very well-mannered. One day he met a sage who was regarded as very wise indeed.

"The youth said to him:

" 'I am very restless and I cannot stop running from one place to another. It's the way I am and people think it strange. I wish I could be happy and I wish I could settle down.' The wise man listened to the boy, thought for a while, and replied: 'I understand your condition, and I can help you. But if you want me to be of help, you must not question the remedy that I am going to prescribe.' 'O wise sage,' he replied, 'of course I would not question your orders. I shall follow them exactly even if it means I do nothing else in the remainder of my days.'

"The wise man then said: 'You must take to the road and travel far and wide. On your travels you must search for the happiest man in the world. When you find him, you must ask him for his shirt.' It sounded like an unusual treatment, but the young man had made a pledge to do as he was asked, and so he said farewell to the sage, and took to the road.

"He traveled north, and he traveled south, and he traveled east, and he traveled west, and he met all sorts of people. Some of them were rich, others very poor. Some were brave and others were cowards. And he asked them all if they knew where he could find the happiest man in the world.

"The youth got many replies. Some people said to him: 'I am very happy, but there is someone much happier who lives over that hill,' and other people said: 'Leave us alone or we will knock you down.' The young man searched throughout his own kingdom, and traveled to the next kingdom and the next. Days became weeks, and weeks became months and then years. He didn't rest for a moment. Until, quite exhausted by the search, he stopped to rest under a tree on the edge of a great forest, and slipped off his shoes.

"As he sat there, he heard laughter. It was so loud that the birds did not roost, but circled round and round. And it was so thunderous that it caused the leaves to fall off the trees. Anyone else would have been shocked by the sound, but the young man—who by now was not quite so young—grew very excited. He slipped his shoes back on and followed the sound of laughter.

"The forest was thick and dark. It would have been silent, too, was there not the rumbling sound of laughter coming from the distance. The man followed the sound and, presently, he came to a lake. On the lake there was an island, and on the island stood a small house. The laughter seemed to be coming from the house. The man could not see a boat, and so he jumped into the water and swam over to the island.

"Dripping and cold, he went up to the house and knocked on the door. There was no answer, but the laughing did not stop. So, plucking up his courage, the man pushed the door open. Inside, on a carpet, sat an old man. He wore a big turban on his head, the color of strawberries. He was laughing so wildly that tears were rolling down his cheeks. The seeker crept up, until he was standing at the edge of the carpet. He said very quietly: 'Excuse me, Master, but I am from a kingdom far from here, and I have been sent to find the happiest man in the world, and you look remarkably happy to me. Please tell me, is there anyone happier than you?'

"The laughing man pulled a handkerchief from up his sleeve and blew his nose. 'I am very happy,' he said, howling with laughter again, 'and I can tell you that I certainly don't know anyone as happy as me. Hahahahaha!' 'Then sir, could I ask you a favor?' 'Yes, what?' 'Would you take off your shirt and please give it to me?'

"At that point the old man laughed and laughed and laughed and laughed. He laughed so much that all the animals in the forest called out in fear. 'My boy, if you had taken the time to look at me,' said the sage, weeping tears of laughter, 'you would have seen that I am not wearing any shirt at all.'

"The young man's eyes widened as he realized it was true. He was about to say something, but the sage was unwinding his turban. He unwound coil after coil, laying the red cloth on the carpet. It was only as he got to the end that the man realized the truth: that the sage was none other than the wise man who had sent him on his journey in the first place.

" 'Tell me, O Master,' said the young man, 'why didn't you inform me you were the happiest man in the world at the start? It would have saved me a lot of time and bother.' 'Because,' said the sage, 'for you to be calmed, you needed to experience certain things, see other things and meet various people. I knew it would be a long process, but if I had told you at the beginning what it would involve, you would have run away and would never have been cured.' "

WHEN HE HAD finished the story, I thanked the police officer. Then I sat in silence. He didn't try to speak, as if he understood that the tale was working away at me. I heard the door of the apartment open and close, and knew I was alone. I felt calm, very calm and, in a way I could not quite fathom, I felt more complete. I just sat there, my mind racing. Then, something happened that I find awkward to explain. My chest began to warm up. It got warmer and warmer until it was no longer warm, but quite hot. My mouth had been closed. It was forced open and a blast of air was sucked in. There was nothing I could do about it. My eyes were wide open, my hands bright red.

And all the while "The Happiest Man in the World" worked away. Like a bank robber cracking a safe, it twisted an invisible dial in my chest, until it had gained entry to my heart. I still do not understand how it worked or quite what happened. But I felt the story penetrate deep through the layers of tissue and muscle with ingenious ease.

I could feel it in there, safe in its own sanctuary. At the same time I knew the story had always been there, been with me. It was lunacy, of course, for there are so many stories in the world and such slim probability of finding the one in your heart.

As I was going over the odds stacked against fortune, the door to the apartment opened again. It was the policeman. I had quite forgotten I was taking refuge in his home. He had bought kebabs. The room filled with the aroma of roasting lamb.

"The story is inside me," I said, as he opened the package.

He nodded very gently and smiled. "It's inside us all," he said.

ONCE BACK IN Casablanca I rooted through my books for any mention of the streams. There were none, not even in Westermarck's thousand-page magnum opus *Ritual and Belief in Morocco.* I strolled out into the garden at dusk and petted my dogs, lazing on the lawn. The air was perfumed with datura flowers, the sky still and steel-blue. Marwan had just arrived for his shift. He clambered through a hole in the hibiscus hedge and shook my hand. I wished his family well.

"Thanks be to God," he said. "We can afford my wife's cataract operation now. She will see clearly again." He paused for half a breath. "*Inshallah*, if God wills it," he said.

I asked him if he had ever heard of the streams of words, stories, running underground.

"Yes, I have," said Marwan. "They keep the world level, and when they hit a stone they burst up into a spring."

"But there's no water in them," I said. "So how could you have a spring?"

Marwan patted down his gray hair with a hand. "They are not springs like that," he said. "Change your thinking. Then you will understand."

"I will try," I said.

"The springs are places of wisdom, sometimes where a saint has lived, taught, or died. They are places where stories are told, and where healing is done. The 'water' in them, the words, the stories, are energy, and they are knowledge."

"But why can't I find any mention of these streams in any books?"

The carpenter glanced down at the grass and then up at my face. "This is an ancient tradition," he said. "It is part of the fabric of our country. As you live here longer you will see that, in Morocco, there are many things you will never find in books."

IN JUNE I traveled to Afghanistan to film the documentary about my search for the lost treasure of the country's first modern king, Ahmed Shah Durrani. The journey was wrapped in worry, not so much my anxiety for the danger we faced, but worry I knew Rachana would be feeling at home. Most of the time I felt sick in my stomach, sick at the thought of her feeling sick for the thought of me. The flight from Casablanca to Kabul took me across North Africa, the Middle East, and to the crossroads of Central Asia. I found it incredible to think that the airplane didn't pass over a single non-Muslim land, that the early followers of Islam had covered the same ground in the century after the Prophet's death, converting as they went. I tried to imagine the battle-worn champions of Islam finally arriving at the azure waters of the Atlantic, their Sea of Darkness.

Many of the tales I found in Morocco had been brought from the Bedouin heartland of Arabia. A great number of them must have originated even farther east, from Persia, India, or Afghanistan. North Africa's pilgrimage route stretches through Morocco and down into Mali, as far as Timbuktu, and across Algeria and Libya, to Egypt. For well over a thousand years, pilgrims have traveled the path in caravans across the desert, in fear for their lives. It's easy to imagine them huddled in caravanserais and under the stars, their camels hobbled around them for warmth, telling and retelling tales.

Just as pilgrims made the Hajj from the Maghreb, they traveled from the east as well, from as far as India and beyond, from China's province of Xinjiang. To go on the pilgrimage at least once in a lifetime is one of the Five Pillars of Islam, a solemn duty of every Muslim. The reason is, of course, to pledge devotion to God at the Kaaba, Mecca, the birthplace of the Islamic faith. But the impact of people traveling over centuries in wave after wave, heading to the holy city and back to their far-flung lands, has been even more profound.

Almost like bees pollinating flowers in gardens far from their hives, the pilgrims have had an extraordinary effect in spreading knowledge and Islamic culture over a vast region. Works of mathematics, astronomy, chemistry, and the arts were disseminated and studied from China to Morocco. In the same way, the matrix formed by the pilgrims and their routes dispersed stories, too, scattering them across much of the known world. The effect has led to a cultural harmony and a likeness in design, whether it be in Morocco, Arabia, Iraq, or northern India.

The Americas have been affected by Arab culture, too, in ways that are sometimes overlooked. In my travels through Mexico and Latin America, I have found the belief in *Mal de Ojo,* the Evil Eye, and have seen terracotta tiles and "Moroccan" architecture, cuisine, and other traditions, brought west by the Spanish conquistadores five centuries ago. Spanish culture is, of course, steeped in medieval Arab culture, an underbelly awaiting visitors with observant eyes.

MY ONE RECURRING dream now is of the prisoner who was chained in the cell beside mine. I used to hear him groaning at dawn, after a night in the torture cells. Once, toward the end, I was led back to my own cell without a blindfold and caught a glimpse of him. He was crouched, huddled in the corner, his face hidden by black beard, his hands wrapped in blood-soaked bandages. Unlike mine, the cell was painted with large black and white spirals. They covered the walls, the ceiling, the floor, and even the bars. For a fleeting moment we caught eye contact. My fear was echoed in his gaze. I don't know who the prisoner was, or what he was guilty of doing, but there was a sense of understanding between us.

The journeys through Afghanistan, and the film we made there, helped me to have closure on the nightmares I suffered after being released from neighboring Pakistan.

We never found the lost treasure of Mughal India in Afghanistan, a treasure reputed to be valued at current rates at more than five hundred billion dollars. But in many ways, we found far more.

The legend goes that, falling ill with cancer, Ahmed Shah concealed the vast hoard of gold and precious gems in a cave system. He supposedly ordered the men who had been charged to conceal the loot to be executed, along with the horses that transported the treasure into the caves. We may not have found the fortune itself but, in a cave system near Bamiyan in central Afghanistan, we came upon dozens of human skeletons deep in a mountain. In one of the tunnels, even farther into the mountain, we found the bones of horses.

On my travels through Afghanistan, there were two small episodes that pricked my consciousness like smelling salts. The first was while visiting the magnificent Friday Mosque in Herat, located on the western edge of Afghanistan. The building is celebrated throughout the Islamic world for the fine mosaics that adorn its façade. I had heard that beside the mosque was a small workshop in which master craftsmen continued to cut mosaics as they had done for almost a thousand years. I asked if I could visit the craftsmen and immediately found myself ushered into their atelier.

Half a dozen old men were chipping away at glazed tiles, making the mosaics. They didn't look up, just kept on chipping with their hammers, their heads wound with turbans, their legs crossed.

Drawing closer to get a good view of their work, I noticed something, something that I found quite astonishing. I was at the far end of the Islamic world, almost as far as I could have been from Morocco. But the hammers used by the craftsmen were identical to the ones used in Fès, where they are called *manqash*.

The other incident that touched me was while sitting in a *chaikhana* at Balkh in northern Afghanistan, where Alexander the Great had made his headquarters in the third century B.C. The room was thick with conversation, and with wood-smoke from the samovar. I got chatting to a Pushtun who was in the carpet business, transporting Turkomen rugs down to his native Qandahar. There was a lull in the conversation. We sat sipping our tea, pondering our circumstances. Then, as happens in Afghan teahouses, the trader touched my knee.

"I will tell you a story of Mulla Nasrudin," he said. Nasrudin is, of course, the Afghan incarnation of Joha, the Arab folk hero. The Nasrudin story that the carpet dealer recounted in Balkh was one that had been imparted to me a few weeks before, by a student in Marrakech.

This is how it went:

One day Mulla Nasrudin knocked at his neighbor's door and asked him if he could borrow his biggest cooking pot, as his in-laws were coming for dinner. The neighbor, who was a very greedy man, resisted, but eventually agreed. The next day, Nasrudin returned the pot and thanked the neighbor. After handing it over, he gave the greedy neighbor a smaller pot. "What's this for?" said the neighbor. "Oh," said the Mulla, "you see, while your big pot was with me, it gave birth to this little pot. As it is the offspring of what is yours, I am giving it to you."

The greedy neighbor was very pleased at getting a second pot for nothing. So, the next time that Nasrudin came over and asked to borrow his big pot, he was only too happy to oblige. The day after, the neighbor hammered on his door and demanded his pot back. Nasrudin opened the door. "We have established, have we not, that a pot can give birth to another pot?" he asked. The neighbor nodded his head, hoping for another free vessel. "Well, just as one pot can give birth to another pot, a pot can also pass away. I have the unfortunate task to inform you that at ten o'clock last night your big pot dropped dead!"

chapter twenty-five

Much travel is needed before a raw man is ripened.

Arab proverb

Three days after my return from Afghanistan, I received a call from Waleed in Fès. The line was very bad. I could hardly make out what he was saying.

"I will call you back," I said.

"No, do not hang up!" spat Waleed.

"Why not?"

"Because the air is filled with words," he said. "Millions of conversations. How do I know that you will find me again?"

"Then shout what you want to tell me."

"Monsieur Tahir, there is something very important!"

I swallowed hard. When a Moroccan tells you something is important, it generally involves asking the favor of a loan.

"Please explain."

"Can you keep a secret?"

"Yes, what is it?"

"There's a house," Waleed replied. "A house in the medina. It's for sale. But you must not tell a soul."

"Look, I don't have any money," I said. "I've already got a house in Casablanca, and it's taken up all my money. I'm broke."

"You don't understand, Monsieur," said the voice amid the crackles and distortion.

"Yes, I do."

"No, no."

"What don't I understand?"

"This house is very different."

"How?"

"It's very old."

"But all the houses in the medina are old!"

"It's different from all the others," he said, repeating himself.

"Tell me, how is it different, Waleed?"

"Because it's the House of the Storytellers," he said.

AT FIRST, FINDING the story in my heart filled me with a new kind of energy. It was as if I had tapped into a reserve of power deep inside me. Rachana noticed right away. She said I seemed happier about myself, that I was calmer. She was right. I was more content than I had been in a very long while. But at the same time, finding my story had been something of an anticlimax and I found myself confused. It's often like that in life. The search for something tends to create its own energy, so much so that when you eventually find what you think you have been searching for, you feel shortchanged. I began to ponder the matter a great deal, wondering why reaching a conclusion could be such a dissatisfying experience. The more I thought of it, the more depressed I began to feel. It was then I remembered something my father had once told me. He was observing how people would come to him for answers, and how—when they were presented with an answer— they often felt miffed, as if they deserved more. He said to me: "It is not that the answer is wrong, but that the seeker does not yet realize its value." I had asked if he could elaborate. He said he would do so, that he would answer my question with a story:

"Once upon a time there was a farmer's wife. She was out in an orchard picking apples from a tree, when one of the apples fell down a hole in the ground. She tried to reach it, but could not. So she looked all around for someone to help her, and she saw a little bird sitting on the branches of the tree.

"She said to the bird: 'Little bird, please fly down the hole and bring the apple back to me!'

"The bird said, 'Tweet! Tweet!' which, in bird language, means, 'No, I won't!'

"The farmer's wife was angry at the bird, and she said, 'You are a very naughty little bird!'

"And then she saw a cat. She said to the cat: 'Cat, cat, jump up at the bird until he flies down into the hole and brings the apple for me.'

"But the cat just said, 'Miaow, miaow!' which, in cat language, means, 'No, I won't!'

"And the farmer's wife said, 'You are a very naughty little cat!'

"Just then she saw a dog, and she said to the dog: 'Dog, dog, please chase the cat and so she jumps up at the bird, so that he flies down the hole and brings back the apple for me.'

"But the dog said, 'Bow-wow-wow!' which, in dog language, means, 'No, I won't!'

"And the farmer's wife said, 'You are a very naughty little dog!'

"Just then, the farmer's wife spotted a bee. And she said to the bee: 'Bee, bee, sting the dog so that he chases the cat, so that she jumps at the bird, and he flies down the hole, and fetches the apple for me.'

"But the bee just said, 'Bzz-bzz!' which, in bee language, means, 'No, I won't!'

"And the farmer's wife said, 'You really are a very naughty bee!'

"Then she looked around and she saw a beekeeper, and she said to the beekeeper: 'Beekeeper, beekeeper, please go and tell the bee to sting the dog, to chase the cat, to jump at the bird, so that he flies down the hole and fetches the apple for me.'

"And the beekeeper said, 'No, I won't!'

"And the farmer's wife said, 'Good gracious, what a naughty bee-keeper you are!'

"And at that moment, the farmer's wife saw a length of rope lying on the ground. And she said to the rope: 'Rope, rope, tie up the beekeeper until he tells the bee to sting the dog, to chase the cat, to jump down the hole, to get the apple for me.'

"The rope did not say anything at all. It just lay there on the ground. 'Oh!' exclaimed the farmer's wife. 'What a naughty, naughty rope you are!'

"Then the farmer's wife looked around and she saw a fire. She said to the fire: 'Fire, fire, please burn the rope so that it ties up the beekeeper, so that he tells the bee to sting the dog, to chase the cat, to jump at the bird, to fetch the apple for me.'

"The fire didn't say anything at all.

" 'You are a very naughty little fire!' said the farmer's wife.

"She looked around again, wondering what to do, when she saw a puddle of water. So she said to the puddle: 'Puddle, puddle, please put out the fire, because it won't burn the rope, because the rope won't tie up the beekeeper, because he won't tell the bee to sting the dog, to chase the cat, to jump at the bird, to get the apple for me.'

"But the water in the puddle took no notice at all. And the farmer's wife said, 'My oh my, what a naughty puddle you are!'

"And then she saw a cow. And she said to the cow: 'Cow, cow, please drink up the puddle, so that it puts out the fire, and it burns the rope, and it ties up the beekeeper, and it tells the bee to sting the dog, to chase the cat, to jump at the bird, to fetch the apple for me.'

"The cow said, 'Moo, moo, moo!' which, in cow language, means, 'No, I won't!' And the farmer's wife said, 'Oh, good gracious, what a very naughty cow you are!'

"And then the farmer's wife looked around one last time and she saw the little bird sitting in the tree, the bird which had started all the problems in the first place. And she said to the bird: 'Little bird, little bird, please would you peck the cow for me?' And the bird said, 'All right then, I'll peck the cow but don't expect me to fetch the apple for you!' And the naughty little bird pecked the cow, and the cow started to drink up the puddle, and the puddle started to put out the fire, which began to burn the rope, which started to tie up the beekeeper, who started to tell the bee, and the bee started to sting the dog, who started to chase the cat, who started to jump up at the bird, who had pecked the cow.

"And then," said my father, clearing his throat, "the wind flew down the hole and brought back the apple for the farmer's wife."

OTTOMAN TELEPHONED ME at the end of the week and asked if I had time to meet him. He said that he wanted to spend an hour or two with me, remembering our mutual friend Hicham Harass. The next evening, we met in a fish restaurant down at the port. The last trawlers were heading out into the black Atlantic waters for the night. On the quay the fishermen were gathering up nets, checking them for tears. Ottoman was already in the restaurant when I arrived. He shook my hand, placed it over his heart, and thanked God for my safe return from Afghanistan.

"You must write a book to show the West there's more to the Arab world than Al-Qaeda and suicide bombers," he said.

"Do you think they will listen to me?"

"They must listen," said Ottoman.

"I see the East through one eye, and the West through the other," I said. "I understand how they both feel, but I don't know how to tell one about the other."

"There's a way to teach," he replied, "it's so subtle that the student doesn't realize he's being taught anything at all."

"How does it work?"

"By silent teaching, a kind of sleight of hand," he said. "In the way that a teaching story seeps in and sows a grain of wisdom. You don't see it coming, and don't know it's there until it's working for you."

Ottoman broke a roll and smothered it with butter. "We have used this method for centuries in the Arab world. You have been brought up with it—taught to use it—like the rest of us."

"My father was obsessed with teaching stories," I said.

"Of course he was," Ottoman said. "We are all obsessed with them. They are our culture, the way we learn."

Right then, sitting there with Ottoman, I had an idea. What if I could start my own kind of College of Storytellers, like my father had kept going until just before his death, to promote teaching through stories as he had done?

An enormous platter of fresh fish was ushered to the table. Ottoman chose the finest fillet, squeezed lemon juice all over it, and placed it on my plate. He could see his idea was soaking in. The waiter set a bottle of red Mèknes wine on the table. I poured two glasses. We looked each other in the eye, clinked glasses.

"To our teachers," said Ottoman.

THE NEXT DAY I took the train down to Fès. As we rumbled across the even brown fields of farmland, the House of the Storytellers occupied my thoughts. I am not a person who finds it easy to stick to a quiet life. I become preoccupied with things, with ideas and with dreams. The more I try to force them out of my head, the more they take root. The only remedy is to face the fantasy head-on, to dive into it.

I found myself thinking about my father and the extraordinary effect he had on people. He was almost incapable of having a normal relationship, for he touched people very deeply. I think part of it lay in the way he observed people. When he encountered someone, he would say certain things or act in a certain way and then watch what response his behavior elicited.

Sometimes people despised him as a result, or went crazy, just as Slipper Feet had done. Other times they listened to what he said and went off to apply his advice. Such people were the ones he held in the highest regard. Others became obsessed with him, or begged him to be a guru figure, something that went against everything he believed in.

A few people were touched by him in ways that still fascinate me.

My parents always had someone to drive them around in England and abroad. A list of long-suffering gardeners ferried us back and forth from Tunbridge Wells to the farthest reaches of Morocco. As far as my father was concerned, being driven was the perfect arrangement. He got taken from A to B and was free to talk to the gardener all the way there and all the way back.

Then one day my mother took her driving test and passed. So as not to be humiliated, my father rushed out and signed up with a driving school himself. He was in his fifties. He took dozens of lessons, and began a strange and sometimes comical relationship with Mr. Slaughter, the driving instructor in Tunbridge Wells.

After many dozens of lessons and several failures at the test, my father passed. A party was held and celebrations continued through days and nights. The driving license was tossed in a drawer and was never used once. It was a symbol of ability rather than a document for the roads.

Years passed.

My father continued to be driven about by my mother, and more increasingly by me. We spent hundreds of hours crisscrossing London together in the hours before dawn, searching the capital's markets for Arabian antiques.

Then one afternoon an urgent message arrived. It was garbled and confused. Mr. Slaughter the driving instructor was gravely ill. He was on his deathbed and was about to expire. But before he crossed into the next world, he wanted to see one man again…a former pupil from Afghanistan.

My father rushed down to Tunbridge Wells, where he found Mr. Slaughter attached to hospital tubes, barely clinging to life. He sat at the bedside and held his teacher's hand. They hardly exchanged words. The time for conversation had come to an end.

The next day Mr. Slaughter died.

AT Fès, I found Waleed sitting on a wall opposite Bab Er-Rsif. He was picking his teeth with a stick, memorizing a document about land tax.

"I do not know you well, Monsieur Tahir," he said, "but I have seen how you think."

"How do I think?"

"Your head is like a billiard table, and your thoughts are like the balls going in every direction," he said.

"Dynamic?"

Waleed put away the document. "Chaotic," he replied.

We threaded our way through the maze, dodging a thousand carts heaped with little pink flowers, televisions, and snails. I had asked Waleed to take me directly to the House of the Storytellers. Although he had been keen on the telephone, he wasn't so enthusiastic now that I was in town. He said the place was in bad shape, that there were problems with the neighbors, that it was too hot to explore the medina. I couldn't understand why he was stalling.

He stopped at a dim metal foundry and shouted a question to a man working a wrought-iron curl at the forge.

"What's the matter?"

"The house is locked up," said Waleed.

"Can't we get the key?"

"Not until tomorrow."

"Then what can we do now?"

"We'll go and see Abdou."

"Who?"

"My friend Abdou."

"Where?"

"At Glaoui Palace."

When we packed up and left England, I looked forward to living in a land where I could allow my delusions to run wild. I was lured by the idea of available parking, affordable restaurants, bright sunlight, and the possibility of having my underwear ironed. But there was something more appealing than any other delusion—to drop by a palace for tea.

Waleed said the Glaoui dynasty had been one of the great survival stories of Morocco, until they were excommunicated after siding too closely with the French. I had read their story in Gavin Maxwell's fine book *Lords of the Atlas,* but had no idea there was anything left of their empire. Waleed stopped at an imposing yet plain double-fronted door, crafted from a sheet of rusted iron, peppered with studs. He slammed a hand to the metal and called out.

"No one's home," I said.

Waleed banged the door again. "Wait, it's a big place, and Abdou doesn't move fast."

Then the door opened. A figure was standing on the threshold. He wasn't what I expected. Indeed, he took me by such surprise that I stepped back into the road. Abdou had the look of a man who had escaped from our world—a world of the banal—into another far more fantastic realm. You could see it in his eyes. They were hollow, and at the same time they were distended, a little maniacal, as if he had glimpsed a great secret. Abdou was average height, had an impressive crop of Afro hair, an emaciated body, and feet that seemed not to touch the ground, but rather hover above it.

Waleed leaned forward and kissed his hand. A moment later, we were inside the palace, following Abdou as he hovered through the immense stark entranceway, down steps, and into the Disneyland of his mind.

Moroccan mansions are all about surprise. They invite the visitor through an unassuming door, through a passage that, like an *amuse bouche,* seeks to heighten one's eagerness for the main plate. The entrance was large enough to receive visitors on horseback. It was dark, illuminated by miniature windows high up on the massive stone walls. At one time there had been birds, perhaps doves, kept in a cage there. But, like the other features, they had served their time and gone.

Abdou glided forward without emotion. He turned left, stepped down through doors. I followed him with Waleed, and we found ourselves in a courtyard of tremendous size. Cloisters ran down opposite sides, lined with grand arches, one after the next. In the middle of the great courtyard was a pool, edged in rusting *fer forgé*. The excessive heat had caused the water to evaporate, much to the distress of the twenty or so ducks which were attempting to get afloat on the slime. Nearby, tethered by a chain, was one of the most ferocious and furriest dogs I have ever come across. The chain was long, but not quite long enough to savage the ducks. The animal's life was spent charging forward at full speed, until the chain snapped tight and choked it. The afternoon was so hot, and the dog's coat so thick, that it could only mount three or four rapid attempts to get the ducks before it was forced to seek refuge in a cardboard wigwam that Abdou had made.

The palace had once been one of the most opulent addresses in Fès, until, that is, the Glaoui's disgrace. Their lands and properties were confiscated. The leading members escaped into exile if they were lucky, or ended up dead, or behind bars if they were not.

Abdou lived in the palace alone. He explained with some pride that his last name was Glaoui. I assumed he was part of the family.

"He's not a real Glaoui," Waleed said, reading my thoughts. "He's one of the servants. They used to take their master's family name."

We toured the palace, taking in the splendid mosaic walls and floors, the grandeur that was slipping easily from wrack to ruin. Abdou had turned one of the great salons into his studio. He was an artist, painting cosmic fantasies on glass, behind which he installed miniature pink Christmas tree lights. He was a musician, too, as well as a sculptor, and had built a grotesque leering statue from musical instruments.

The great courtyard led to a kitchen of unsettling starkness and size, and through into another spacious courtyard.

Waleed said it had once been the harem.

"Don't you ever get frightened living here alone?" I asked.

Abdou dug a hand into his Afro and pulled out a paintbrush.

"I have my work," he said distantly.

"He seems a little psychotic," I whispered.

"He's a genius," said Waleed calmly.

"I'm sure he is."

"Genius is a tightrope," said Waleed. "It calls for perfect balance."

I didn't quite understand what he meant, but it sounded profound.

"Does anyone ever buy his art?"

"Of course not," said Waleed sternly. "That proves what a genius he is."

THAT EVENING, I went alone to the Restaurant Sheherazade in the new town. It was a Moroccan version of *Fawlty Towers*, packed with foreigners, all pretending they were enjoying the inedible food. The swing doors flapped open. Robert Twigger burst in, scanned the room, and swanned up to my table.

"Vile, isn't it?"

"What?"

"That gunk on your plate."

"It's the coq au vin," I said.

"Like hell it is."

"How's the search for the dwarf race?"

Twigger pulled up a chair, sat down, and dipped a crust of bread in my sauce. "A bit like the coq au vin," he said.

"How's that?"

"The more you put up with it, the better you imagine it is."

"Got any leads?"

"One or two."

"Folklore?"

"Yeah."

"Haven't you got to get up into the mountains sometime? After all, that's where lost little people are likely to be."

Twigger picked a bone from my plate and stuck the end in his mouth. "You're right," he said. "But I'm a sucker for what anthropologists call 'imagined advancement.'"

"What's that?"

"It's when you spend so long trying to progress at something where the odds against you succeeding are fifty billion to one, that you lull yourself into a false sense of security."

"You lie to yourself?"

"That's right. Everyone's struggling to keep the lie alive."

"Like in 'The Emperor's New Clothes'?"

"Exactly," said Twigger, tossing the bone back onto my plate. "Or like pretending to the waiter that the coq au vin didn't taste like grilled rat."

THAT NIGHT, AS I rested my head on the pillow, I had a flashback. I was in my early teens, walking with my father through the woods at our family home. He seemed to take great comfort in being surrounded by trees, and would stop from time to time to pull a creeper away from a seedling, or to clear a clump of thick grass that was smothering a shoot.

"Only a few of these saplings will reach maturity and grow into trees," he said. "They all have the same chance, but some succeed while others, most of them, will fail."

We walked on across a carpet of bluebells, and down to where the woods met grassland. My father pointed to a young tree growing on the open grass.

"That oak was planted on the day you were born," he said. "An acorn was put in a pot and covered with a little light soil. Look at how well it's doing," he said. "There's great hope for that tree. But there's always a threat—it could be hit by blight, have its roots flooded, be struck by lightning. Do you see?"

"Yes, Baba."

"Tahir Jan, we have passed on to you certain information," he said. "It may be dormant now, but with time it will wake up, take root, and lead to growth."

I didn't reply. At the time I felt a little swollen with pride that anyone would have bothered to nurture my development with such care. At the same time I felt a tinge of resentment that I couldn't be like all the other boys I knew—carefree.

It has been almost twenty years since I last saw the oak tree planted as an acorn on the day of my birth. I think about it sometimes, as if there's a strange bond between us, and I wonder if it now has seedlings of its own.

Over the years I have tried to allow the values to shape me, just as I have begun passing them on to Ariane and Timur. I have come to understand the real value locked in the teaching stories passed down by my father to me, and by fathers and mothers to their sons and daughters across Morocco and the Arab world.

It is the value of selflessness.

My father never knew my children. He died four years before Ariane was born. Inside my heart there may be the story of "The Happiest Man in the World," but there is sorrow as well. I am grieved that half of the generation that produced me did not see the generation I have produced. But then, they have met in a more profound way. My father is inside my children as he is inside me, just as is everyone who ever held the baton in their hand.

AT TEN THE next morning, Waleed took me through the medina to the House of the Storytellers. The route was so complicated that I had little chance of ever finding the place if I did buy it. There was a passing joke in the old city of a foreigner who had bought a sprawling medieval palace then gone out to buy some milk for the tea. He had hurried home with the milk, but had never been able to find the house again. It was a good joke, but I could easily imagine it being true.

We turned right off the jewelry bazaar, and weaved back through narrower and narrower streets, until we came to a murky passageway. It was less than five feet high, and had sides that seemed to be closing in.

"Follow me," said Waleed.

I did and found myself in a confined opening, facing a door.

"Is this it?"

"Wait and see."

Waleed knocked. An extremely old man opened the door, smirked confidently, and led the way in. I have visited dozens of houses in the medinas of Marrakech, Mèknes, and Fès. Many have charm, a sense that they are jewels waiting to be revived. A few boast features that impress or amaze—fabulous fountains, magical views over the old city, tombs, or even slave quarters. But none I had seen until then had matched the atmosphere of the House of the Storytellers.

The floor plan was not large, about the size of the salons at Dar Khalifa. But there was a presence, a sensation of something so grave and so important that it connected anyone who entered with a formidable chain of history.

The owner led us into the main courtyard. The tiles were a harlequin of orange, white, and black and were so old that the colors had been worn in places, exposing the terracotta. The walls were adorned with striking carved plasterwork, phrases from the Qur'an.

"When was this built?" I asked.

"About eight hundred years ago," said the man.

"Who lives here?"

"Just me. My family are all dead."

"What's its history?"

"People used to come here to talk."

"To tell stories?"

"Yes, stories. They would sit here and listen and they would learn." He paused, touched a wrinkled hand to his head. "They would learn about good and bad," he said.

He led me through the small kitchen, to a staircase hidden behind the stove. There was no electricity, and so he set fire to a newspaper and carried it like a burning torch. We ascended into a forest of wooden staves, which were holding up the roof.

"Is it dangerous?"

The old man waved a hand, fanned the flames.

"Not at all," he said, as his foot went through the floor.

We were standing in a small cavity, a room, tight and calm.

"What is this?"

"This is where boys studied the Qur'an," he said. "It was a

madrasa. I learned the Qur'an in here sixty years ago. I sat over there with my friends. The imam would come from the mosque and beat any of us who made a mistake."

"Did he ever beat you?"

The ancient choked out a laugh. "Every day," he said.

The newspaper's flame went out and we fumbled our way back down the stairs.

I stood in the courtyard elated, wondering if I had the energy to transform a ruin into a center for people interested in learning from stories.

"It would cost a lot to renovate it," I said, thinking aloud.

"God gives to those with a purpose," said the old man.

"I don't know if I could raise the money," I said.

The man pointed to the floor of the courtyard, to a spot where the terracotta was especially worn. "Down there, under the ground," he said, "there's a treasure."

I looked at him, witnessing the margin between fact and fantasy. "Do you believe that?"

"Of course," he replied. "I believe it because it's true."

"Then why haven't you stopped everything and dug down to the treasure?"

The ancient rubbed his eyes. "Imagine the problems a treasure would bring me," he said.

A FEW DAYS later I was home at the Caliph's House with Rachana and the children. The guardians had clustered around me on my return from Fès and said that the stork had come to Osman in a dream.

"How did the dream go?"

Osman pushed forward and motioned something flat, at waist height.

"I was on a magic carpet last night," he said, "right here in the garden. It was just about to rain, and there was a breeze, very gentle, but getting stronger."

"What did the carpet look like, Osman?"

He thought for a moment, flicked his eyes shut. "It was beautiful," he said, "with strange patterns on it, and it was very soft."

"Where did it take you?"

"Out over the Sea of Darkness, to another land. We flew and flew, the carpet steady like the ground. After many hours we came to an island. It was all alone in the ocean. The carpet dropped down and landed on the beach. I climbed off and I saw a tree, a tall palm tree, at the edge of the beach. There was a huge stork nest at the top of the tree. I ran over and called up to the stork that was sitting on the nest."

"What did the stork say?"

"He asked me if I worked at Dar Khalifa. I told him that I did. 'Then you must help my brother stork,' he said, 'because he is trying to build a nest on the roof there.' I said that we had tried to build the nest for him, because we like storks. Then..."

"Then what?"

"Then the stork flapped down to where I was standing. He told me to close my eyes. I did. When I opened them, the stork was the most beautiful woman. She held out her hand to me."

Osman blushed.

"Tell him what the stork woman said to you," prompted the Bear.

"She said, 'Osman, the son of Younes, you shall go to Paradise.'"

THAT NIGHT WHEN I tucked Ariane and Timur into bed, they asked me what story I was going to tell.

"It's a story about a little boy and a little girl who were loved very much," I said. "They lived beside a great ocean, known by some as the Sea of Darkness, in the most magical house in the world. The house was in a kingdom where people understood good from bad, and where they knew about honor, duty, and respect. And they learned about these things because every night all the children in the land would listen to their fathers who sat on the edges of their beds, like I am doing now, and told them stories of princesses, magic, and wondrous things.

"Sometimes there were problems in people's lives," I said, "but everyone was ready to face them, because they had a secret knowledge, a sense of selflessness, that had been passed on from one father to the next for thousands of years."

"Baba, what was the kingdom called?"

"It was called Morocco," I said. "And the little boy and the little girl who lived there, lived in the land of *Arabian Nights.*"

I kissed Ariane and Timur good night.

They were both already fast asleep.

Glossary

A Thousand and One Nights: a large collection of stories, also known as the *Arabian Nights,* of unknown authorship deriving from Arabia or, more likely, from many Eastern lands. The stories vary in length and number, and were first introduced to Europe at the start of the eighteenth century by the French writer Antoine Galland. The most celebrated translation was that of Sir Richard Burton, in the 1880s. During the twentieth century the stories were read by children more frequently than adults, as well as being discovered by Hollywood, which created films based on the characters such as Aladdin, Ali Baba, and Sindbad.

Aisha Qandisha: a female Jinn often associated with misfortunate happenings within Moroccan homes.

Alf Layla wa Layla: literally "a thousand nights and a night." The Arabic name for *A Thousand and One Nights.* See *A Thousand and One Nights.*

Alhamdullillah: "Thanks be to God."

Antar wa Abla: a pre-Islamic Arab folk hero and his wife, of whom there are many fantastic tales told, traditionally recounted in poetry.

Arabian Nights: see *A Thousand and One Nights.*

argan oil: an oil rich in fatty acids extracted from the fruit of the argan tree, which grows exclusively in southwestern Morocco.

As salam wa alaikum: literally "Peace be upon you"; a greeting given between people in Morocco and across the Arab world whenever they meet. It is a duty for Muslims to greet others when they enter a room, etc.

Assemblies of Al Hariri: regarded for eight centuries as the greatest treasure in Arabic after the Qur'an and the Hadith, the *Assemblies* are regarded as one of the classics of Sufi literature. They were written by Al Hariri of Basra (1054–1122), who is variously described as a silk-merchant and a high official of the Seljuk monarch Malik Shah.

b'saf: Moroccan Arabic, literally "a lot" or "so much."

baba: literally "father." Used as a term of endearment by children in place of "Daddy." Also used as a term of respect for an old man.

baboush: popular goatskin sharp-toed slippers worn by men and women in Morocco, in yellow or other colors.

Bahr Adulumat: literally "Sea of Darkness," Arabic name of the Atlantic Ocean.

baraka: literally "blessing" or "blessed."

Berber: the native fair-skinned people of North Africa, or their language (although, more correctly, their language is divided into different dialects).

bidonville: French word for "shantytown," literally "tin-town."

Bismillah: "in the name of God," said by Muslims before starting or finishing many actions, such as eating, driving, sitting down, and so on.

Bollywood: the famous Indian movie industry, based at Mumbai (formerly known as Bombay).

bwana: Swahili word for "man."

café noir: French term for "black coffee," referring to the strong black coffee drunk especially by men at cafés, usually served in small glasses.

Caliph: the successor to the Prophet Mohammed; used also to refer to a governor or a man with considerable political power.

caravanserai: a lodging place for people and animals, typically found on the outskirts of Arab towns. See *fundouk.*

chaikhana: a teahouse in Afghanistan or Central Asia.

conquistadores: Spanish conquerors of Central and South America, especially the repressors of the Inca and Aztec cultures.

couscous: a dish of steamed semolina, extremely popular in Morocco, usually served with stewed vegetables and meat. Can be eaten at any time, but is usually reserved for guests or for the midday meal on Friday.

daal: staple Indian dish made with lentils.

Damascene: of Damascus, referring especially to metalwork in which gold or silver writing or pattern is laid on top of a steel base. Also refers to other forms of craft heralding from the Syrian capital, especially intricate marquetry and other forms of woodwork.

dar: literally "house," as in Dar Khalifa, the "Caliph's House."

datura: a member of the potato family, native to Latin America, but found across North Africa, with large trumpet-shaped flowers. Regarded for its hallucinogenic properties by medieval European witches and by Amazonian shamans.

dervish: a mystic, often a Sufi, following a path of poverty and self-imposed austerity. Frequently dressed in patched robes.

dirham: the currency of Morocco. There are currently about 10 dirhams to 1 U.S. dollar; and about 16 dirhams to the British pound sterling.

div: a magical creature, either disguised in human form or seen as a monster.

efrit: a demon or creature with magical powers.

Evil Eye: belief that by looking at a person, one is capable of sending ill-fortune. The belief is widespread in Arab folklore, especially in Morocco, and is found in Latin cultures as *Mal de Ojo*. See *Mal de Ojo*.

fantasia: display of horsemanship popular in rural areas in Morocco, in which participants charge their horses while attempting to fire their antique weapons at precisely the same time.

Fassi: a native of Fès; often refers to one of the diaspora from that city who can be found in other Moroccan cities, notably Rabat and Casablanca.

fundouk: see *caravanserai*.

Gauloises: one of the most popular and iconic brands of French cigarette, a blend of dark Arab tobacco. See *Gitanes*.

Genie: Westernized form of Jinn: See *Jinn*.

Gitanes: an extremely popular brand of French cigarette. Like *Gauloises*, it is made from dark tobacco, and can be smoked with or without a filter.

gnaoua: member of a spiritual African brotherhood, found in the south of Morocco, famed for their rhythmical music.

gommage: the process of scrubbing the body at a hammam, either oneself or by a professional masseur.

Hadith: traditions relating to the deeds or to the sayings of Prophet Mohammed. There are several collections of Hadith, gathered in the years after the Prophet's death by his followers and transcribed. The Prophet's example in all things is considered correct, and the Hadith is regarded as a blessed text in itself.

Hajj: the Islamic pilgrimage to Mecca; one of the Five Pillars of Islam, a duty expected of all Muslims at least once in their lifetime.

halqa: literally "a circle." Used to describe a gathering of storytellers, or also the opening of an enclosed courtyard home, to the sky.

hammam: a traditional Turkish-style bath, with one or more steam rooms at different temperatures. Most Moroccans visit a hammam at least once a week and the activity is a central part of Moroccan culture. See *gommage.*

harem: a section of a traditional Arab home reserved for women.

hudhud: Arabic word for the hoopoe, regarded as a magical bird which sat at the right hand of King Solomon.

imam: the leader of the Islamic prayer. In Islam there is no religious hierarchy as in Catholicism or Christianity. The imam's duty is to lead the prayer and also to call the faithful. See *muezzin.*

Inshallah: literally "If God wills it." Used to clarify any action or event that will come in the future.

Jan: a suffix added to a name, denoting a close association to the person using it.

jelaba: long, flowing robe worn by both men and women in Morocco.

Jinn: a fraternity of spirits created by God from smokeless fire and mentioned in the Qur'an, who, Muslims believe, inhabit the earth along with humans. Unlike us, they can change their form, and supposedly appear at dusk and sunrise especially in the form of cats. See *Jnun, Genie.*

Jnun: Moroccan term for Jinn. See *Jinn.*

Joha: medieval Arab folk hero, known throughout the Arab world and Central Asia, as well as in Central European countries. Also known as Hodja and Nasrudin. See *Nasrudin.*

Kaaba: the central stone at Mecca, to which practicing Muslims pray five times each day. A circumambulation of the Kaaba forms a central part of the Hajj as well. See *Hajj.*

kaftan: long flowing gown worn by Moroccan women.

Khalifa: Arabic word for "Caliph." See *Caliph.*

kif: marijuana resin. Grown widely in the Rif Mountains but prohibited by Moroccan law.

madrasa: literally "school"; often referring to an Islamic school, teaching the Qur'an.

Maghreb: literally "the West." Refers to Morocco, and to the first Islamic prayer of the day, held at sunrise.

Mal de Ojo: see *Evil Eye.*

manqash: a heavy sharp-edged hammer used for cutting mosaics in Morocco. Identical to a tool used for the same purpose in Afghanistan.

Marrakchi: a native of Marrakech.

medina: the old city, especially referring to tight, narrow streets set out in a labyrinth, as in Marrakech or Fès.

milh: Arabic word for "salt." In Sufi terms it refers to the goodness of mankind.

moualem: literally "master," refers to an expert in a traditional craft.

muezzin: the person who calls the faithful to prayer. Sometimes incorrectly used to refer to the actual call to prayer. See *imam.*

Mulla: literally "Master," especially used by Sufis to denote someone who has reached higher spiritual understanding.

Nasrudin: also, Mulla Nasrudin. Afghan name for the Arab folk hero Joha. See *Joha.*

pederasty: antiquated term for homosexuality. As used by Sir Richard Burton in his "Terminal Essay" in *A Thousand and One Nights.*

pied noir: literally "black foot." Term used to describe the residents of European descent living under (especially) French colonialism, or in its aftermath, in North Africa.

Pillars of Islam: the five duties of all Muslims. They comprise attesting to the belief that there is "One God and Mohammed is His Prophet," giving charity, performing the Hajj, praying, fasting during the holy month of Ramadan.

Pushtun: race in southern and southeastern Afghanistan, as well as western and northwestern Pakistan, tall in stature and with a proud warrior spirit.

Qur'an: the Holy Book of Islam, revealed over a number of years to the Prophet Mohammed by the Angel Gabriel.

riad: literally "garden"; refers to the name of a courtyard home in which the central yard is planted with flower beds and trees. Based on the idea that Paradise is a garden.

Sahrawis: people who live in the Sahara.

savon noir: literally "black soap," a mentholated paste derived from olive stones, used in a hammam.

sehura: literally "sorceress."

Shukran: Arabic for "Thank you."

Sotadic Zone: hypothesis created by the nineteenth-century explorer and academic Sir Richard Burton (See *A Thousand and One Nights*), comprising the Americas, North Africa, Asia Minor, and Central Asia, as well as parts of the Far East, where Burton believed that homosexuality was endemic.

souq: literally "market," referring especially to a traditional market in Morocco or elsewhere.

Sufi: an adherent to a mystical fraternity, believed to have predated Islam, but found most commonly in Islamic countries, with a large associated literature, and a belief that stories can pass on information, wisdom, and values.

tagine: a popular Moroccan stew, named after the round conical vessel in which it is cooked. Also incorrectly used to refer to any dish prepared in such a vessel.

tarboush: a hard felt- or velvet-covered hat, usually in maroon or green, known incorrectly in the West as a "fez."

Tuareg: an ethnic group, possibly of Berber origin, residing in the southern deserts and in the Sahara.

vizier: literally "bearer of burdens"; referring to a high-ranking adviser or minister, especially during the time in which *A Thousand and One Nights* was set.

zaouia: a center of reflective study often built beside the tomb of a religious figure or saint.

Recommended Reading

Arabian Nights

Les Mille et une nuits, contes Arabes
Translated by Antoine Galland, 1704–17

The Thousand and One Nights
Translated by John Payne, 1882–84

A Plain and Literal Translation of the Arabian Nights Entertainments, Now Entitled the Book of the Thousand Nights and a Night
Translated by Richard F. Burton, 1885–88

The Thousand and One Days: A Companion to the Arabian Nights
Miss J. Pardoe, 1857

The Arabian Nights: A Companion
Robert Irwin, 1994

The Arabian Nights and Orientalism
Edited by Yuriko Yamanaka and Tetsuo Nishio, 2006

The Earlier History of the Arabian Nights
D. B. MacDonald, 1924

The Arabian Nights: A Structural Analysis
Ferial Ghazoul, 1980

Story-Telling Techniques in the Arabian Nights
David Pinault, 1992

The Teaching Story

Caravan of Dreams
Idries Shah, 1968

The Pleasantries of the Incredible Mulla Nasrudin
Idries Shah, 1968

World Tales
Idries Shah, 1979

Tales of the Dervishes
Idries Shah, 1967

The World of Nasrudin
Idries Shah, 2003

The Way of the Sufi
Idries Shah, 1968

Arabian Fairy Tales
Amina Shah, 1989

Kalila and Dimna
Retold by Ramsay Wood, 1980

Problems, Myths and Stories
Doris Lessing, 1999

The Past We Share: The Near Eastern Ancestry of Western Folk Literature
E. L. Ranelagh, 1979

Antar and Abla
Diana Richmond, 1978

Arab Folktales
Translated by Inea Bushnaq, 1986

Art of Story-Telling
Mia Gerhardt, 1963

The Secret of Laughter
Shusha Guppy, 2005

Illustrated Children's Books by Idries Shah

The Farmer's Wife
The Man with Bad Manners
The Boy Without a Name
The Lion Who Saw Himself in the Water
The Magic Horse
The Old Woman and the Eagle
The Clever Boy and the Terrible, Dangerous Animal

The Silly Chicken
Neem the Half-Boy
The Man and the Fox
Fatima the Spinner and the Tent

Morocco

Morocco: A Traveller's Companion
Margaret and Robin Bidwell, 1992

Marrakech: Through Writers' Eyes
Edited by Barnaby Rogerson and Stephen Lavington, 2006

Wit and Wisdom of Morocco
Edward Westermarck, 1931

Saints and Sorcerers
Nina Epton, 1958

Lords of the Atlas
Gavin Maxwell, 1966

Cadogan Morocco
Barnaby Rogerson, 2000

Ritual and Belief in Morocco
Edward Westermarck, 1926

Miscellaneous

Love with a Few Hairs
Mohammed Mrabet, 1986

The Devil Drives: A Biography of Richard Francis Burton
Fawn Brodie, 1967

A Rage to Live: A Biography of Richard and Isabel
Mary S. Lovell, 1998

Dwarfs of Mount Atlas
R. G. Haliburton, 1891

The Songlines
Bruce Chatwin, 1987